The l

The author of numerous articles, two edited volumes, and six books, four of them about European integration, **John Gillingham** is a long-standing but respected critic of the Brussels institutions. Gillingham holds a doctorate in History from the University of California, Berkeley, and is a fellow at the Harvard Center for European Studies. His work has been translated into several languages. He is the recipient of numerous honours and awards, among them the American Historical Association's research prize in International History, and is listed in *Who's Who in America*.

# The EU
## *An Obituary*

JOHN GILLINGHAM

**VERSO**
London • New York

To my dear brother, Paul Muir Gillingham, MD

First published by Verso 2016
© John Gillingham 2016

1 3 5 7 9 10 8 6 4 2

**Verso**
UK: 6 Meard Street, London W1F 0EG
US: 20 Jay Street, Suite 1010, Brooklyn, NY 11201
versobooks.com

Verso is the imprint of New Left Books

ISBN-13: 978-1-78478-421-8
ISBN-13: 978-1-78478-423-2 (US EBK)
ISBN-13: 978-1-78478-422-5 (UK EBK)

**British Library Cataloguing in Publication Data**
A catalogue record for this book is available from the British Library

**Library of Congress Cataloging-in-Publication Data**
A catalog record for this book is available from the Library of Congress

Typeset in Sabon MT by Hewer Text UK Ltd, Edinburgh
Printed in the UK by CPI Group (UK) Ltd, Croydon, CR0 4YY

# Contents

# Introduction: A Re-examination of the European Union

The present crisis of the European Union makes it painfully evident that the history of the EU must be re-thought, re-cast, and re-written. More is at stake than merely setting the record straight. At one and the same time vast and parochial, the existing research on the EU not only defines the current intellectual parameters of the subject and provides the language that shapes discussion: it also establishes the contexts of policy-making, guides political action, and opens new sources of legitimacy.[1]

This is the case for two special reasons. Directly or indirectly, the European Union has funded the bulk of the scholarly literature written about it. For most of its life, and even down to the present, the EU has also been the beneficiary of an ideology of Europeanism – a secular faith that it is an ordained agent of human progress. The many scholars, commentators, assorted experts, and like-minded journalists who have spent careers doing EU research, are nearly all devotees of the Euro-cult. To be sure, they can at times be critical – and in light of current events are more so than previously – but only for the most part in order to better serve the cause. Doubters are still unwelcome. Such heretics have yet to make serious inroads into the legacy of EU scholarship. The makers and shakers in Brussels have stood, and still stand, behind the massive establishmentarian intellectual enterprise, and symbiotically profit from it. The same cannot be said for the rest of us. The loop between thinkers and doers must be broken if real progress is to be made in reforming the EU and in dealing with its legacy.

Three influential theories have sustained belief in the EU as something historically transcendent; while all differ fundamentally in the interpretation of the integration process, each posits a similar teleological outcome: a federal Europe. None of them has much purchase. Nevertheless, an alternative paradigm has yet to replace them. The earliest and most prominent among such conceptual approaches, functionalism, holds that European integration, once set in motion, would have 'spillover effects' that carry over from one economic or political sector to another, eventually pervading the body politic. One might have expected this process to move predictably forward over time, yet this has never been the case. Progress has been at best sporadic and at worst absent for prolonged periods. The author of functionalist theory, which dates from the 1950s, the political scientist Ernst Haas, later repudiated it; recent revival attempts, no matter how desperate, have got almost nowhere.

A second theory, liberal intergovernmentalism, developed by another political scientist, Andrew Moravcsik, in the late 1990s, explains the integration process as the outcome of optimal bargains struck between state actors. He has little to say about how institutions operate and nothing about their possible failures. He tells a success story. It is hard, in light of the EU's plight, to take the notion seriously.[2]

A third reigning approach is somewhat different in character. Formulated in the early 1990s by the historian Alan Milward, it maintains that the integration process is best understood as a necessary and beneficial strengthening of the welfare state and, as later elaborated, further posits, as the other theories do not, that the EU will develop from an elitist into a mass project. The connection between Milward's two theses and the contours of actual EU history (and that of its predecessors) is only incidental.[3] A deep, abiding, widespread, and fiercely defended faith that the integration process will eventuate in a united social democratic Europe is what sustains such ideas.[4] Convictions die hard.

To summarize the discussion, all three outworn theories rest on serious misperceptions that beg for correction.

This inquiry into the EU's history will make no triumphalist presumptions. It will instead reassess the EU's past in an effort to discover what went wrong, how it might yet be righted, and what might come next. One must, at the outset, view the subject from outside-in rather than, as previously the case, from inside-out. An epiphenomenon of stronger historical forces, the European Union's growth and development has, by and large, occurred exogenously – through international drivers of change: intermittently by shifts in superpower relationships and continuously by the seemingly inexorable expansion of world trade as mediated through new global economic, political, and organizational contexts. This force, and not the EU, is the prime mover of the integration process.

The gradual erosion of the power inherent in national and regional political institutions, as well as their supersession by ever-larger and deeper markets, is closely related to the ever-increasing flow of imports and exports. The growth of international trade reflects the development of an increasingly dense and complicated interdependence between states and corporate institutions; within such institutions themselves; and between markets and institutions. The trend has constituted, and continues to pose, a growing threat to bureaucratic EU system-builders who, put on the defensive, have raised political stakes in a futile effort to dam the tide. Europe suffers as a result.

As for contexts, the original one was the setting of postwar Europe, whose most significant features were the American Grand Design, the revival of Germany as well as Europe, and the Cold War. The next context resulted from the so-called monetary regime change – the breakdown in the 1970s of the Bretton Woods world financial system, which had been set up in the final months of World War II and was anchored in the Dollar–gold standard. The collapse of this system ushered in an era of neo-liberalism as well as, regionally, the two-edged sword known as the Single European Act of 1986. Its sequels were the conclusion of the ill-conceived Maastricht Treaty (1992), the launching of an abortive constitutional project, and the fatal decision to adopt the euro as a single currency. The cyber revolution provides the context in today's crisis Europe. Together with the revival of China and India and their return to the mainstream of world history, it presents immense technical and geo-political challenges to a European Union debilitated by a loss of authority, archaic operating methods, and bad judgement.

European Union adaptation to change sometimes commands respect, but more often does not. On the one hand a powerful engine of potential betterment, but on the other hand deeply flawed, the EU is the product both of human decision-making and institutional design and operation. The EU's history has neither followed a prescribed course nor been moulded by a single template, or even several of them. Without either a constitution or other single founding document but the outgrowth of several treaties and many informal understandings, it lacks a strong backbone. To complicate matters further, the EU also operates opportunistically outside such frameworks in a legal and institutional never-never land.

Its development can be characterized as having been mutable, polymorphous, and refractory; as an organization the EU has consequently altered over time, assumed different forms and acquired new functions, yet nevertheless remains stubborn and resistant to change. This very formlessness may, paradoxically, be a source of long-term strength. If the EU has re-made itself before, it might be able to do so again. Any such makeover will, however, have to be drastic.

Unnecessarily complex and inefficient, the EU's operational mechanisms are enveloped in semantic confusion. To explain how the Brussels machinery works, or fails to, one must whenever possible eschew jargon, avoid legalese, be wary of public relations packaging, and consider unacceptable the official excuse that abuse of meaning is the inescapable consequence of the *sui generis* character of the integration project.

The latter assumption is untenable. The EU is an international organization, which, like others created in a utopian spirit, is subject to the constraints of history, and therefore fallible. In assessing its strengths and weaknesses, one must not only scrutinize the EU as an institution but examine alternative courses of development and weigh impacts. Its present sorry state was not predetermined, but due to a history of unsound thinking, bad attitudes, poor policy-making, and inertia. The EU is the product of individual minds and actions, but also of path-dependent, dysfunctional, and ossified institutions. This legacy must somehow be overcome.

The three parts of this book reflect the themes running through the uneven course of EU history. They are: Myth as Method, Behind the Curve, and Lost in the Future. The EU may not yet be dead but only defunct. Its survival, as in the past, nevertheless requires rigorous and even painful adaptation to the powerful long-term global forces that drive the world forward. Future reform may well involve a change of mission, re-structuring, and sharp reductions in the EU's power and influence as an institution. The story of the EU can no longer be about goals attained, or even, as in recent revisions, goals deferred, but of decline. The EU has a long record of policy interventions along broadening swathes of human affairs, of failing ever more consequently in the attempt to implement them, and of inflicting correspondingly greater harm as a result. It is a dead weight that must be lifted if national cultures are to flourish and Europe regain the confidence to meet the challenges of the future.

The fast-breaking events of Autumn 2015 call this future into question. They made a mockery of EU pretentions, condemned already faltering policies to failure, and launched a public assessment of the very need for it. The Volkswagen cheating scandal on standards of diesel emissions exposed the emptiness of Brussels' claim to serve as the world's conscience on climate policy and undermined its credibility as a regulator. Overshadowing this humiliation, the escalating refugee crisis provided stomach-churning evidence of the EU's powerlessness in a field in which it asserted exclusive jurisdiction: internal European security. The grisly 13 November suicide bombings in Paris shocked the citizenry of the member states into a pained awareness that the Schengen policy of open borders jeopardizes public safety. They also had far-reaching policy implications: reversed the Commission's anti-US tech policy – the spearhead of its economic programme – for the sake of better cyber surveillance; necessitated massive new (and unproductive) investment in policing and welfare; resulted in a de facto devolution of power from Brussels to the member states; turned public opinion sharply to the right; and triggered a search for alternatives to the EU itself.

Its fate may well be determined by Brexit, the possible withdrawal of the UK from the EU. It now seems likely that Prime Minister Cameron, who promised a referendum on Britain's membership, will not manage to wrest from Brussels the far-reaching concessions needed to placate a wary electorate. A Brexit victory could split the EU, decentralize it, or in some measure do both. A British exit could also trigger a reconfiguration of the European Monetary Union and delegitimize the body of European law and regulation known as the *acquis communitaire*. We seem, in short, to be at a turning point in Europe's post–World War II history.

*13 December 2015*
*Harvard Centre*
*for European*
*Studies*

# PART I

## MYTH AS METHOD

The most appealing, persuasive, and oft-repeated defence made in praise of the European Union is unambiguous and twofold. It credits the EU with the peace and prosperity enjoyed by Europe since 1945. It is a sweeping claim, all the more powerful in light of the catastrophic first half of the twentieth century. To challenge it is to cast doubt on accepted certitudes about our own era. The EU is still considered by many to be the greatest historical achievement of the present age. This judgement should not be accepted uncritically. To know where one is headed, one should know where one has come from. An examination of the formative years of the European institutions can promise few conclusive answers but might at least raise serious questions about the EU which, if troubling, provide clues as to how past and present problems have arisen. It may even contribute something to their solution.

It took more than bricks and mortar to rebuild Europe after World War II. Faith was also needed – in a better future and in a roadmap leading to it, and, to sustain such faith, a founders' myth. To track down the historical origins of present problems one must take a close look at the setting in which the EU came to life, the motives that led to its creation, the short-term consequences of the choices then made, and the long-term problems that grew out of them. We will find that Jean Monnet, the iconic George Washington of the integration process, launched his big projects against a background of Cold War politics in order to deal, as a Frenchman, with the German Problem. Military security was his foremost concern. The institutions he designed were hierarchical, centralized bureaucracies, unaccountable to the public but outfitted with the trappings of representative democracy. The results were less than optimal, and had certain of his plans succeeded they could have been disastrous. Nonetheless, Monnet left a legacy of hope and expectation that remains alive even today.

Monnet did not have the integration field to himself. He shared it with other architects of the new Europe, a group of like-minded senior civil servants representing France, Germany, and the Benelux countries. Their purpose in coming together was to strengthen commercial ties with a resurgent West Germany, a sensible aim in line with long-term economic trends and consistent with peacetime requirements. Yet the institution they built, the customs union christened as the European Economic Community (EEC), was not the only or necessarily even the best vehicle for the ends they sought.

It might have been possible both to organize a broader economic union and reduce political risk. The EEC included an executive authority vested with ill-defined powers that opened the door to trouble. The struggle that soon broke out between this office and the six founder members of the EEC would result in gridlock lasting for years. Even as political integration became stuck in its tracks, economic progress continued. Europe enjoyed a twenty-year recovery boom, which resulted in industrial modernization and the rise of the consumer economy. Although the European Economic Community contributed little to this remarkable growth, the claim that it did so went unchallenged, and the EEC became indelibly associated in the public mind with prosperity. Another myth had been born. Meanwhile, underlying political problems persisted in Brussels. The most serious of these was the elitist and undemocratic character of the new European institutions. Monnet's successors would fail to deal with this legacy.

# CHAPTER I

# A Complicated Early History

To appreciate the full significance of the epochal Schuman Plan announcement of 9 May 1950 – in retrospect the harbinger of the better days to come – one must begin with a reminder of the condition of Europe at the time. World War II had, of course, ended five years earlier, but memories of it were very much alive. Loss of life, destruction of property, material deprivation, physical dislocation, and general disruption shaped public outlooks everywhere on the European continent; a nasty negativism was their hallmark, and hostility their expression. Underlying such attitudes was also a profound longing for personal security and an eagerness to return to normal peacetime conditions, as well as a desperate hope for a better future.

Robert Schuman's eloquent words, delivered in a radio address of 9 May 1950 promised a dramatic breakthrough. Warning that 'Europe will not be made at once, or according to a single plan . . . but through concrete achievements', he proposed the creation of a new international authority to manage as a single unit, and independent of national control, the heavy industry of France, Germany, and the rest of Western Europe. Thus conceived, the European Coal and Steel Community (ECSC) was founded the following year. It marks the official origin of the integration process.[1]

*Jean Monnet and the Postwar Years*
The Schuman Plan – indeed the very text in which it was announced – was the handiwork of the most remarkable and now controversial figure in the history of the EU, Jean Monnet.

Much of the subsequent course of the integration process is associated, for better or worse, with his memory. Central to it is the notion of the so-called 'Monnet Method', which initially was deemed consistent with the theory of functionalism, as developed behind the scenes by Ernst Haas and a team of Monnet's close collaborators. As is often the case with other protean figures, his legacy has been co-opted, complicated, obscured, and confused by devoted admirers, who all too often invoke his name to sanction policies of their own. The 'Monnet Method' has thus been debased to a meaningless catch-all that in practice has become a by-word for advocacy of technocratic governance.[2] Yet the myth of Monnet-as-Seer survives. What – exactly – then, did Monnet mean to accomplish? How should one assess his successes and failures or imagine what might have happened had he brought his plans to fruition?[3]

Monnet was partly responsible for creating the cult surrounding his memory. Contrary to the image projected of him as a modest, even unassuming man, who worked selflessly day and night from behind the scenes, inching the integration process forward one step at a time towards the Promised Land – he spared no effort to establish his reputation as a titan of public life, power-broker *extraordinaire*, and visionary. His influential *Memoirs* – actually the collective labour of a carefully selected group of favoured academics and associates – describe a career characterized by an unbroken string of triumphs; setbacks almost never entered the picture. Lest this message be forgotten, he set up a private foundation in Lausanne, Switzerland – the *Archives Jean Monnet pour l'Europe* – to house his papers. They consist of the documentation used in his memoirs, from which was carefully culled evidence inconsistent with its central thesis. For those who want to find it, the French national archives is the place to look.[4]

Monnet's greatest creations – the European Coal and Steel Community and the French Plan de Modernisation et d'Équipement – depended upon his having disciples at the summits of power in the public administrations of the United States, Britain, France, West Germany, and elsewhere, whom, by force of vision and will, he engaged in the service of his ideas. Their successors would long remain guardians of the flame, act in his name, and preserve his memory.[5]

To take the measure of Monnet's achievement, one must recall the special conditions obtaining in postwar Europe that made him the indispensable man. American power was overwhelming and few other Europeans had either the personal connections or the know-how to tap directly into it. But there were limits to what he could accomplish. His projects did not hold the field alone, and some would prove unworkable. This was by no means necessarily a bad thing. Monnet viewed democratic decision-making as a hindrance to technocratic efficiency. In the new atomic age, this opened the door to a host of potential evils, many of which, thanks to the unviability of his plans, never materialized.

A sound claim can be made that it was the founding of the European Economic Community (EEC) in 1958 rather than the 1949 Schuman Plan announcement that marks the real beginning of the European project, and not just, as was described at the time and since, its 're-launch'. The enduring value of the EU dates from this event. The nature of the new EEC – its configuration, methods, and rationale – represents a rejection of Monnet's design for European institutions. This was strategic in conception and centred on the security of France. Contrary to conventional wisdom, politics and economics, at least in the civilian sense, were only of secondary interest to him. Monnet's schemes reflected the experience and threat of war. In contrast, the EEC's organizers were concerned primarily with the material welfare of Europe and thus their work remains germane to the problems facing the EU today.[6]

How, if realized, might Monnet's plans have altered the subsequent course of European history? The projects he devised and promoted – the European Defence Community (EDC), Euratom, and the Multilateral Force (MLF) – though today almost forgotten – were extraordinarily ambitious and very reckless. Monnet proposed nothing less than integrating Europe around the nucleus of what would have become a military industrial complex twinned to the one then developing in the United States. Much in play during the Eisenhower and Kennedy years, these failed endeavours damaged American Cold War policy. Had they succeeded, the consequences would have been dire.

*Washington's Grand Design Confronts European Reality*
President Roosevelt had a definite vision of the postwar world. It was an image, writ large, of America under the New Deal. He foresaw an international order governed under law, with open markets and a close relationship between state and economy. A future United Nations – policed by the Big Four of the US, UK, USSR, and China – would provide a framework of world government. An International Monetary Fund would restore currency convertibility, and a free trade organization promote commerce in a world without tariffs. Supporting such an international architecture would be restored nation states resting on mutually reinforcing relationships between government and economy.

Such a vision would, of course, never materialize. For one thing, FDR did not foresee a Cold War; nor did he take sufficient account of what was happening in China. Nevertheless, his basic ideas, at least those dealing with economics, not only framed policy in the aftermath of World War II but, as modified over time, provided the essential structures for the new capitalistic era of freedom and prosperity that eventually opened up in the West. In the short term, however, the American plans for the future confronted two main obstacles. One was the defeated former enemy, the other the prospective future one. This called for a policy of 'double containment'.[7]

Within this mix, Germany was, for good reasons, a French obsession. Jean Monnet said openly what all Frenchmen feared: that another war with the dreaded enemy would end France's history as a great power. Monnet knew whereof he spoke, and he had the experience and connections needed to take corrective action. Back in World War I Monnet had represented the French on the Allied agencies that were set up to regulate world trade in grains, minerals, and shipping. In the 1920s he operated at the interface of finance and government as a bond underwriter representing Wall Street in Europe. An early advocate of preparedness in the 1930s, Monnet left his homeland before the Fall of France, but instead of joining the Free French under De Gaulle, served as British representative in the US Lend-Lease programme. He also became the official planner of the (chiefly propagandistic) American 'Victory Program', and, crucially, later took charge of economic affairs for the provisional French government in Algiers. In this capacity he provided a conduit for US military assistance to the postwar French government. The American connection was the source of his influence in France. Thanks to his access to well-placed Washington policy-makers, he could not only influence American policy from the outside, but shape it from within.[8]

After the war, Monnet headed the French Plan, whose design and methods of operation were inspired by the US war economy. He was subsequently the de facto negotiator of the Blum Loan of 1946 and, more important still, the French delegate to the Marshall Plan, which he influenced at the top level. It was no accident that the famous aid programme required the establishment of analogues of the French Plan in the other beneficiary nations. Nor was it by chance that the Plan received about half of France's Marshall Plan aid, something that did not necessarily endear Monnet to jealous French political operatives.

Within the parameters of France's security policy, Monnet, a political realist, was a voice of moderation. Initially, the French hoped to carve up the ex-Reich into medium, bite-sized states like those Napoleon once organized for the Confederation of the Rhine. With the advent of the Cold War, the beginnings of recovery, and the growing likelihood of German revival, French aims focused increasingly on the Ruhr, home to the coal and steel trusts thought in France to be the mainspring of the Reich's economic and political power. French policy had two specific goals: to restrict German steel production and to pre-empt the coal supply needed to fuel their economy, especially the planned modernization of the nationalized metallurgical industry.

In 1947 the three Western occupation governments therefore set up the International Ruhr Authority (IRA) with these ends in mind. The IRA set limits to German recovery. The American decision to restore sovereignty to the new Federal Republic once made, Monnet determined that France should maintain control over the Ruhr but exercise it not by means of the occupation statutes but 'in the name of Europe'. Once the ex-enemy had regained respectability, and France bolstered its strength, a relationship could be established on the basis of equality. The Schuman Plan organization, the eventual European Coal and Steel Community, was to be the vehicle of this transition.[9]

Long before any such stage had been reached in the negotiations, a totally unexpected event occurred in a faraway place, the former Hermit Kingdom, that threatened to wreck them. To Washington, the invasion of South Korea by the Communist government in the North made no sense except as a feint to divert American attention away from Europe. It thus triggered a snap decision to begin re-arming the young Federal Republic at once, and accelerated a second one already in progress to station 200,000 US troops in Europe under the auspices of the North Atlantic Treaty Organization (NATO).

To rescue the coal–steel negotiations from certain failure, Monnet came up with an even bolder proposal than the Schuman Plan. This was the Pleven Plan announced on 24 October 1950, named after the prime minister *du jour*, a long-standing associate of his. In the name of France, Pleven called for nothing less than the organization of a future European armed force of 100,000 men composed of European units integrated nationally down to the lowest feasible level of organization, presumably the brigade. It was to be called the European Defence Community (EDC). Consistent with French views, it was to be officered by the French themselves until the completion of German rearmament at some remote date, and provisioned by a modernized French munitions industry. The proposed armed force would not, however, be able to act independently; it was to be incorporated into NATO strategy and command.

The Pleven Plan initiative saved the Schuman Plan negotiations. The coal–steel authority opened for operation in June 1952. By then, however, EDC had eclipsed the ECSC in Allied diplomacy. The coal–steel pool retreated into the background. The ECSC provided the means by which Germany could regain control of industry in the Ruhr and thus to end the occupation. In that sense, it was a diplomatic triumph for Germany. Otherwise it barely got off the ground. Contrary to expectations, it had little impact on either the conduct of business in heavy industry or in the balance of power between Germany and France. Trust-busting did not take place. Producer relations in coal and steel had not been competitive for many years, but, from the producer standpoint, were regulated satisfactorily by private laws and conventions – cartels – in a tradition dating from the 1920s that had remained intact during the recent war. In 1953 an international steel cartel was revived.[10]

The big problem facing the managers of mine and mill was that business itself was no longer very good; nor was heavy industry still the lead sector in the armaments field. The era of coal and steel had already given way to an atomic age with higher and quite different strategic requirements. Economically as well, the days of the big trusts were numbered. Cheaper fuel could be shipped to Rotterdam from Virginia than delivered locally from the Ruhr. Henceforth European steel mills would all be built near ports to access cheap overseas supplies. In the meantime, oil and electrical power rapidly displaced coal in traditional markets. By 1955 the mining industry of Western Europe was in the throes of mortal crisis. A few years later the steel producers would be in the same boat. The ECSC would eventually be folded into the EEC.[11] It was not, as is often still maintained, an integration model.

## The European Defence Community and Euratom

Although the European Defence Community (EDC) project, the outgrowth of the Pleven Plan, eventually collapsed, the massive diplomatic onslaught set in motion to advance it became a focal point of Cold War thinking. The failure of the EDC project was definitive. Nothing on such a scale has ever been undertaken under EU auspices. Until now, Europe has lacked an armed force of its own and depended on NATO and the American nuclear umbrella. The EDC was, as conceived, not intended to play more than a supporting role in NATO, yet the political implications of Monnet's plans were huge. They would have locked a militarized Europe into satellite status in a one-sided trans-Atlantic partnership.

At the core of the EDC proposal was the so-called Commissariat, an armaments procurement agency vested with a mandate to sponsor a new (largely French) defence industry, which was to have at its disposal a common budget large enough to make Europe self-sufficient in conventional weaponry. Over time, the treaty would have allowed for the manufacture of nuclear weapons, if only, according to the protocols, by France. More troublesome still, this 'defence community' was to be clothed in something larger, a European Political Community (EPC), outfitted with embryonic but expandable powers of state. In organizing both the ECSC and the EDC, Monnet circumvented the representative institutions of the French government, an approach justified as unavoidable under the circumstances. He relied on Foreign Minister Schuman to keep the politicians at arm's length. The parliamentary institutions incorporated into his plans were to have worked the same way, and above all to be kept from interfering in the international security sphere. The assembly of the ECSC, a shadow organization, was to assume the legislative functions of the proposed EDC to give it a democratic veneer; its powers were advisory. The Commissariat was to have been its executive and to exercise control over fiscal policy. Had the EDC–EPC plans come to fruition, the new Europe would have been saddled in its formative years with a supranational defence ministry acting as a government, responsible to no authority but a sham parliament – and least of all to the public. Its survival would have depended upon perpetuating the arms race with the USSR. Such an organization would have sapped the strength of democracy, perpetuated the Cold War, and crushed an independent European spirit.

Although now largely forgotten, the EDC was the central issue in inter-Allied, and especially American, diplomacy during the years between its initialling by foreign ministers in May 1952 and its eventual rejection by the French Assembly in June 1954. Nonetheless, the only real enthusiasts for the EDC project were to be found in the US State Department, more specifically, among the devoted band of Monnet's supporters that other State Department officials ridiculed as 'The Theologians'. Secretary of state and chief of American security policy, John Foster Dulles was the Grand Poo-bah of the new dispensation. Dulles was a long-standing personal friend of Monnet. A super-rich lawyer, he bailed Monnet out of bankruptcy in the 1930s, and always spoke reverentially of 'Jean'.

President Eisenhower guffawed when Dulles first introduced the plan for the EDC: the General could hardly imagine that a military force so organized could do more than trip over its own two feet. But after the secretary of state enlightened him to the fact that the EDC had little to do with actual war-fighting and much to do with 'building Europe', as well as, more importantly, integrating it into the Atlantic Community, Ike came around. Henceforth, the president backed the EDC proposal to the hilt. In this respect it would set a precedent. In the next decade, the Multilateral Force (MLF) initiative of Kennedy's would, upping the ante, call for a new, and quite useless, integrated nuclear-armed navy for the explicit purpose of joining the old civilization to the new. The initiative was part of an even more far-reaching proposal for binding Europe to the American New Order, John F. Kennedy's 'Grand Design'.

The Theologians were, in any case, grimly determined to see the EDC matter through. Their diplomacy, a combination of private browbeating and public coercion, culminated in Dulles' extraordinary 'Agonizing Re-appraisal' speech, which threatened a US troop withdrawal from Europe in the event of non-ratification. Having renounced for all time Germany's interest in becoming a nuclear power, eager for anything that would advance the schedule for conventional rearmament, and bent upon ending the occupation, Chancellor Konrad Adenauer, gave the EDC proposal lukewarm support. Already possessing their own atomic weapons, the British were indifferent to the proposal. The high command of the French armed forces, then bogged down in the war in Indochina, emphatically opposed it, as well as any other measure that might impinge on France's determination to join the nuclear club as soon as possible.[12]

Objections from this quarter were muted until the fall of Dien Bien Phu, at which point France's dependence on US military assistance, which had covered the costs of the war, was no longer critical. Thereupon, to nearly universal relief, the French National Assembly let the EDC treaty die. Dulles cried at the news. His point man and special envoy for European integration in the two-year-long struggle for ratification, the ultra-Monnetist David Bruce, despaired that the French *Non* meant the loss of Western Europe. He professed to hear champagne corks popping in the Kremlin. Within months, however, West Germany joined NATO – with no one the worse for it.[13]

Monnet learned two obvious things from the failure of the EDC project. One was that coal and steel no longer counted for much in the balance of power. The other was that ambitious projects like the EDC had little chance of success without popular support. Thereupon he organized the Action Committee for the United States of Europe. It served several purposes: to act as a think tank, to promote the careers of promising national political figures predisposed to Euro-federalism, and to serve as a lobby group.

The Action Committee was an attempt to build networks as effective as those Monnet had relied upon in the past. The new one, however, was formed to guide Europe's future. In that respect it was a measured success. Thanks to it, Monnet would become an icon of integration – to his devotees *L'Inspirateur* (The Inspiration). At the same time, veterans of the Action Committee would move Europe in a different direction to that which he might have had in mind. Control would no longer be exercised in executive fashion as in the postwar period, but to some extent be shared. The parameters of policy-making had shifted.[14]

Seen in retrospect, the EDC episode was indicative of the dialogue of the deaf that was becoming commonplace in the relationship between the superpowers. The Soviets were popping no champagne corks, but instead running scared after the death of Stalin on 1 March 1953. Confusion reigned, followed by a struggle for power that concluded with the execution of the current top dog in the leadership, Lavrenti Beria. Beria's fatal mis-step was to reverse the collectivization of the East German economy decreed by Stalin in the final months of his life, a sensible move but fatal for Beria. Stalin's policy had triggered the flight of 500,000 people, including important cadres, to the Federal Republic. Beria began to speak openly of Stalin's crimes and even advocate German neutralization. Prime Minister Churchill, backed by Foreign Secretary Eden, sensed that the time for an overture had come and thought an attempt at détente timely.

Preoccupied with the EDC issue, Dulles refused to believe that the stirrings in the Bloc were anything other than a ploy. Soviet actions should have suggested the contrary. Even after Beria had been shot, the Kremlin continued to back away from Stalin's harsh policy – curtailing the forced exportation of German goods, proposing an end to collectivization, and assenting to a 'sharp increase' in the production of consumer goods. The foolish East German Politburo, having recently committed to stepping up the pace of 'progress towards socialism', found itself summoned to Moscow for a dressing down. None of this did any good. Rioting broke out in June 1953, not only in Berlin, which made the headlines, but sporadically throughout the DDR. It would last for months. Still Washington sat on its hands. A year-long chance had been missed to end the division of Germany, revise the postwar settlement, and perhaps even set in motion reforms like those which eventually brought about the collapse of the Soviet Union. Such possibilities were never seized upon because Dulles, a captive of misperception, was obsessed with the EDC.[15]

## The Origins of the European Economic Community

The failure of the EDC project gave rise to a new round of negotiations within the year that would lead to the European Economic Community (EEC), the eventual EU. This outcome was not inevitable. In fact, it was considered the least likely of two other possibilities, each of which was in play concurrently. The first of them, and the one estimated to have the best prospects of realization, was the Monnet-authored, American-championed, and, (with qualifications) French military-supported proposal for an atomic community, Euratom. The design reflected Monnet's security concerns as well as a characteristic emphasis on the sectoral, the hierarchical, and the superficially democratic. Euratom was to have enabled the six founder members of the ECSC to regulate the European atomic energy industry. In theory, its scope was limited to civilian uses. In practice, military applications were not ruled out, at least for France. Monnet's personal ambitions extended far beyond those of the French generals. He wanted a European A-Bomb.

The crunch problem in the Euratom talks was enriching uranium to weapons grade standard; only the Americans could afford to build plants suitable for such a purpose; in Europe, national resources would have to be pooled. At issue were matters of cost-sharing and nuclear parity. The complicated and time-consuming negotiations led to a dead end. No one, not even the Germans themselves, wanted to lift the self-imposed nuclear ban. After much quibbling, the French, still at an early stage in the development process, remained determined to forge ahead with plans to build the Bomb. The eventual Euratom would be little more than a record-keeping agency. The episode is, however, more than an historical might-have-been. The tenacity of Monnet's advocacy for the atomic pool, supported as it was by the French military establishment and the Monnetist cabal in the State Department, gave France a strong bargaining lever in a parallel set of ongoing negotiations, those, namely, for a Common Market.[16]

The negotiations for the Treaty of Rome (1958), which eventuated in the EEC, began in Messina, Sicily. Running alongside them, as well as beside the Euratom track, was yet another set of negotiations, led informally by Britain, for a free trade area (FTA). The EEC was designed as a customs union with a common external tariff, whereas the FTA, a somewhat less ambitious venture, merely eliminated trade barriers between contracting states. The theoretical importance of this difference remains the subject of a long-standing debate between economists. The only salient differences between the two organizations was that the European Economic Community had a political component, a commission of unspecified powers, and was meant to be run as a joint venture with a restricted membership. It was, in this sense, a successor to the coalition of the six founder members of the ECSC. Membership in FTA was open to all Marshall Plan nations.[17]

The Treaty of Rome, the EEC's charter, made no mention of political federation as a future aim of the EEC, but contained language no more specific than that of 'laying the foundations of an even closer union among the peoples of Europe to ensure the economic and social progress of their countries by common action to eliminate the barriers which divide Europe'. What this commitment would entail in practice would remain in dispute up to the present day.[18] As for the proposed FTA, membership was unrestricted, and it had no stated political aim. Yet both organizations sought to stimulate growth by increasing trade. At several points they might have merged. Political bargaining determined their varied outcomes.

The success of both the EEC and the FTA, which would later become EFTA (European Free Trade Area), rested on a case famously made by Gottfried Haberler in his inaugural address as president of the American Economic Association, 'Integration and Growth of the World Economy in Historical Perspective'. According to Haberler, there was nothing altogether new about post-World War II integration, which he defined as 'closer economic relations between the areas concerned'; rather, it represented the most recent of three great waves in this long-term trend, the first of which took place at the national level beginning will trade expansion in the eighteenth century; the second wave occurred internationally, through free trade in the nineteenth century; the third one, associated with increasing economies of scale, began after 1945.

Intervals between such waves occurred, he admitted, as a result of tariff increases and the outbreak of wars, but even they could only slow down the ongoing integration process. The Great Depression provided the only exception to this pattern of long-term growth, but he ascribed it to 'horrendous miscalculations', not 'secular stagnation'. Haberler took comfort in the expansion of world trade, which had tripled in the three years after World War II and grown at 6 per cent annually in the 1950s and 1960s, faster than ever before. Every major industrial power enjoyed impressive increases in exports and imports. According to him, these gains stemmed from the elimination of a 'jungle of internal and external direct controls' dating from the years of depression and war. He added that the removal of such shackles 'released great energies which led to the spectacular rise in output and consumer satisfaction'.

The freeing of trade constituted a movement towards worldwide integration that, in his view, preceded and overlapped the regional reduction of trade barriers in the European Common Market (EEC) and other similar schemes; there can hardly be a doubt, it follows, 'that up to (1965) the quantitative effects of trade on world wide integration and liberalization have been much greater than those of the much more discussed and advertised regional schemes'. The future is not without its dangers, he added. Protectionism of one sort or another always being tempting, Haberler warned of a recent rise of it in the EEC. He expressed further qualifications about the dollar–gold currency-pegging of the Bretton Woods system. Such concerns would prove to be far-sighted.[19]

Haberler's remarks can be interpreted as a back-handed compliment to Ludwig Erhard. Like Chancellor Konrad Adenauer, a devout Catholic from the Rhineland, Erhard was a non-mainstream figure whose background might otherwise have consigned him to the fringes of policy-making. His career was an unlikely one for a German living under the Nazis. He was a consulting economist to a retail association. Erhard rose within the proto-government of the occupation era as a compromise candidate independent of powerful rival political factions in the conservative party, the Christian Democratic Union.

Ludwig Erhard was the author of the June 1948 currency reform that sparked recovery and symbolically ended the miseries of the occupation. He stood alone in his advocacy of what, had it failed, would today be derided as 'shock therapy'. But his policies worked, and there was no alternative to them. At a single stroke he wiped out the internal debt, drastically curtailed the money supply, de-controlled prices, and lifted all but the most essential regulations. Since Nazi-era controls had broken down irreparably, only the market could send the necessary price signals to buyers and sellers.

With economic recovery also came revival of the restrictive practices embedded in Germany's organized capitalist traditions. Erhard countered them by unilaterally cutting tariffs and keeping the external value of the Deutschmark (DM) as low as politically feasible in order to stimulate competition in the German market. The results were impressive. German GDP grew from an index of 100 in 1950 to 162 in 1958. Foreign trade nearly tripled over the same period. The rise in intra-European trade was greater still. West German imports grew in both absolute and relative terms. The Federal Republic became the largest export market for France, Sweden, Austria, the Netherlands, Italy, Belgium, and Denmark. German productivity rates increased rapidly, inflation rates fell (which dampened inflation elsewhere), and unemployment disappeared. A model of liberalization and market-based policy-making, Germany had become the economic hub of Western Europe even before the EEC was founded. Unsurprisingly, the primary objective of the negotiations at Messina, and its successors, was to strengthen and perpetuate this role.[20]

In his eloquent remarks, Haberler also tipped his hat to two institutions which had reduced bottlenecks to trade expansion. They were the European Payments Union (EPU), which restored the convertibility of national currencies, and the General Agreement on Tariffs and Trade (GATT), as well as its near-neighbour, the Organization for European Economic Cooperation (OEEC), which specifically dealt with trade-restricting quota arrangements. Both the payments union and the trade forums originated in connection with the Marshall Plan, and each was a valuable precursor to the negotiations for the EEC and EFTA. Though the histories of GATT and OEEC are uneven, they have grown over time as engines of liberalization into today's World Trade Organization (WTO) and the Organisation for Economic Co-operation and Development (OECD).

The EPU was a temporary mechanism for overcoming the dollar shortage and reducing trade distortions dating from World War II and the two decades prior to it. The value of all major European currencies, Britain then being a partial exception, was destroyed by wartime inflation, which made them unsuitable for trade finance. Only the dollar was left to cover the costs of importing the raw materials, machinery, and foodstuffs needed for Europe's economic recovery. The United States was the main source of such goods. Thus a severe dollar shortage choked off growth. The elimination of economic distortions was a secondary purpose of the EPU. Participants in it had to accept the Marshall Plan's Code of Liberalization. The EPU was a dollar-backed clearing house that enabled an exporter to be reimbursed in his own currency. Soon becoming convertible, the DM replaced the dollar as EPU bank capital and in trade. The ease with which interstate commerce could now be conducted, together with the price convergence encouraged by liberalization, contributed to trade expansion, particularly within Europe.[21]

GATT's mission was, as the name implies, to reduce the tariff barriers that had prolonged the Depression. To this end it made acceptance of the most favoured nation (MFN) principle the ticket of admission for its eventual twenty-three members. It also launched three negotiating rounds between 1947 and 1950, which reduced tariffs to levels below those of the prewar period, which the MFN then extended to all contracting parties. Germany set the pace in tariff reduction. A bid made in 1953 to phase in further 30 per cent cuts across the board made no progress, but the policy was later adopted by the EEC. GATT would revive with the so-called Kennedy Round of the late 1960s, and later, in the so-called Uruguay Round, become a powerhouse of liberalization.[22]

In the 1950s, however, the OEEC had a greater impact. Its task was to eliminate so-called non-tariff barriers (NTBs), which often took the form of import quotas. Agreements to eliminate 50 and eventually 75 per cent of them were reached in 1950 and 1951, respectively. NTBs, which could take myriad forms, would re-appear with regularity during economic downturns, were tenacious, are a bane in the Single European Market, and have remained foci in the negotiations for the proposed Trans-Pacific Trade Pact (TPAC) as well as the Trans-Atlantic Trade and Investment Partnership (TTIP). Advances in managing the troublesome NTBs were nonetheless made by the 1950s.

The discussion rounds that produced the EEC involved parallel talks among the six founder members of the ECSC and a long list of former Marshall Plan aid recipients outside it for a free trade area (FTA). Deeply engaged in the Euratom issue, the US generally favoured the EEC over the FTA, but otherwise followed a hands-off policy. Complicated and at times confusing, the talks took unexpected twists, and had an indecisive outcome. The founding of the EEC produced no equivalent to the éclat that followed the Schuman Plan announcement, and no clear-cut national division of opinion within Europe between the customs union and FTA options. On the contrary, with the possible exception of France, organized parties within each country favoured one side or the other, and large numbers of others, even among elites, were confused, indifferent, and wary. The publics of the participating states remained, as usual, in the background, their sentiments disregarded, except for the lingering suspicion of Germans, which ultimately had to be taken into account by the negotiators.

Advocates of liberalization could, in the main, live with either the EEC or free trade options, but preferred, in any case to 'go with the English'. Bound to *dirigisme* and suffering from Malthusianism, the French stood alone in rejecting liberalization, a card Robert Marjolin, representing France, played to great advantage. The other five negotiators strongly favoured the opening of markets, and thus the whys and wherefores at the talks turned on technicalities rather than matters of principle. Even though he knew that Euratom had no legs, and in fact enjoyed little support outside of official circles, Marjolin's repeated threats to terminate the EEC talks led the other parties to make two important concessions which, being hardly in the spirit of Europeanism, benefited only France. One was the inclusion of the French overseas empire in the proposed customs zone, a bonbon for colonialists. The other was to write into the founding treaty provisions for a Common Agricultural Policy (CAP).[23]

No need existed for such a thing. Each founding member state had its own price-support system for foodstuffs. The concession also violated the rules of both GATT and the OEEC. As Marjolin, who negotiated the deal, fully understood, CAP was a straight payoff to French farmers (who ironically had never lobbied for such a thing), albeit one sugar-coated for their counterparts elsewhere in the EEC. Erhard, who had supported the free trade negotiations all along, baulked at the CAP provisions. Disinterested in economic issues and committed as ever to Franco-German cooperation, Adenauer simply overruled him: it had to be the EEC or nothing.

Yet the future of the EEC, at least in its original form, was far from assured. Negotiations with the free trade association (FTA), although led indifferently by Britain, continued, and quite possibly could eventually have been concluded. Since, for a period of several years both parties would be bound to agreements made with GATT and OEEC, trade between the two entities was conducted on an MFN basis of equality for an interim period. There was not much occasion for disagreement. The European Commission had little statutory power, but it surely would have been diluted in a broader organization. Yet this threat would never materialize: the new French president Charles de Gaulle abruptly ended French participation in talks with the British-led trade association, which thereupon transformed itself into the European Free Trade Association (EFTA). It included seven nations: the United Kingdom, the three Nordic countries, Austria, Portugal, and Switzerland. In terms of economic performance, there was little to distinguish between the EEC and EFTA.[24]

Debate among economists about the comparative merits of one or other of the options – free trade area or customs union – reached an early stand-off. One point, however, seems indisputable: the trade area – which was open to all Marshall Plan nations – would have been substantially larger and its potential benefits correspondingly more widespread. The unresolved issues concerned the political side – whether a supranational executive authority was either necessary or desirable. It is a matter that elicited much discussion but little agreement, and would soon be bitterly contested not between EFTA and EEC, but within the EEC itself.

The Treaty of Rome, the foundation document of the EEC, is best described as a 'liberal framework agreement' for a customs union regulated by a 'competition principle', that forbade trade discrimination in any form. Articles 85–94 are at the core of the Community's charter. They set out precise rules for marketplace behaviour and specifically ban abuse of dominant positions by trusts and through state aids as well as public corporations. They also set standards defining both anticompetitive conduct and allowable exceptions to it. These provisions reflect the legal doctrine incorporated into the Basic Law of the Federal Republic and are embodied in a 1957 antitrust regulation that enshrines the competition principle as guarantor of essential rights vis-à-vis concentrations of both public and private power.[25]

Though not a delegate to the several pre-EEC conferences, Erhard deserves moral credit for the inclusion of competition law into the treaty – a special contribution of the Federal Republic. Though a practical man and by no means doctrinaire in outlook, Erhard's policy-making bears the distinct stamp of ORDO-liberal thinking. ORDO was a specifically German school of economic thought that viewed competition as essential to the break-up of the Nazi state-capitalist system, while, at the same time, putting paid to dreams of world conquest. Germany, said a leading ORDO-light, Wilhelm Roepke, 'should become another Belgium'. While Erhard did manage to attach a representative of the German Ministry of Economics to the European Commission, ORDO doctrine has had little subsequent influence in Brussels.[26]

At the same time, the competition principle has been incorporated into EU law in a manner similar to that of the commerce clause of the American Constitution: it has leveraged court authority to enforce sound marketplace behaviour into a legal mechanism that strengthens and broadens the power of a federal government, or in the EU case, a would-be federal government. This turn was unseen by the drafters of the Rome Treaty. The European Court of Justice (ECJ), a carry-over from the ECSC, was included in the EEC as an afterthought, but, as events would prove, a shrewd one. Without the ECJ's ability to enforce laws nationally, the European Union would have been an empty shell.

The statement, made advisedly, must be understood in consideration of the crucial fact that CAP, the farm price-support system also built into the treaty, would, until the 1980s, pre-empt three-quarters of the EU's annual revenues. Unless new sources of funding could be tapped – something hardly possible – little wiggle-room would remain for EU policy-making. It is not surprising, in light of this fact, that other priorities adumbrated in the treaty have been starved for funds and, except rhetorically, largely left out. Social policy has been the main victim of the farm price-support system.[27]

Monnet's influence on the European Economic Community settlement may have been indirect, but it had lasting consequences. The Action Committee (AC) for the United States of Europe, which he had set up after the rejection of the EDC treaty, was at work even before the inauguration of the EEC. Since many of its leading figures had been recruited from the ECSC, the Plan, and other Monnet-inspired projects, and later entered the European Commission, it is all but impossible to distinguish the AC's influence from that of the formal European institutions. Although the goal of the AC was to 'Europeanize' policy-making, in the early phase of its activities, it served as a liaison between Monnet and Washington.

The AC interventions had two main results. In an effort to head off possible FTA dilution of the EEC – that is, the inclusion of its six founder members into a larger organization of former Marshall Plan nations, which were still joined in the OEEC – Monnet succeeded in persuading a well-disposed US State Department into transforming what had until then been an exclusively European institution to one with diffuse international responsibilities. Thus the OEEC became the OECD (Organisation for Economic Co-operation and Development), whose new responsibilities were to include foreign aid to emerging nations. This manoeuvre – whose underlying purpose was diversionary – was a remarkable sleight-of-hand feat.

But the AC did not end its work there. Apparently discouraged by the lack of progress at the EEC, it picked up on Monnet's abiding concern with the atomic issue. It did this, according to Walter Yondorf, 'under the Innocent title of "The Beginnings of a Joint Policy on Nuclear Questions" ', which urged the United States not to wait 'until Europe has achieved political and military unity before dealing with (the matter) in common accord'. It was mistaken, the report continued, for the US to negotiate bilaterally with European nations on atomic issues, since 'only a joint effort by the United States and Europe, which would require Europe to share in the necessary efforts, resources, and burdens, could assure the latter's participation in vitally important decisions relating to the common nuclear defense, arms control, and disarmament'.[28] The Monnet men were swimming in treacherous waters.

## JFK's Grand Design

Overshadowing the early years of the EEC was the presence, even more overbearing than during the Eisenhower years, of the new Democratic administration of John F. Kennedy. Kennedy's design made Roosevelt's look modest by comparison. Its result would have been a trans-Atlantic condominium ruled from Washington, with the EU, and what remained of the West, brought in as junior partners. The plan was a species of ultra-Monnetism too extreme even for The Inspiration. Its pathetic outcome marks the high-water mark of American ambitions with regard to Europe. These were frustrated during Kennedy's lifetime and even before the Vietnam War degenerated into a tragic quagmire, which, as it turns out, permanently relegated Europe from priority number one in American policy to uncertain status on a lower rung of the ladder.

A speech delivered by Kennedy on the Fourth of July 1962 in Independence Hall in Philadelphia was the touchstone of the new administration's policy. It enunciated a new Declaration of

*Inter*-dependence based on partnership between the old civilization and the new. Set against the background of a Cold War, where temperatures were perilously beginning to rise, it was a mighty – even hubristic – attempt to wrap solutions to all outstanding problems relating to Europe in a single giant package. A proposed Trade Expansion Act (TEA) provided the wrappings.

The bill was drafted by George Ball, Monnet's most prominent American disciple in the JFK years. It was meant to provide the president with what has since been called Fast Track authority to circumvent Congress and conclude omnibus foreign trade bills with a single in–out vote, as opposed to what otherwise would be a long, tedious, and most likely unsuccessful procedure. TEA had a special feature. It was to take effect only after the US and the EU together controlled 80 per cent of world trade, a condition that would not obtain unless Britain – then negotiating entry into the EEC – were allowed to join. The bill passed, its fate then shifting to the hands of the imperious de Gaulle, and the somewhat hesitant British prime minister, Harold Macmillan.

As bait, but also a possible solution to the problem of nuclear proliferation, the Kennedy people – in this case meaning above all The Theologians in the State Department – devised an astonishing proposal: it called, once again for a multinational European armed force, this time, however, not an Army but a Navy armed with deadly new Polaris missiles. This so-called Multilateral Force proposal took different forms – first linked to nuclear submarines similar to those going into service in the US, and later to surface ships. Such an armada, it was hoped, would discourage the French from proceeding with their own deterrent, rope in the British (who already had theirs), and slake the (mistakenly) perceived German thirst for nuclear status. As with the EDC, crews would be composed of men representing different NATO nations but still be subject to US command and control.

President de Gaulle publicly sneered that the MLF would be better named the Multinational *Farce*. Laughter resounded in Europe.

For reasons that have yet to be convincingly explained, in December 1962 the American secretary of defense, Robert McNamara, allegedly for cost reasons, without forewarning cancelled the Skybolt air-to-ground missile programme which the UK had counted upon to keep its ageing bomber fleet in service. The US had earlier encouraged the British to drop their rocket development programme, with the assurance that the Skybolt system provided a cheaper alternative. The consequences of the betrayal were disastrous for the British prime minister, who flew to Nassau for an emergency meeting to set the situation aright.

There a conference took place that sealed Britain's fate. Kennedy promised to furnish the UK with the new Polaris missile system in order to save Macmillan's face – and his government. This appeared to be a huge concession and, without anything further being said, might have been. With a range of 2,600 miles, and armed with sixteen missiles apiece, the forty-ship American submarine fleet gave the United States an invulnerable second strike capability. Put another way, the USSR could not hope to win a nuclear war against such a force, either then, or, as it turns out, ever. Correspondingly, the US soon unilaterally and drastically reduced the size of its atomic arsenal.

Nuclear policy had become a plaything of diplomacy. Left unsaid in the Nassau protocols, and unnoticed, was an additional secret clause signed by the British, assenting to a two-key firing procedure, which, at a stroke, stripped Britain of nuclear independence. The new missiles could only be used with American permission. The British left empty-handed in a deal that, inadvertently, also gave de Gaulle just what he had sought: an excuse for blocking UK admission to the EEC on the spurious grounds that it would be a Trojan Horse for an American takeover of Europe. The British, for their part, would have to wait another decade to get in. TEA was dead.

The collapse of Kennedy's plans for Europe brought a symbolic end to a one-sided relationship that was, in any case, normalizing. The European economy was expanding apace; the American stumbling. The fundamental reason for this, as reflected in the rising payments imbalance – a matter especially worrying to the US president – was less a lack of economic competitiveness than – even prior to the mounting costs of the Vietnam War – strategic overstretch. Continued growth in Europe on the one hand and inevitable American pullback on the other translated into opportunity for Europe to advance the integration process on its own. De Gaulle was determined, however, that the EU would not lead the charge.[29]

*Empty Chairs*

Walter Hallstein may not yet fully qualify as a great European, but he surely was an influential one. Monnet's hand-picked appointee to the post of president of the European Commission, Hallstein had cut his teeth in the Schuman Plan negotiations. A professor of law, he was the most rigorous, systematic, and influential thinker in the immediate circle of The Inspiration. Determined to set his stamp on the new institution, he developed an integration teleology, a legal doctrine, and an assertive line of argumentation pointing to the inevitability and irreversibility of the integration process. This too became part of the founders' myth, which, it can be said, Hallstein turned into dogma.

Professor Hallstein harboured a chiliastic vision. He had little doubt that the integration process would unfold quickly, in a matter of years, not decades, and fully expected to be installed as president of Europe. Yet he faced a dilemma. The treaty grants few powers to his office. These he had either to seize from the Council of Ministers, representing the member states, or have thrust upon him by foreign parties, meaning Washington.

Hallstein deserves credit for one major accomplishment: he secured recognition from GATT as tariff negotiator on behalf of the EEC member states. This was an important precedent. The Common Agricultural Policy, however, remained sacrosanct, and the Council managed it. Hallstein's economic authority was limited to enforcing competition rules.

Hallstein feared that unless he established the powers of his office the EEC would dissolve into a free trade area like EFTA, either merging with, or even being swallowed up by it. To become the nucleus of a future European government, the Commission would have to take over management responsibilities from the member states' national bureaucracies. This required French-type indicative planning, in his view less an economic preference than a political necessity in service of a higher cause. To this end, he invented a dubious legal rationale. It rested on a misleading assertion that ipso facto by acting internationally the treaty-signers had intended to create a federation. He thus titled his memoirs (in German) *The Uncompleted Federal State*.

The European Court, he added in his commentary, has subsequently ratified this line of approach, and 'is performing a truly constructive, not to say creative task of law-giving, interpretation, and guidance'. Hallstein pressed for a constitutional convention to codify recent integration progress, but at the same time recognized that the process was what he calls a *création continue* with every step creating new situations, problems, and needs, 'which in turn demand yet another step, another solution to be worked out on a European basis'. Integration in the fields of economic and social policy should be extended, he asserted, 'to defense and foreign policy', and, consequently, 'there should be no restrictive interpretation as regards the outside world'.

Hallstein envisaged a Commission similar to Plato's Guardians, 'unselfish servants of the community who live for the joy of service', and who alone can produce good government. As conceived by him, the Commission should cease to be a mere appendage of the Council, which, as a literal reading of the treaty might suggest, had to approve legislation. Nor, he added, was the Commission's authority limited to taking the initiative in drafting proposals; it was rather 'The Guardian of the Treaties, an honest broker standing outside national interests'. On this point, he insisted, 'the survival of the Community depends'. The Commission should therefore not need approval from the Council on any measures necessary to implement the treaty. He added that 'any reserve powers that the Council may have during the period of transition should be gradually reduced'. He was determined that the Commission would serve as the brains of the EEC.[30]

Hallstein soon found himself on a collision course with the Council, and in particular with General de Gaulle, who deeply resented his pretentions and the pomp with which he surrounded himself on 'state' visits. Dispute over the budget was the immediate issue, particularly whether the Commission would have its 'own resources' or have to request annual contributions from the Council; the change, advocated by Hallstein, would have allowed the Commission to tap CAP revenues. By bringing the matter before the Assembly (a parliamentary talking shop) and, presumably, the public, rather than, as customary, settling matters behind closed doors, the president of the Commission threw down the gauntlet. The notorious Blair House Speech, delivered in Washington, in which Hallstein spoke of Europe as a single nation was the last straw for de Gaulle. But rather than destroy the EEC and sacrifice the CAP, the French merely walked out of Council meetings for six months, bringing operations to a halt.[31]

De Gaulle justified his actions at a September 1965 press conference. Ridiculing those who 'dreamt' of a European federation, a 'project devoid of all realism', and mocking 'the embryonic technocracy, mostly foreign' setting up in Brussels, he called for a return to 'a path of organized cooperation'. He demanded no less than total overhaul of the treaty. What he got instead was the Luxembourg Compromise, which granted veto power to each country represented on the Council. The Commission and the 'community method' championed by Hallstein were both routed. Brussels would be nearly paralysed for the next twenty years. But the integration mythology lived on. Even so, at the end of the decade, when the first stirrings of revival were perceptible, and the integration process resumed, it was under different auspices and without the benefit of teleology, theology, ideology, or even heavy-handed propaganda. Practicality was back, at least for a time.[32]

## Economic Growth

West European economic growth in the 1950s and 1960s – 3.5 per cent in the first decade, 4.5 per cent in the latter – was stupendous and has never been surpassed. It derived fundamentally from a phenomenon of 'catch up' to the most advanced industrial economy, the American, and from the ruins not only of World War II but of the Great Depression. The latter were more than physical in nature: international financial and commercial systems had to be restored and previously sheltered autarchic domestic economies made competitive. The lineaments of world capitalism had to be sewn together.

The EEC's role in this process can be described as perhaps necessary but hardly sufficient. As an economic unit, the EEC was not, of course operational until 1960. It had no hand in generating growth prior to that year. This growth had three primary sources. Initially it involved overcoming physical bottle-necks to production – destroyed factories and power plants, broken bridges, congested waterways, worn-out railroads, displaced labour forces, and so on. The second phase was one of putting together the financial and commercial networks needed for the market economy. The third concerned the organization of domestic economies, and how they could best promote economic growth.

There are several reasons, apart from the obvious one given above, for assigning only a modest role to the EEC in this twenty-year process. The first one concerns the state of economic science. No satisfactory way has yet been discovered to measure either the growth impact of 'integration', itself a slippery concept, or of the EEC. Such estimates as have been made vary from .1 to .15 per cent. The best estimate is that between the mid-1950s and mid-1980s the Common Market may have increased economic growth by 3 to 4 per cent, and the Single European Market Act by another per cent. The contribution of the monetary union having been negligible, Perry Anderson concludes that over the past half century the EU has boosted European economic growth by no more than 5 per cent.[33]

The path-breaking work of Jacob Viner remains the starting point for economic analysis of the EEC/EU. Noting that, by definition, a trade regional association is a second best (when compared to global free trade), he posited that such an association could be either trade-creating or trade-diverting. Viner and his successors, while leaving the ultimate conclusion open, have generally inclined to the former view in the case of the EEC. For the 1950s, however, and only to a lesser extent thereafter, it has been hard to differentiate its impact from that of EFTA as well as to distinguish the EEC from the broader networks of commercial and financial institutions which preceded and set the context for its operation. It has, moreover, proved impossible to assess the *dynamic* as opposed to the static effects of the integration process. How did it influence the thinking of investors, innovators, political decision-makers, and so on? How did it translate into action? What came of such activity? Finally, what of its morphology? What do politics or economics or both have to do with its formation?[34]

A further spate of issues arises when the operations of the regional (as opposed to the national or international) are disaggregated nationally and growth rates then compared. The only way out of the intellectual thicket is to approach the matter historically. Words must fill in where numbers cannot provide satisfactory answers. Thus, in the most widely read work on the present subject, the magisterial *European Economy since 1945*, Barry Eichengreen, a UC Berkeley political economist, assigns a starring role to an 'extra-market' phenomenon called 'coordinated capitalism', his term for what others call 'organized capitalism'. The category includes both the mixed economy welfare state of the post-World War II era and a few cases prior to it, the proto-welfare states of the Nordics and the corporatist economies of fascism, including the former Reich. The theory is questionable.[35]

Eichengreen fully acknowledges West Germany's pre-eminent role in spurring growth in the 1950s, but downplays the importance of Erhard/ORDO policies in it. Instead he praises the tripartite cooperation between industry, labour, and the state dating from World War I, which was updated and strengthened under national socialism. He sugar-coats the pill a bit by making favourable references to the 'Third Way' followed by the Nordics and the Benelux nations, only later to backtrack to express praise for the 'corporate capitalisms' of Franco, Salazar, and Mussolini, which also date from the 1930s. What these share in common was wage restraint, in his view the secret ingredient in the economic policy stew. Thanks to it, good profit margins produced high rates of investment, labour peace, social stability, and low inflation in the 1950s and, to a lesser extent thereafter.[36]

In the 1960s, his account proceeds, France and other previous laggards took up the slack and, in spite of a slowdown in the Federal Republic, growth rates increased until, at the end of the second half of the decade, the first signs of breakdown appeared. In the 1970s and henceforth, for reasons he cannot satisfactorily explain, the once successful European growth model gradually fell apart, and with it also the important supporting role of the EEC/EU in the story. The evidence does not hold up the theory.

Strong growth also occurred in countries where labour relations were poor, inflation high, and currencies volatile. Other 'coordinated capitalisms', notably the UK, Belgium, and Norway were deep in the pack. It follows that the sources of economic success or failure must be located elsewhere.

What happened in the 1960s provides a clue as to where they might be found. In this decade, France provided the model. As in the previous one, changes at the national level far outweighed the importance of anything set in motion by Brussels. The French contribution was not in the form of indicative planning (*dirigisme*) that Monnet-designed and directed as substitute for the 'coordinated capitalism' of the Germans, but a turning away from it. Colbertian by disposition but pragmatic by necessity, de Gaulle, at the instigation of his prime minister, Antoine Pinay, appointed Jacques Rueff minister of finance. Thereupon ensued an astonishing, unexpected and, as events would prove, one-time wave of genuinely liberal reform in France. It produced growth rates of 6 per cent.

In Eichengreen's eloquent words, 'An economy no longer saddled by controls and cartels responded energetically to the reforms.' On 1 January 1960, when the Rueff Plan came into effect, 90 per cent of all trade with European markets and 50 per cent of trade with the Dollar Zone were freed. The Plan tackled the country's chronic fiscal deficits by limiting public sectoral pay increases to 4 per cent, cutting subsidies for nationalized companies, and eliminating pensions for able-bodied ex-servicemen. It addressed inflation inertia by abolishing index linking except in the case of the minimum wage. Capital formation was encouraged by tax provisions allowing the accelerated depreciation of fixed investment . . . and (that) scaled back . . . protection afforded small farmers. The results were out-migration from agriculture, rising farm prices, and elastic supplies of labor to industry.[37]

Stimulated by franc devaluation, French companies consolidated in order to capture scale economies on export markets.

Gross fixed investment rose from 17 to 22 per cent per capita over the previous decade. The French car industry expanded faster than the Japanese. In short, Jacques Rueff was the Erhard of France. The French example had healthy repercussions elsewhere.

The Italians opened to the world, and exports grew at a rate of 12 per cent annually. Even the traditional slow movers advanced. Thanks in part to EFTA, Norway's engineering industry, which employed a third of the industrial labour force, went international. The Danish government ceased to coddle its small firms and rationalized them to cope with trade liberalization. To the same end, Belgium provided tax and loan benefits equal to fully one-third of gross capital formation and reduced capital restrictions for private banks. Even super-Catholic and arch-conservative Ireland joined the liberalization parade. So, too, did both Iberian economies, where 'catch up' – aided, as Eichengreen insists 'by government oversight of labor markets to prevent excessive wage push' – had just begun. In Spain, the 1959 Stabilization Programme unified the exchange rate and eliminated structural distortions.[38] In Portugal, joining EFTA made a crucial difference: growth spurted from a European average of 3.5 per cent to a phenomenal 7.5 per cent by the early 1970s. Exports rose from 15 per cent in the 1950s to 26 per cent by 1973. In both cases these reforms were essential prerequisites for entry into the European Community.

The contribution of the EEC/EU in the 'Twenty Glorious Years', as they became known in France should be considered in light of other more important factors. Among them are the expansion of the labour supply, due both to flight from the Soviet Bloc and the recruitment of guest workers; the shift from farm to factory, which yielded huge gains in productivity; and improvements in specifically European technologies. The American contribution should also not be overlooked. The raw numbers are impressive but do not tell the whole story. As a matter of policy, the US accepted both trade and currency discrimination as dictated by the higher priority assigned to building an Atlantic Community and strengthening Japan, thereby providing a huge boost to exports. This imposed direct costs on American producers and indirect ones due to loss of foreign markets.[39]

Military aid (Under the Mutual Defence Assistance Programme), relieved NATO's European allies of a quarter of their defence costs. American foreign aid to Europe totalled about 11 billion over the over the decade – a rough equivalent to the Marshall Plan. Of at least equal importance were amounts spent by NATO troops and their dependents in Europe.[40] Supplementing these sums by 1960 were ever-increasing inflows of private capital, heavily weighted for the first time to FDI, or foreign direct (as opposed to portfolio) investment. Burgeoning American multinational corporations were a major beneficiary of them. So-called Eurodollar markets, offshore pools of investment funds, accompanied the rise of the multis, as did the spread of transnational banking in Europe and the development of modern capital markets.

The mega-companies would have huge impacts. One of them – as evident in Jean-Jacques Servan-Schreiber's 1967 best-selling *American Challenge* – was to trigger intellectual protest of an American buyout of Europe. But there was more to the matter than that. The multis also accelerated transfers of new technologies and advanced managerial methods. These were already considerable thanks to the Productivity Missions dispatched by the Marshall Plan, which continued to operate in the 1950s. Moreover, the 'American Challenge' unleashed a wave of company mergers, domestically, across Europe and the Atlantic alike. It would be mistaken to conclude that this consolidation had a galvanic impact; its influence was evolutionary, long-term, and continuous.[41] The spread of the giant corporations should not be equated with Americanization. European business did not copy US models so much as adapt them to their own configurations and strategies. They, along with European affiliates of

American companies, began vigorously exporting to the US, aggravating what by 1960 was becoming a mounting concern in Washington with the trade deficit. It was a forceful reminder that the days of US hegemony in Europe were drawing to a close. The heavy hand had been lifted. The time had come for Europeans to do things their own way. Yet the integration process hit a low point in the 1970s and would make little progress for another twenty years.

# CHAPTER 2.

# The Dark Years

The stand off in Brussels during the 1970s did not mean that the integration progress had ceased altogether. It did, however, entail finding new ways to move forward. The route would not be easy to identify. Public enthusiasm for the European project was slight and insufficient to fund additional tasks. A conflict of interest existed between national corporatist alliances, on the one hand, and would-be European counterparts on the other. The tumultuous events of the decade – protests, stagflation, terrorism, and political de-stabilization – moved Hallstein's Capital of Europe to the sidelines. The student riots of May and June 1968 in Paris were the signs of things to come – triggers rather than causes. Copycat examples of the student unrest that had plagued American campuses since the mid-1960s, the French protests in turn soon had imitators in Germany, Italy, and elsewhere in Europe, as well as far-reaching political repercussions. Protesters brought down de Gaulle in France, though not the Fifth Republic, and weakened the authority of governments elsewhere. Strong systems, as in Germany, survived essentially intact. Weak ones, like Italy's, did not. But mounting social unrest became a major problem throughout Western Europe and would continue to be until economic growth resumed in the 1980s.

*Europessimism*
The problems facing Europe ran deep. The oil price shocks of 1973 and 1979 symbolized the miseries of the decade but were by no means their primary cause, which can be attributed to the widening payments and budget deficits run by the United States

beginning in the late 1960s. These triggered successive attacks on the Greenback, which in 1971 brought down the Bretton Woods system of dollar–gold parity, and, along with it, the national regulatory machinery that had buffered domestic economies from international pressure (exogenous shock). Wild swings in currency parities became the new normal. Defensive measures soon cropped up to contain the damage – money printing to ease the pain of adjustment and new forms of domestic and international protection to hold back the tide of foreign competition. The result was the ugly-sounding phenomenon of stagflation – low growth combined with high inflation, which fanned the flames of labour militancy, undermined the resistance of governments to it, and put excessive strains on welfare states. Such headaches triggered the search for better methods of dealing with the crisis. It would take years of trial and error in learning how to apply them.[1]

Beginning in the early 1970s, the president of France and the chancellor of Germany met together in the European Council, an informal, extra-treaty body created to advise Brussels on policy and, specifically, to mount a combined defence against irresponsible decision-making in Washington. To this end, the new Council would piece together a European monetary system. The Council also deserves much credit for orchestrating Britain's admission to the EEC. Constructive cooperation was the keynote at its sessions and sealed the first Franco-German partnership based upon real equality.[2] These were all good starts. Elsewhere, notably toward the end of the decade in Britain, still bigger things were afoot that would take years to unfold. They included bold approaches to accommodate change and to create wealth. Europe in the 1970s was not only the scene of destruction, but of *creative destruction* that would undo the old and usher in the new.

The surveys undertaken in the 1960s by the famous political scientist Karl W. Deutsch are the best available guides to contemporary public opinion on European integration. The results were not encouraging. He and his team found that, while economic change had increased state interdependence and growth, this had not been accompanied by corresponding alterations in behaviour and attitude. Non-Germans continued to mistrust Germans and preferred the British as alliance partners. Only Germans exhibited much enthusiasm for building Europe. Among the vast majority elsewhere indifference prevailed. Deutsch doubted that the future would be much different. Prospects for anything resembling political federation were dim. It would follow that a substantial increase in the EEC budget was not on the cards. Such was in fact the case.[3]

What could be done to advance the European project? The economic thinker Frederick A. Hayek formulated a theory to explain why a system of interstate federalism could only succeed if anchored in free markets and free institutions, whose interaction prevented a stultifying identity of interests between the state and economy. The existing system of mixed economy welfare states of the period ruled out such a path of development. Bela Balassa was the first major economist, and also the last one, to propose an economic logic of integration, whereby in five successive steps it would shift from an economic phenomenon to one with political effects, but the theory met with scepticism on the grounds that the final two of the five involved policy decisions. There is, in short, no morphological economic theory of integration. How did it then resume?[4]

The Hague Summit of 1969 often features in the EU literature as having breathed 'fresh air' into the integration process but did little of the kind. While it made reference to a future monetary union as a policy aim for the EEC, as set out in the so-called Werner Report tabled there, it was short on specifics about how to arrive at the goal. Hans Tietmeier, later president of the Bundesbank, called it 'an attempt to reconcile the irreconcilable'. The Dutch delegate at the summit did him one better, characterizing it as ' a compromise not in the sense that member-states resolved their differences by meeting each other on intermediate positions, but rather they agreed on documents which they felt left them free to push for their own preferences'.[5] In his respect the Report would be a trend-setter.

After the Hague Summit, the Commission sponsored a spate of studies which indicated that what had begun as a myth and been turned by Hallstein into an ideology had hardened into a deeply ingrained way of official thinking: frontal in approach, blind to alternatives, and increasingly out of touch. Such reports typify the state-centred, planning-oriented thinking of the period, and their findings are similar. They all attack what was termed the 'administrative deficit', the first of many such subsequently discovered 'deficits' which Brussels would have to fill in to complete a pre-cast design.[6]

The Werner Plan required, according to a British policy review, 'a new centre of decision-making with decisive influence over the general economic policy of the community and with responsibilities extending to . . . social spheres'. A Commission report of May 1973 echoed this emphasis, calling for an investigation 'along a wide front', including regional, structural, industrial, and social policies, as well as an expanded budget, a central government, massive resource transfers, and a much enlarged administrative machine. Envisaged was 'a Community (with) clear policies on pricing, growth and income distribution, inflation, employment, social benefits . . . and many of the central questions of national politics'. It was, finally, 'necessary to regain control over the Community economy as a whole, which '(otherwise) will be lost at the national level' and thus be 'subject to sharp and politically unacceptable disequilibria'.[7]

A panel of six distinguished economists, all of them subsequently prominent in EU affairs, convened to make specific recommendations to advance the integration agenda. They published its findings in 1974. The recommendations went far beyond the mere coordination of national budgeting called for in the Werner Report. It plumped for *dirigisme*: the 'composition and direction of public spending needs to be analyzed (in terms of) distortions of competition, the contribution to growth, the regional allocation of resources, and the relief of inflationary pressures lest governments compete for private investment at the expense of public investment'. The latter, it follows, 'contributes more to social amenities and the quality of life than does industrial competitiveness'. The MacDougall Report, the most thorough and radical of the period, concluded that to advance the EEC from its 'pre-federal' condition, it would have to extend its authority into new industries and devise 'structural and redistributive policies designed to bring about convergence in economic performance between member states and regions' without which 'further integration of any kind would be unattainable'. This required tripling the tax yield from 0.7 per cent of GDP to 2.2 per cent, a political impossibility.

None of these recommendations were adopted. The cause of integration stasis, as explained in 1980 by Ulrich Everling, a recently retired senior German civil servant attached to the Commission, was obvious. It had less to do with money than member state resistance. The Treaty of Rome called upon the states to harmonize laws in order to eliminate trade barriers, but nowhere had this happened, because the Commission could only coordinate policy, not enforce it. The lack of implementing machinery, he added, doomed a monetary union. The attempt to coordinate economic policy by industrial policy – the EEC philosophy during the decade – was futile. Complicating coordination problems were disparities among the member states in economic philosophy, administrative methods, 'structures', and regional standards of living. 'Procedural tricks' such as the introduction of weighted voting would only increase confusion, he added. Everling concluded that, to survive, the EEC had to become more than an administrative association (*Zweckverband*), but he was at a loss as to how to proceed.[8]

The core of the problem is that only 'negative integration', meaning governance by 'thou-shalt-not' rules of competition policy, had any chance of success as an approach to economic integration. 'Positive integration', entailing policy by directive from Brussels, was a non-starter, because, '(it was) systematically constrained in those areas where national interests diverge and when, in the absence of legitimate majority decisions, opposition cannot simply be overruled'. In addition to which, such market correcting policies, according to Fritz W. Scharpf, harm consumers and reduce firm profitability.[9]

*Monetary Regime Change*

The disruptive event now referred to as the monetary regime change eventually made all the difference. It undermined the state-centred Bretton Woods system in effect since 1945, in which governments controlled international capital flows, thereby making it possible to regulate domestic economic activity and channel public money into the welfare state. By detaching the dollar from gold, President Richard Nixon inadvertently destroyed the Bretton Woods system. He gave little thought to the consequences of his financial decision. It turned entirely on domestic politics. By the late 1960s the dollar was seriously overvalued and the payments gap was widening ominously. To reverse ongoing runs on the US currency required sharp increases in American interest rates, the slowing down of the economy, and an increase in unemployment. Convinced (incorrectly) that a rate boost in 1959 had cost him the 1960 presidential election, Nixon vowed not to let history repeat itself in the upcoming 1972 contest.

The decision to cut the dollar off from gold resulted in an immediate 10 per cent drop in the value of the currency, on top of which the president laid on a 10 per cent import surcharge to protect American producers and slapped on wage and price controls to suppress inflation. Nixonomics was addictive.

Presidents Ford and Carter also inflated their ways out of slow-downs. By the end of the decade, the dollar had depreciated 50 per cent against the Deutschmark. This relinquishment of responsibility by the hegemon was the beginning of a cycle of beggar thy-neighbour-policies that would course through the decade at the behest of a succession of policy-makers.[10]

The real problem facing the international system was the excessive growth of the American money supply. But Nixon cared nothing about it. Although his action undercut the ability of Washington to enforce financial policy, the power to do so was already being eroded by the recovery of private international finance. As governments gradually relinquished controls in the 1950s, and once convertibility had been restored, financial institutions could deal directly in foreign money markets. The change led to substantial capital movements between countries. The most fungible of commodities, money can be transferred at a keystroke, limiting the power of government regulation. Such 'disruptive' flows could not, however, be prevented without rein-stating the old inefficient restrictions.[11]

Trade liberalization widened the horizons of businessmen, internationalized investment, and expanded financial markets. New kinds of international offshore credit and capital facilities – called, for lack of a better term, Eurodollar markets – had sprouted up. Their amplitude, workings, and impacts were little under-stood. Government control over finance, as well as the money supply, had been correspondingly reduced. Central bank interven-tion to restrict capital flows could easily be circumvented through private channels. In a nutshell, Nixon not only cut off the Europeans from American financial hegemony, he undercut the power of governments to regulate markets and flows. The short-term conse-quences were currency turmoil and the rise of protectionism. Over the long run, however, the opening of private financial markets would be the curtain-raiser for a new era of growth and prosperity for the US, Europe, and the world at large.[12]

## Neo-mercantilism

The European economic problems of the 1970s originated in a breakdown of labour discipline. The 1968 protests in France touched off a wave of strikes across Europe which enfeebled governments settled by conceding inflationary wage increases. Costs rose and productivity fell, as did growth. Fiscal deficits increased and trade shrank. Efforts to reverse the situation by tightening corporate relationships failed time and again, as they had in most cases previously. The slowdowns had counterparts in international commerce, where protectionist policies were regressive and destructive. The increased exposure to world trade resulting from the end of dollar–gold currency pegging aggravated existing troubles, not least of all because the defence mechanisms used both domestically and internationally were unsuitable and counterproductive. The decade was indeed dismal.

By 1980 over half the commodities traded on world markets were regulated by convention or cartel. The international protectionism of the 1970s was particularly pernicious. In addition to quotas and tariffs it involved 'coherent systems of industrial protection, each with its increasingly pronounced and entrenched characteristics'. These were generally private or quasi-public in character, regulated loosely, and associated with producer associations. In the words of Jan Tumlir, the chief economic advisor to the OECD, they were 'expanded sectoral . . . industrial protection systems'. Two important new devices – so-called VERs (Voluntary Export Restraints) and OMAs (Orderly Marketing Arrangements) – were a new form of private cartel in which exporters 'voluntarily restricted foreign sales', the most notorious among the many of them was one limiting the sale of Japanese cars in US markets. It raised prices for American buyers and restricted new market entrants in Japan, but, ironically and unintentionally, forced the nation's exporters to move upmarket.[13]

Then, too, new international agreements appeared – for textiles, shipbuilding, and steel – which set output quotas, discriminated against newcomers, especially in the developing world, and raised prices. Since foreign trade connects national price structures to international price systems, without whose signals comparative advantage is lost, the indirect costs of protectionism outweigh the direct ones captured by reductions in bilateral trade flows. They also lead to distortive investments that seed problems for the future. The interdependence of open markets and constitutional government further bodes ill for both when one or the other is absent. Trade protectionism, in other words, fostered neo-mercantalism and neo-corporatism, and vice versa, in national politics as well as at the EEC, over the decade.

It would seem to make little sense to speak of neo-mercantilism in the land of Colbert, the finance minister of Louis XIV, who fathered the policy. The state dominated the economy of France. Electric utilities; the natural gas and nuclear power industries of oil, coal, and steel; telecommunications, and much of the electronic and information technology industries; and the defence and aviation industries – all were in its hands. The remaining sectors were heavily subsidized and never far from the fallout of administrative order, directive, and regulation. The economy of France was the least open of all the six founder members. The liberalization of the late 1950s undermined the effectiveness of national planning, as the economy became exposed to foreign trade. The third Plan (1957–61) all but broke down.[14]

Thus in the 1970s the policy shifted from directing overall economic growth to subsidizing critical industries by the selective use of credit, profit guarantees, and subsidies. The 'Grenelle Agreements' concluded with the unions to end the stand offs of May and June 1968, raised the minimum wage by 35 per cent, reduced the working week by 10–15 per cent, gave union cells special organizing privileges in the factory, and built inflation into the economic system. A quick devaluation provided only a short-lived 'pick-me-up'. Rising inflation soon reached double digits and remained there for the rest of the decade. Growth fell from 4.6 per cent (1969–73 to 3.0 per cent (1973–79). Unemployment nearly doubled over the same years to 6 per cent.

The Barre Plan of 1976 offered a brief reprieve from indexing, inflation, and devaluation. It linked expansionist policy to the medium-term payments equilibrium; in other words, restricted growth. The Plan harkened to a future of economic partnership with the stable Federal Republic, the first hint of what would mark an epochal shift in French policy.[15] At the time France began to glance eastward, and the Federal Republic become more aware of its European responsibilities, the German model of concerted action was losing its allure. The anti-inflationary maintenance of high German interest rates elevated the value of the Deutschmark at the cost of economic expansion and lowered growth and investment rates. Cross-subsidization increased, Voluntary Export Restraints spread though the economy, and domestic quota arrangements proliferated. About 15 per cent of industrial imports were subject to tariffs and NTBs. Subsidies and tax benefits rose to 10 per cent of turnover, most of it going to sunset industries.

Labour-management relations broke down in a dispute over co-determination (*Mitbestimmung*), heretofore restricted to the coal and steel industries, but which the union federation wanted to extend throughout the economy. The unions then renounced 'concerted action', the cornerstone of the tripartite system. Future wage bargaining would be tough and include, as concessions to the union, employment guarantees, quality-of-life considerations, and delays in introducing labour-saving devices. Wage costs would become the highest in the world. German economic performance would be subpar for two decades.[16]

It makes little more sense to talk about neo-corporatism in Italy than it does neo-mercantilism in France. Mussolini proudly invented corporatism. Giant state-owned trusts, closely allied with the reigning Christian Democratic Party (CD), dominated the economy from 1945 to the 1990s. Clientage was the core managerial principle. Entrepreneurship survived only as 'islands' (almost entirely in the north) in a sea of regulations and corruption. In 1973 the Italian Communist Party reached a 'historic compromise' with the CD, which up to then had ruled alone since World War II. The purposes of this deal were, quite simply, to stave off a slide into civil war and to choke off a right-wing coup d'etat. The costs of the compromise were excessive. Wages rose over 11 per cent annually and employees received guarantees of lifetime employment, which actually increased in frequency over the decade. Productivity plummeted. Rates of inflation more than doubled, and the lira fell 40 per cent against the Deutschmark. Much of industry operated at a loss and investment stagnated. Successive governments reacted by pouring money into the state sector. The economy grew thanks to off-the-book sales and devaluations.[17]

Britain's anaemic economic performance was indeed persistent and, since World War II, getting worse by the decade. The Conservative government of Harold Macmillan was the first to adopt modernization as a top priority, as well as the first to approach the EEC. Neither the one nor the other made much difference. The governments of the 1960s and 1970s were characterized by repeated and concerted drives by each of the main two political parties to stimulate the economy. Two obstacles stood in the way of success. The first of them was the overvalued pound, which, under the Bretton Woods system, was pegged too high to the dollar, but even after its breakdown was supported at artificial levels, in theory to protect the City, but in practice in a misplaced effort to keep what was left of the Commonwealth intact.

The other problem was poor labour morale, as manifested in chronic striking. To turn the economy around, successive governments drew lackadaisically on a broad policy-making palette, here on French indicative planning, there on German corporate governance, but nothing worked. Only one government really tried to make a difference. Edward Heath (1970–74) bargained hard to clinch a deal for an income policy with the powerful Trade Union Congress (TUC). A convinced Monnetist, in 1972 Heath also negotiated Britain's membership in the EEC. It did no good economically or otherwise, and, for the next few years, Britain had little influence in Brussels. Heath's undoing was an attempt to cut wages, albeit in accordance with the terms of the recent wage policy bargain concluded with the unions: the result was a long miners' strike that he was determined to break.

He called an election to win a parliamentary majority for his hard line – and lost it. Labour was back, with the second Harold Wilson cabinet, followed by the James Callaghan cabinet. Amid work stoppages and a breakdown in public services, the International Monetary Fund was called in to administer a diet of austerity. It was too late. As Callaghan put it,

> The cozy world we were told would go on forever, where full employment would be guaranteed at the stroke of the Chancellor's pen, cutting taxes, deficit spending – that cozy world is gone . . . We used to think that you could just spend your way out of recession to increase employment by cutting taxes and boosting government spending, I tell you in all candor that that option no longer exists. And insofar as it ever did, it did so by injecting inflation into the economy.[18]

The stage was set for the appearance of Margaret Thatcher.

## A Most Imperfect Union: Structure and Policy at the EC in the 1970s

The European Community (the name change occurred in connection with the British enlargement) was in the 1970s by no stretch of the imagination even a 'partly built house' and surely not, as myth would have it, a proto-government. It lacked the essential attributes of a state, the power to collect taxes, frame a budget, and force compliance with its decisions. Its resources were bounded. It was not sovereign. Powers that it claimed as its own were subject to the judgments of national courts. Executive power was divided – between Council, Commission, and, in a purely nominal sense, the so-called Parliament – and the relationship between them was complicated, cumbersome, and, at least to the public, opaque. In the absence of a democratic mandate, the EC lacked legitimacy.

The aforementioned institutions must get at least *pro forma* recognition in these pages, but in the period under discussion they were of little importance. The 1970s did not feature public power struggles like those in the Hallstein era. The funding situation left little room for new programmes. The times were inauspicious. The institutional machinery created by the treaty was stalled. Decision-making, to the extent that it happened at all, took place in a new ad hoc body, the European Council, and was made privately by two men, the German chancellor and the French president. To be sure, important legal precedents were set, but, as if by stealth, their weight would only be felt in the future.

Brussels was, in reality, a small-scale, foundering operation that could be economically influential only by dint of its affiliation with more powerful private interests – so-called 'industrial policy' being thus the only option open to it. One thing still worked in its favour – the power of myth, which lent to its transactions a significance they did not deserve, but which, at the same time, won the loyalty of those serving the cause of Europe. As for the EC itself, it was an institution on a mission but without the means to pursue it and with major obstacles facing it.

The biggest one, which, being treaty-based, could not be surmounted, was the Common Agricultural Policy (CAP). This has been so universally damned that criticism of it is hardly worth repeating: its costs and inequities are well understood. Less so are its implications for the development of European institutions. CAP consumed three-quarters of the budget, and tightly constricted technocratic policy-making.

The first priority of the Commission had always to be the obvious one of building up its own power, however possible – no easy task for a general staff without an army to command. Thus policy-making was twice warped: by the incumbent legacy of the CAP and bureaucratic imperative. Wise decisions were thus never easy to arrive at, even in a period of relative inactivity. There was one exception to the rule: the inclusion of the United Kingdom, Denmark, and Ireland in 1973 – the first enlargement – put the EC on the right course. Otherwise, policy-making success was limited to 'negative integration', adhering to fundamental principles as enforced by a set of thou-shalt-not competition rules. Anything more ambitious had to contend with crippling conflicts of interest or, if enacted, the likelihood of adverse effects. Its one apparently successful initiative of the period, the Davignon Plan for the steel industry, actually underscores the point.

If, prior to the 1970s the EEC could be crudely defined as a customs union with price supports for farmers and plenty of hot air emitted in the name of Europe, the neo-mercantilism of that decade enabled the Commission to extend its competence into the field of industrial policy. Nothing in the treaty foreshadowed such a role: far from enforcing competition rules, industrial policy encouraged the organization of producer cartels, most actively in three sunset industries – shipbuilding, textiles, and steel – thereby setting examples which spread pervasively into the broader economy, including automobiles, defence, and chemicals. By the mid-1980s, the special relationships of one kind or another would extend through much of European industry, and plans for more of them were high-priority items on the Brussels agenda.

In shipbuilding, which was plagued with chronic overcapacity, high levels of subsidization, and serious competition from Japan (and soon Korea), the Commission negotiated VERs to 'rectify' the situation: the Japanese agreed to hike prices by 5 per cent in order to let European competitors outbid them. This was not enough, however. Averaging 5 per cent in 1972, subsidies had to be increased to between 20 and 30 per cent in France, Italy, and Britain, lest downsizing take place. The sick industry remained on life-support for another decade.

Textiles were a more complicated matter, with many producers in many countries. The international Multifibre Agreement (MFA) had allocated national quotas in 1974, albeit with disastrous results for French and British mills. Working in cooperation with COMETEXIL, the producer association, the Commission negotiated bilateral VERs with thirty of the main exporting nations as a condition for the renewal of MFA in 1978. In the special area of synthetic fibres, where a handful of European producers controlled 80 per cent of the world market, but which suffered from excess capacities of 30 per cent, the industry formed a cartel in clear violation of the competition rules. The Commission looked the other way. The drastic expedient worked temporarily; textile imports, which had increased by over 20 per cent in 1976, fell by 6 per cent the following year. Over the decade, however, 750,000 European jobs disappeared.[19]

The Commission made its biggest impact in the steel industry. The overcapacity that plagued European foundries in the mid-1960s did not lead to market rationalization in which, across the Community, efficient producers would eliminate the uncompetitive. Instead it resulted in overinvestment in national champions, requiring heavy subsidies and cartel formation for survival. The ECSC closed its eyes to such flagrant violations of both the Paris and Rome treaties. Facing new competition, however – much of it from production units using a new 'minimill' technology nearly all of which were concentrated in the Brescia region of northern Italy – cartel defences buckled. In 1965 the producers turned to Brussels for help, more specifically to what remained of the

ECSC, then in the process of merging with the EC. No aid was forthcoming until the various national producer associations formed Eurofer, a stronger organization than the international cartel already in being, which – though already more powerful than anything previous – was a coalition rather than a governing body.

The collapse of steel prices in 1976 spurred the industry into action. In anticipation of such an event, German producers had prepared 'rationalization schemes' in which, with aid from the government, survivors would compensate those who had to be sacrificed. The French followed a similar path, as did, subsequently, all the other national groups but the Italian, who were still adding to capacity. At this point, Viscount Etienne Davignon, the commissioner for industry, assumed responsibility at the request of Eurofer for 'modernizing' the industry Europe-wide. The Davignon Plan had several components. It required the shutdown of the *Bresciani*, pegged prices to the costs of the least efficient Belgian, state-sector Italian, and nationalized British and French producers, and continued to provide state aids for retraining and conversion.[20]

After markets again weakened in 1979, formal production quotas were introduced, and a long-term plan for the phase out of excess capacity entered into force. What had begun with 'voluntary production quotas' had, by 1980, evolved into a 'full-scale compulsory system armed with inspectors, reporting requirements, and fines'. Davignon's office became the de facto planning authority for the industry, in brief the 'something new' otherwise missing in the EC Commission of the 1970s. It stabilized the European steel industry in the short-term, reduced the competitive provision of state aid, and brought about a permanent reduction in excess capacity, but at the expense of the efficient producer, the modernizer, and the manufacturer – and at greater cost and over a longer period of time than necessary.

As a result, Europe missed the minimill revolution taking place in the United States. A stepchild of American protectionism in the 1970s, the minimill has become the surprising source of a steel industry renewal, and is today responsible for more than half its output. One firm, NUCOR, is now among the top producers in the field. It has also been the industry pacemaker. The firm was built by an outsider named Ken Iverson, who in the 1970s built a number of modest works in various parts of the country around an updated version of a German electric arc furnace technology developed to produce low-value bars and structural steel shapes. Thanks to process refinements, however, this changed. Since the early 1980s miinimills have been able to manufacture the full range of steel products, normally at costs far below those of the integrated operations of European mills. Many firms transformed themselves from minimills to 'market mills', and from regional to specialized producers. Traditional 'price making' gave way to 'price taking', as competition heated up nationally, lowering costs across the manufacturing industry.[21]

Minimill economics are quite different from those of the traditional steel industry, and the same is true of its externalities. The minimill is based on electric arc furnace production. It starts with scrap steel rather than with coal and ore, omits both coking and metal-making in the blast furnace, and, consequently, is faster, cleaner, and less expensive than the previous technology. The minimills need not be located close to supplies of ore and coking coal. Because of the high energy content of scrap they save fuel. Little labour is required to operate them; pay is high. Scrap, wages, and electricity are, in descending order, the main cost factors. Proximity to markets is also a major consideration; the new mills are consequently scattered across the country, reducing transportation costs. Furthermore, it takes only two years to build a minimill – not five as with an integrated work; capital costs per ton are only a quarter as great; and labour costs only a fifth. These gains are reflected on the balance sheet. Whereas the traditional sector of the industry is chronically in the red, the minimills have been money-makers.

The improvement of minimill product and process has occurred without either in-house or sponsored research. New technologies have been developed on-site. Though tinkering and 'ad hocery' often leads nowhere, the steel industry results speak for themselves. The minimill provides a model case of entrepreneurial success, and should give second thoughts to advocates of sectoral planning and industrial policy as well as give pause to protectionists, especially those of Brussels still in the saddle.

## A Less Imperfect Union

The question that overhung the European Community (EC), as the EU was known during the dismal 1970s, was not how progress would be made towards federal union, but whether it would survive as a viable institution. It could not vaunt its role as engine of prosperity, because there was none, nor claim credit for maintaining peace in Europe, because détente with the Soviets was under way and disorder bordering on anarchy and civil war posed a very real and frightening threat much closer to home. There was, to be sure, no demand to dismantle and shut down the EC, because there was so little public interest in it. There was plenty of chatter in Brussels about ending the energy crisis, but no meaningful action; Europe's would-be government was an irrelevancy to the *Sturm und Drang* of global oil markets.

Only at the end of the decade, moreover, did it become apparent outside the corridors of Brussels' growing bureaucracy that a serious effort was being undertaken from there to cope with the world financial crisis. Earlier efforts were derided both in the press and private conversation. Under the circumstances, anything that could maintain circulation in the sclerotic circulatory system of the Eurocracy was to be appreciated; hope, there and elsewhere, was in damnably short supply at the time. The

Davignon Plan – the only new task of importance undertaken by the EC over the decade – came in for praise, though its long-term implications were then unknown – but otherwise the record of the EC was, within recent memory, a blank slate.

Yet all was not ill in these unhappy years. Early signs appeared of change to come, not least as it affected the integration phenomenon. A new forum, the European Council, came into being to end the gridlock that jammed the machinery put in place after the Treaty of Rome. By far the most significant institutional innovation since 1958, the Council would give rise to the first efforts to coordinate European monetary policy. The development of European law was also important. A process of 'constitutionalization' took hold in the EU courtroom, and its influence would grow accordingly, whether for better or worse. Finally and unexpectedly, the worlds of both international trade and global finance expanded, became more intertwined, less state-dependent in their operation, and more formidable as agents of transformation, and, it must be added, destruction. None of these developments was unambiguous in character, pointed to specific outcomes, or precluded others. Rather they were each only factors in play. High politics would set the course for, and determine the fate of, the Brussels institutions.

The European Council is an EU anomaly. Its importance grew out of problem-solving, not by the assignment of a mandate, a so-called 'competence' in Euro-speak. It had in fact been given responsibilities in the areas of both energy and transportation, neither of which amounted to anything. The Council did, however, come to grips with the financial turmoil that wracked the 1970s, or at least made a good attempt to do so – a validating chapter in the history of the EU. It began a tradition that could be built on.

The Council does not fit well into either the customary EU narrative or the institutional structures put in place to run the EEC/EC. It did not, in fact, even legally exist until incorporated into treaty law in the Single European Act of 1986. What became the European Council grew out of successive summit meetings of the heads of states and government convened on an occasional basis, beginning after General de Gaulle's resignation, as a forum for discussing long-term policy issues and, beyond that, to supply the leadership lacking at the Commission. The setting was traditional, informal, and diplomatic. The meetings were confidential. Officially, no notes were kept. Staff did not attend. Participation was neither required nor necessarily limited to EEC member states. The Council's very existence attests to the polymorphous character of EU history. It need not in fact have existed as an institution. Its importance turned on personal relationships.[22]

During the years of Georges Pompidou's presidency and Willy Brandt's chancellorship, which coincided, little was accomplished at the Council other than on an agreement reached on British entrance into the EEC/EC. In other matters the two men were often at daggers drawn. Terminally ill with cancer, Pompidou favoured *les grandes gestes* and expressed support for a slew of proposals to reignite the integration process. He baulked, however, once Brandt put the subject of an elected parliament on the committee agenda; this was a strict Gaullist no-no. Brandt had raised the matter simply to vaunt his democratic credentials and to allay residual West European concerns about the serious side of his policy – the *Ostpolitik* that was to open the path to German reunification.

There was, in brief, no meeting of minds between the two men at the early summits, which were noteworthy chiefly for pompous press releases. The Werner Report of 1969 should be thought of in light of this fact. While calling for some form of monetary union, it left the big questions unanswered. Should it provide for a single currency or fix parities between European currencies? Was policy coordination by central banks adequate, or would a new European banking authority be necessary? Would a single monetary policy drive economic convergence or the lack thereof destroy it? Was a new superstate necessary to make it viable? The search for answers to such questions would devolve by default to the new forum.

The Economic Council would come into its own as a policy-making body only when, coincidentally, two strong and like-minded pro-Europeans, Helmut Schmidt and Valéry Giscard d'Estaing, became respectively chancellor and president of their two countries in 1974, and its influence faded rapidly when they were replaced by Helmut Kohl (1982) and François Mitterrand (1978). Its responsibilities were taken over in the 1990s by a succession of intergovernmental conferences, huge, sometimes disorderly semi-public convocations with much adverse political fallout. They bore little resemblance to the old Council.[23] The Schmidt–Giscard partnership marked the real beginning of the Franco-German duopoly that underpinned EU policy-making for another twenty years, and, in that connection, put France on a course of economic convergence with the neighbour to the east which, though intended to strengthen French independence, in fact would slow growth, and, over decades, gradually shift the locus of decision-making away from Paris towards Berlin.

Under the aegis of the Council, the first step towards European monetary unification took place. It involved creation of the so-called Snake, and more specifically the arrangement referred to as the Snake in the Tunnel. The snake in question was the various European currencies, which were allowed to slither around one another, now in one direction, now in another – all of which was to take place within a broader, metaphorically tubular band defined by fluctuations of the dollar. The European currencies in question were those of the original member states, plus those later admitted: Britain, Ireland, and Denmark. Under pressure of hurricane-velocity financial storms, however, the tunnel soon collapsed and the snakes ceased to slither, yet the experiment by no means failed. It advanced European monetary cooperation significantly.[24]

The next stage in the development of a common policy would come towards the end of the decade with the creation of the European Monetary System (EMS). Prepared in secret by Schmidt and Giscard d'Estaing, the plans reflected the determination of the French government to keep France on a course of economic convergence with Germany, as well as the willingness of Schmidt to accommodate this end, even if in defiance of the conservative Bundesbank. Both decision-makers, it should be added, represented, if only virtually, distinct economic blocs: Schmidt the strong small neighbouring northern nations bound economically to Germany, and France the other weaker ones in the rest of Europe. Rather than deal with potential complications, Schmidt and Giscard acted on their own, on an emergency basis, and without informing even their national banks and finance ministers.

The EMS was novel. It was, like the Snake, a loose currency parity system, but its features included a new unit of account, the ECU, and a stabilization fund, as well as a 'trigger mechanism' to keep currencies aligned. It automatically set off fiscal loosening in case a currency – namely the Deutschmark – grew too strong. With the franc under threat, the Germans in fact revalued upward (not downward), and the French, in need of face-saving, devalued only slightly in order to reduce the trade imbalance and stay within the parity bands. The German concession signalled a new willingness to sacrifice for the cause of Europe. There began a long, painful, and sometimes grudging – although by no means steady – Europeanization of German monetary and fiscal policy. Whether in fact it helped or hurt the interests of the Federal Republic is hardly an issue that can be settled in a few words. The same is true of an even larger and equally difficult question: Has it been good for Europe?[25]

The creation of the EMS also raises a third and more intangible issue: Should policy-making in such matters be dealt with behind closed doors? An answer was not pressing in the 1970s, and the decisions arrived at did not have long-lasting conse-quences. Yet Schmidt and Giscard moved monetary policy further away from public control than ever before. In retrospect, more thought should have been given to the importance of this prece-dents. But who would have guessed, given prevalent Euro-pessimism, that the stakes would be much larger in the future? Though weathering occasional battering, the EMS survived. It has now become respectable to argue that, as a result, the European Monetary Union (EMU), with its single currency, was unnecessary. One lesson should, in any case, have been learned from the experience of the EMS: the success of a single monetary system presupposed a similarity of economic condition among participants, in the absence of which the weak would be forced either to suffer or to drop out.

The 'constitutionalization' of law – a third important devel-opment of the period – must be apostrophized because a prepon-derance of legal opinion considers the process of EU law-making less than legitimate. The German Court has, for instance, elabo-rated a doctrine of 'conditional acceptance' of its authority. The European Court of Justice (ECJ) is another EU institutional afterthought, one created by a single clause in the ECSC treaty and later incorporated into the legal structure of the EEC. Its statutory authority was specifically limited to adjudicating between European institutions and their relationships with the member states. The subsequent spread of its jurisdiction beyond this well-defined area of responsibility rests on the 'implied powers' doctrine imputed by Hallstein, as well as ultimately on a teleological interpretation of EU legitimacy, according to the Cornell University Law Professor Jeremy Rabkin.[26] The notion presupposes unwarranted intent on the part of the founders: that the lack of specified powers acknowledged the 'incompleteness' of an implied contract to complete an eventual European federal union.

The legal expert Karen Alter places the ECJ in a somewhat different light. She represents it as a mere 'messenger . . . [for] political bodies [and] . . . responsible for enlarging [their] roles in European politics'. In short, the ECJ is a creature of the EU, and serves it over and above some higher principle [rule of law]. This puts the court 'in the strange position of exercising the authority of a constitutional court – without a national government or a national constitution or anything like a cohesive nation behind it'.[27] Explanations as to how this unsettling state of affairs came about usually emphasize two main points. One is that the court stepped into the breach to implement regulations and directives that the Commission could not enforce on its own. The other explanation is that the national courts, particularly supreme courts, generally – though by no means always – favour the ECJ's ambitions, even though, counter-intuitively, these have been realized at the expense of member-state law.

The legal cornerstone of ECJ power is the supremacy doctrine as enunciated in the famous van Gand en Loos case (1962), the first in a line of precedents holding that EU law takes priority over national legislation, and even constitutional courts. There are no evident limits to the accretion of EU judicial authority, according to Diarmuid Rossa Phelan: 'Any time the constitution of the EC has been clarified, it has become more federal . . . From the perspective of EC law, the EC is very close to a disguised federal nation'.[28] There is, of course, no European 'supremacy clause' like that found in the US Constitution. The ECJ is answerable only to itself.

The Court's most important political impact has been to strengthen the Single Market, above all through the Cassis de Dijon 'harmonization' judgment that requires a member state to respect prevailing product standards in any other. Critics insist that the Cassis case imparts a 'liberal bias' to community law. This may or may not be true. It is, however, undeniable that the preponderance of its judgments has favoured economic growth over social protection, and in that sense has been consistent with the trend in overall policy.

The ECJ bench consists of one judge, serving a five-year term, from each of the twenty-eight member states. Opinions must be unanimous and dissents are never published; its operations are, in other words, characteristically opaque. It does, arguably, have three virtues. Its existence implies respect for legal principle, and therefore supports an important EU mission: the spread of law to nations which previously have not lived under it. The second point is that the 'legal lever' of EU policy enforcement is better than the bureaucratic one, not to mention more overt and violent forms of coercion. Finally, the intertwining relationships between the ECJ and the national courts provide at least a measure of restraint on the actions of a transnational quasi-governmental institution otherwise responsible to no one.[29]Although on a different track – the legal as opposed to the political – the fate of the European Court of Justice will be determined by the EU. The ECJ is not in fact a legitimate constitutional supreme court, but in essence what it was originally intended to be: an administrative chamber. Any grander notion is a legal fiction.

Exogenous change was the greatest source of hope for the EU during the sorry 1970s. While protectionism slowed down the growth of international trade, it did not stop it. Although no one has yet managed to net out the policy alternatives – free trade versus protectionism – over the decade, strong countervailing forces offset the effects of interventionist policy. Generating them was a new postwar interdependence. American exports grew, from 9 per cent in 1960 to 20 per cent by the late 1970s, and imports from 5 per cent to 25 per cent over the same period. American direct foreign investment grew from $11.8 billion in 1950 to $86 billion in 1980, taking ever-larger shares of GDP. The business expert Helen Milner was the first to prove that the relative 'anti-protectionism' of American producers stemmed not only from the enlargement of trade flows but from the increased degree of firm, especially large firm, interdependence.[30]

She found evidence of a similar 'anti-protectionism' in an unlikely place, namely France, leading to the conclusion that 'firms' preferences shaped the state's activity and initiated policy for the sector'. The Harvard University political scientist Peter Hall took the argument one step further in arguing that, quite unintentionally, the *étatisme* of the French, by being forced to ally with industry in order to increase competitiveness, 'fostered the growth of large, dynamic multinational . . . firms . . . much less dependent on it'.[31] Those who would build big, in other words, would have to contend with an intrinsic liberalization tendency, more powerful even than indicated in increased international trade flows – driven by the marketplace and reinforced in the political arena. The 1970s would provide a mere intimation of change to come. What should, or could, be done?

Two social science giants of the era devised integration scenarios which, one would hope, remain relevant today. They lay out paths to the formation of a democratic and representative federal union in Europe. In his famous Reith Lectures, *Europe: Journey to an Unknown Destination*, the prominent Labour Party economist Andrew Shonfield argued that a future European polity would have to be anchored in public consensus and political democracy. He disposed of no special formulas for achieving this result but, while making a few policy recommendations, warned of possible perils that might be encountered on the way.

One of them was a directly elected parliament for which essential mechanisms, and notably political parties, were lacking; appointments should continue to be made, he thought, indirectly by national legislatures. Another red flag was a powerful central bank, which might de-politicize politics and weaken the representative principle. To coordinate between parliaments at the European and national levels, Shonfield suggested setting up interstate boards composed of delegates from bodies at both levels to implement European law which, he stressed, should be made by national courts acting within the framework of common principle. Shonfield also had little use for the European Commission.[32]

The same can be said of the eloquent plea made in the pages of Ralf Dahrendorf's *Plädoyer für die Europäische Union*, published under a *nom de plume* in 1973, which echoed Shonfield's mistrust of technocracy. A renowned Anglo-German sociologist, Dahrendorf wrote from the standpoint of a concerned German liberal. Deeply committed to European democracy, he also thought it a distant prospect. To get to a 'Third Europe', he argued, required economic growth, which could neither be forced politically nor sustained without the market principle.[33]

He proposed making Europe *à la carte* – one step at a time. New institutions would, however, be necessary to advance the integration process, including a central bank-like board of directors to discipline fiscal and monetary policy and maintain open markets. Aware of the political dangers inherent to assigning such powers to an independent board of experts, Dahrendorf did not endorse the idea of a single currency, but rather advocated political coordination of overall fiscal and monetary policymaking. Until conditions had ripened for European democracy, Dahrendorf recommended that Brussels adopt 'flanking measures' like regional, environmental, research and development, as well as educational policies that could eventually produce consensus. Like Shonfield, Dahrendorf counselled patience. He was prepared to let history take its course.

## Monnet's Legacy

In the 1980s EU history did not follow the leisurely democratic route envisaged by a Dahrendorf or a Shonfield, but instead, during the presidency of Jacques Delors, experienced an integration relaunch aimed at the creation of a European federal state.

The technocratic methods of Monnet and Hallstein would be supercharged and applied on a vast scale. The decision to follow in Monnet's footsteps was bold and even rash. Representative democracy was either an afterthought or all but absent in the design of the military and economic institutions bearing the imprint of his security concerns: the European Coal and Steel Community, the European Defence Community, Euratom, and the American proposal, inspired by him, for a Multilateral Force. The coal–steel pool was the only one of these otherwise alarming projects to get off the ground, and it was unimportant in the big picture. Monnet's plans did not always produce political or economic results. Nor were they necessarily sound.

Monnet's legacy lived on not by dint of demonstrated utility but because he inspired a deep-seated hope that integration – driven from behind by the force of history and pulled forward towards the ultimate goal of a united Europe by the strength of an idea – was assured; getting there was only a matter of putting power in the right hands. It was a seductive appeal and one sufficiently persuasive to enable those moved by it to overlook, dismiss, or accept setbacks as mere speed bumps on the highway to federal union. In fact, this very approach had several adverse consequences that led to denial of institutional flaws; downplaying violations of principle; assuming that the experts know better than the people they should serve; and paying insufficient attention to the forces that were driving change internationally. With history on its side, power in the right hands, and inspiration, progress was assumed to be inevitable and irreversible. The most enduring legacy of Monnet was surely the myth surrounding his work.

The real history of the EU and its forerunners followed a different path than that, either then or now, envisaged by its champions. The European Economic Community (EEC), the embryo of the later EU, was not Monnet's handiwork, or conceived as an essential first step towards a united Europe, but grew out of the collective labours of senior civil servants more modestly intent upon strengthening commercial relationships with the Federal Republic, which by the late 1950s had already become the economic motor of Europe. Although structurally sub-optimal as compared to the competing EFTA, the economic philosophy built into the EEC was sound, consistent with constructive international trends, and promising.

Hallstein's state-building approach was not. His struggle with De Gaulle resulted in two decades of political paralysis. Being hamstrung by the CAP deal, unable to wrest power from entrenched national bureaucracies and organized interests or to increase revenues, both he and his successors struck alliances that made the EEC dependent on big business. Industrial policy thus nudged aside the competition principle upon which the EEC had been founded. Simultaneously, laws made in Brussels, as validated and enumerated by the European Court of Justice, encroached upon fundamental rights of national legislatures, a development that unfolded beyond the purview of an unwary public. These were storm signals.

The European integration process took hold in the 1950s and acquired momentum in the 1960s, but it owed less to Brussels than to collateral and concurrent developments. NATO maintained the peace. Prosperity was due in the first instance to 'catch-up', in the second to American money, and in the third to an expanding labour supply. The economic role of the still-embryonic European institutions was at best slight. The economist Gottfried Haberler was the first to identify the trend – a centuries-long increase in international trade – that drove the integration process in postwar Europe: it opened new markets, created novel methods of finance, and inspired modern forms of corporate organization. Together, such advances strengthened global interdependence, tightened the bonds that connected many forms of human activity across borders, created new sources of wealth, and changed economic contexts. In the early

1970s the latter shifted, quite unexpectedly, with the collapse of the state-centred Bretton Woods system. Opened up was a vast new realm of integration possibility, as well as an immense opportunity for the EU – if only it could be properly grasped – to move from the periphery to the epicentre of European affairs.

# PART II

# BEHIND THE CURVE

To make sense of what transpired in Brussels between the adoption of the Single European Act of 1986 and the rejection of the proposed European Constitution in 2004, it is necessary not only to reconsider the history of the EU but to change the very terms that frame the discussion of it. The era began with a much-heralded relaunch into a new realm of state-building but ended with an aborted mission. This flameout has never been properly explained. Not even admitted at the time, it remains difficult to understand what led to it. This may be due to the shock effect of the Euro-crisis. It is not, however something that 'just happened'. The EU was in poor shape long before the crisis broke. Bad decisions were the root cause. Not by chance, they were made in a vacuum, even divorced from reality itself.

The search for what went wrong will take us through an Alice-in-Wonderland world of strange inversions, directionless wanderings, confused identities, and preposterous riffs. We will show how events of the 1980s and 1990s twisted the course of Europe's recent history. To make this strange journey will require entering a mind-set that seems all the more foreign as the current crisis drags on and the European Union slips into irrelevance. The men then at the helm imagined that they were at the cusp of a Brave New World, when in fact they were, mentally, in an old one. Instead of completing the European Project, they almost wrecked it.

During the nearly two decades in question, Jacques Delors – the most forceful leader since Jean Monnet – tried to turn what had, until then, been largely a paper project into a future European superstate, at once Napoleonic in scope and 'Westphalian' in conception. Reference to the treaty ensemble that ended the Thirty Years War in 1648 is inescapable. It marks the inception of the modern nation state. To construct something similar at the European level was Delors' dream, if only because he could envisage no real alternative to it in the rapidly globalizing world. Jean Monnet, Delors' Inspiration, became an integrationist in order to save France after World War II. Delors became an integrationist, it appears retrospectively, in order to save Europe from the twenty-first century.

'During the last decades of the twentieth century', according to the distinguished economic historian Ivan T. Berend,

> a new chapter opened in world economic history: the robust *new technological revolution* led by information and communication technologies, [which] combined with a near-total internationalization of the world economy, or *globalization* . . . the transition from the 1970s to the 1980s became the real watershed for its breakthrough . . . Around the turn of the century, Europe entered the age of a new civilization.[1]

Being rigidly bound to an outmoded set of ideas, Delors misunderstood the fundamental nature of the world historical process; rather than repeating itself as he assumed, it changes in ways that are difficult to predict. The sands shifted under his feet even as he struggled to secure a toe-hold. Intellectual re-runs like the one he embarked upon are bound to fail in a period of transition from an era of slow-moving big institutions to an era of fast-moving big markets, and from a world run by the West to one in which power will be shared with a revived China and India. New approaches are necessary – starting almost from scratch.[2]

By the 1980s it was evident that the pace, amplitude, and complexity of global change required not only fresh policies but new ways of thinking about politics. Margaret Thatcher is the pivotal figure in the process that eventually must lead to this result – the only political entrepreneur of her generation.[3] The mantra of her many critics has been that 'Thatcherism is not an export product'. This is a serious misjudgement, for two reasons. Her economic pills were cures, not nostrums. Her policies, therefore, had purchase. They spread through much of Western Europe, and were adopted, at least in part, by governments of both the *soi-disant* left and the *soi-disant* right because the grave crisis facing the mixed-economy welfare state left them with no other choice. The link between Europe's problems and Mrs Thatcher's solutions was seldom explicit. It was, if anything, an embarrassment to those who adopted them.

Political rhetoric, at least on the left, remained essentially the same in most European countries and changed significantly in only a few. Although forms may have resembled what they had been, the content often differed. Her challenge to the social democratic tradition turned the tables: thereafter the right tended to be progressive; the left reactionary. The one tried to accommodate the agents of transformation by means of 'market-conforming' policies, the other, whenever possible, resisted them, even as foundations crumbled, labour unions shrank, wages fell, and loyalties weakened.

Eventually, and almost everywhere, the traditional left, however grudgingly, gave way to or merged with a stronger political right, even before the collapse of the USSR turned what remained of socialist dreams into nightmares. The two traditional political wings are, in most countries, today all but indistinguishable at both the national and European levels. The politics of Tweedledum and Tweedledee have taken their toll – giving rise to 'populist' parties across the EU. The most important political distinction in Europe is now between such outliers and the two quite similar centrist parties of state.

A second outcome is a distinctly less happy legacy of Thatcherism. As the first important outspoken nationalistic politician of her generation, she rediscovered how to mine a vein whose depth and richness would be tapped by less responsible politicians elsewhere. This should have sounded a cautionary note for would-be builders of the future Europe. The old Europe of nationalities remained very much alive. The identikit Europeans mocked by Mrs Thatcher in her famous Bruges speech of 20 September 1988 in fact inhabited only a few square miles of central Brussels, and its colonies.

The Europeanists had moved – as events later proved – too fast and too incautiously. The architects of the would-be Europe were out of touch with the public. But no one listened, and the house that Jacques built thus would not stand. What remained in its place were the ruins of his work and the ideology that was its guiding force. To rebuild trust will require a new science of political engineering. The attempt will have to confront mass opposition to the very notion of Europe as a political project.[4]

The results were not inevitable. The challenge of globalization, as the massive increase in financial and commercial interchange was referred to in the 1980s, was difficult but not insurmountable. The governments of every European country dealt with it at different times and in different ways, and achieved varying degrees of success. Such attempts should, however, be taken seriously: they demonstrate that the member states of the EU were not behind the curve, but moving up it. The results belie the extreme pro-EU contention that 'more Europe' is necessary because an irreversible process of attrition has sapped the strength of national governments and effectively destroyed their representative character. Things had then not gone so far; there was life in the old dog still. The challenge of globalization, as met by the member states, provided the sort of collective historical experience – a better one than either war or revolution – in which all viable federal systems must be anchored. The architects of the European project paid no heed to this fact, but plunged ahead in a *Flucht nach Vorne* that would steer the ship of state into treacherous waters and eventually almost sink it. The EU thus missed the best chance in its history to become the moving spirit of a new Europe.

Enlargement was another opportunity lost. A potential source of European rejuvenation, the niggardly manner in which it was implemented neither reconciled the peoples of Europe nor imparted a new sense of mission to the EU. The Single Market – the most vaunted achievement of the integration project – was, moreover, left incomplete. Now bulky and baulky, the machinery of governance remained dysfunctional – a third big problem. New technologies met with suspicion, were bypassed, or had their development foreclosed by administrative and political obstruction – a minor issue at the time, but one with heavy future costs.

Above all, Brussels antagonized the public. The days of 'permissive consensus' – when policy conducted in the name of integration would usually be granted the benefit of the doubt – were over. In the future, the public would no longer be satisfied with vague promises; it would demand results. At a time when, as in the 1950s and 1960s, the EU might have ridden on the coat-tails of prosperity, it foundered. Politics-as-usual was not the culprit, but politics-as-the-*un*usual – a forced march to federal union as directed by tin-eared elitists and bureaucracies run amok. The single most outstanding student of the integration phenomenon, Giandomenico Majone, ascribes the shortcomings of the EU to 'total optimism'.[5] There is a better term for it: arrogance.[6]

# CHAPTER 3

# Neo-Liberalism

The two final decades of the last millennium were, for the world, very good ones. The international economy grew impressively, and avoided serious recessions. China re-entered world history. The Soviet Union collapsed, Eastern Europe was liberated, and Germany re-united. Midway through the period, worldwide trade liberalization progressed, providing a welcome spur to growth. The United States was again dynamic. Europe, however, lagged behind, though less in economic respects than in political.

The history of Europe in the 1980s and 1990s is bracketed by developments in the United States and China, whence would originate the current wave of globalization. It is best understood, according to the author of the most substantial book on the subject, Martin Wolf, as a 'long run process with powerful forces behind it. Economics, conventionally defined, is a crucial component of a wider range of positive sum activities that drive ever-widening exchanges, and with these changes, create bigger and more complex political institutions.'[1] Or, one might add, at least *should* have. There was nothing automatic about the intermediation of economics and politics, and Europe proves it. China's rise had little immediate economic importance as viewed from that vantage point in 1980, but in the year 2000 its share in world exports had risen to 16 per cent, driven by growth rates of 12 per cent annually; it had by then become too big to overlook. All but unnoticed in Brussels, India, though still trailing, was following in China's footsteps.

Although still indistinct, outlines of a multipolar world were emerging. Not many Eurocrats of the day gave much thought to what the astronomical rise of the two ancient civilizations – 1.5 billion and 1.3 billion people – might portend. Instead, the power brokers of Brussels grew increasingly obsessed – the word is not too strong – with the United States as a threat to European values. This was a waste of time and energy. The new prominence of the US did not entail conflict but posed an alternative to what Europe thought it stood for. The new American Challenge derived less from shifts in the balance of power due to the collapse of the USSR than from changes in domestic politics and economics set in motion by the so-called Reagan Revolution.

'Reaganomics' must be properly understood. It does not qualify as a new ideology. The president had none of his own, and his advisors fought bitterly over what such a doctrine might entail. Young Ronald Reagan had risen in the world of broadcasting as a radio announcer specializing in the 'recreation' of sports events sent to him on ticker-tape in a studio, which he dramatized and supplemented with canned crowd noise and special effects. As a Hollywood actor and television salesman, as well as later in politics, his work remained related to, but at the same time was divorced from, reality. Thus he could bring himself to tears by memories of concentration camps he thought he had once seen in World War II, when in fact he had never been closer to a battlefront than East Los Angeles. Thanks to his star quality, Reagan still receives credit for having 'healed' the economy, not to mention for having 'won the Cold War'. He does not really deserve such plaudits. He was not a providential figure.

Reaganomics, according to the president's chief economic advisor, was '. . . a return to basic ideas about creating capacity and removing government impediment to individual initiative that were central to Adam Smith's *Wealth of Nations* and in the classical economists of the nineteenth century [that] has characterized most economic policy analysis during the past two hundred years'. The reforms of the Reagan presidency owe as much to a bipartisan consensus as to the man himself. The dismantlement of the telephone monopoly ('Ma Bell') began in the Carter years (1976–80), as did the deregulation of the airlines and the trucking industry. The break-up of such monopolies owed a great deal to separate antitrust cases that had moved their way through the courts. In finance, the breakthrough measure, long prepared in the Department of Treasury, was lifting 'Regulation Q', which froze interest on bank accounts at an artificially low level; its elimination gave rise to new financial instruments and created new credit resources. President Carter, it should be recalled, and not Reagan, nominated Paul Volcker as chairman of the Federal Reserve system. He was the man whose 'tough love' drove up interest rates, forced the country into recession, and set in motion a wave of 'creative destruction' that turned much of the American Midwest into the Rust Belt. The huge 1981 tax cut, the most important reform of the Reagan era, was in fact a bipartisan bill.[2]

Taken as a whole, the policy package of the Ronald Reagan years worked well. The federal budget stopped swelling. Volcker's tight-money policy drove inflation down from 16.9 per cent in 1980 to 3.2 per cent in 1983. It fell even further after the economy revived. Substantial non-inflationary growth was the rule for the rest of the decade. Wages grew, though not much. The labour force increased, as the number of women employed nearly doubled, and the pace of innovation stepped up. New technologies sprang into existence, triggering wide-ranging changes in business organization and social values. Something new and, for Europe, distinctly disconcerting, was afoot.[3]

### Mrs Thatcher and M. Mitterrand

Mrs Thatcher's attempts to reform Britain were of less interest to progressive intellectuals than concurrent changes in France. There, in 1981, for the first time in the history of the Fifth Republic, a Socialist government was in office, which included communists in the cabinet. Inspired by a uniquely French school of left-wing thought then in vogue, François Mitterrand set out in May with his cabinet allies to build a non-Stalinist version of socialism in a single country. Mitterrand spoke rapturously about a 'rupture with the past'. Planning was to be restored to prominence; whole sectors of industry and finance nationalized; unemployment conquered; wealth and political power redistributed from the top down; and the state administration built up. Worker self-management and solidarity were to strengthen democracy, and deficit-spending was to stimulate growth.

Mrs Thatcher was not a well-known quantity when chosen to head her party in 1975. Few fellow Tories could have fully appreciated the extent of her intellectual debt to a small, isolated, and uninfluential band of men (and a very few women), who were the remaining heirs of nineteenth-century British classical liberalism within the Conservative Party. They comprised a small, ill-regarded dissenting minority. The lodestars of Thatcher, and those who shared her views, were: small government, government under law, and open market capitalism. Three overarching and interrelated objectives drove Mrs Thatcher's policy: to break the labour unions, shrink the state sector, and restore confidence in the currency.

Once in office in 1979 she acted decisively. The aims of her first budget were to cut inflation by reducing the deficit and lower taxes on the wealthy. The government also announced a medium-term financial strategy that targeted spending and borrowing. Next she proposed a long lists of cutbacks. A number of Labour governmental institutions found themselves pole-axed, including fifty-seven quangos. Privatization began in June 1979. The British National Oil Company was told to put a large number of exploration blocks up for sale. Within months, the Corby steel plant went under the hammer and British Leyland got orders to clean up operations or face disappearance. Over the next year the government would sell its stakes in ICL (computers), Ferry Holdings and Ferranti, as well as part of its shareholdings in British Petroleum,

British Aerospace, British Sugar Corporation, and Cable and Wireless. Two years later British Telecom, British Gas, and British Airways were all privatized. Mrs Thatcher broke strikes at the coal mines and in the steel mills in 1980 and 1981, and put down race riots in London (Brixton) and Liverpool (Toxteth).

She was at this point the least popular prime minister in British history, when, in the first quarter of 1982 the economy turned up, along with something equally welcome, a nice little war in a faraway place, the Falkland Islands. Argentina's government of generals started it for domestic reasons unrelated to any purported British provocation. For Mrs Thatcher it was a godsend. The hated Iron Lady became, almost overnight, a hero to Britain's patriots. After winning stunning victories in the 1983 and 1987 elections, she could proceed with building her 'Enterprise Culture'. It included selling council houses to tenants, spreading share ownership, abolishing exchange controls, integrating financial markets and production, reducing industrial employment, reforming labour relations, and ending industrial policy – and amounted to a revolution.

Substantial change had come over Britain by the time Margaret Thatcher left office in 1991. The state-owned sector of the economy had been reduced by 60 per cent, over a quarter of the public owned stock, and 600,000 new jobs had migrated from the public to the private sector. The sluggish British economy turned around – grew faster than any other in the 1980s except Spain. Business industrial investment did likewise. Productivity and profitability shot up as well. Employment grew by over 3.3 million between 1983 and 1990, as did productivity. Margaret Thatcher wrested control of the Tories from the Old Guard, and, effectively, Labour from its counterpart, the unions. In so doing she re-contoured British politics. She was the most important woman in the public life of the country since Elizabeth I.

Margaret Thatcher's victories were decisive. She 'identified the national interest and the general interest of capital with

84

furthering the integration of the British economy into the world economy and (obliged) all other sectors to prove themselves internationally competitive or go to the wall'. The future of the British economy would no longer be tied to manufacturing, but to remittances from foreign investment, the growth of international tradeable services, and the continuation of inward investment flows. Thatcher deprived Britain of 'any coherence it still possessed as a national economic (unit)', but, at the same time, made the UK 'the first of Europe's former great powers to relinquish an illusory national economic sovereignty, maintained at great expense, in favor of an unprecedented acceptance of transnational financial and commercial integration'. Put simply: Mrs Thatcher put Britain at the forefront of European change.[4]

*Mrs Thatcher and Europe*
To come to grips with modernization, the nations of Europe had to grapple with the significance of Thatcherism. Herman Schwartz was among the first political scientists to perceive that international market pressures were not only responsible for a shift towards 'less state but towards a different kind of state', one in which growth replaced full employment as the overall objective of policy.[5] The governments of the era all made serious efforts to manage this transformation with the methods of the Iron Lady. Adjustment was relatively easy for some countries, much harder in others. Each faced different political challenges, but they all tried hard to meet them. Out of this common experience might have developed a tradition of national policy coordination that could have provided a strong foundation for an eventual political union.

The Nordics sought to update the welfare state; the Italians, overhaul their political system; the Spanish, overcome the legacy of Franco; the Germans and French, merge their national economic and political traditions; and the Dutch, redefine their national identity. Yet all moved, albeit at different speeds, along the same track. They had something else in common as well: a shared sense of European-ness, the notion that somehow the troubles of their society could be cured at a higher political level than that of their own nation. These were promising beginnings, but only that. Breaking the mould of national tradition was nowhere costless, and the attempt to do it could raise new problems as well as solve old ones. National convergence, however desirable, could not be imposed from above without exacting a high price. Statesmanship of a high order was called for. Descriptive vignettes of selected individual countries will underscore the point.

*The Nordics*

The Scandinavians had to make the greatest sacrifices in order to meet the demands of the age. Home to a fully developed European welfare state as well as often a model for others, the Danes were the first to struggle with the reform issue, but also the first to adapt successfully to the new realities. With the decision to join the financial Snake in 1973 – the first organized attempt to protect European currencies from American-caused monetary disorder – the Danes definitively pegged their currency to the strong Deutschmark, thereby shifting the burden of adjustment to labour. Central wage bargaining was the first casualty, due in large part to the 'drift' phenomenon, the spillover, in other words, of wage increases into the public and non-tradeable sectors. Inflation resulted, and competitiveness suffered. The conservative Schluter government countered by de-indexing wages, cutting the budget, eliminating the deficit, and curtailing social transfers. Labour costs fell, investment flowed in, and growth resumed. These measures were essentially stopgaps.

More important over the long term was the re-configuration of the welfare state, whose expansion ended in the 1980s. The rationale that guided its operation was no longer universal entitlement but rather based on prudential criteria, targeting those in genuine need. Goldbricking decreased and savings resulted. Henceforth a means test applied to flat-rate social security benefits. It also included a new tax liability for wealthy pensioners, who had previously been sheltered. Facilitating such reforms politically was something real but intangible: a mounting conviction that the existing system undermined a sense of civic responsibility. Thus a new achievement principle gradually crowded out the pre-existing ethic of solidarity, the central administration ceded or returned authority to local and regional government, incentives to promote entrepreneurship were put in place, and competition was introduced into the delivery of public services. These policies did not produce a marketized and Thatcherite Denmark but rather strengthened a proud, egalitarian, and independent nation that managed its own adaptation to change and in so doing protected traditional interests and values.[6]

The Swedish transition was substantially more difficult but would prove to be equally permanent. In Sweden national identity had been conflated with the welfare state. By the mid-1970s the public sector had expanded to 70 per cent of GDP, the highest in the OECD. The union movement (*Landesorganisationen*), which included 85 per cent of the labour force, ran the country. The Rehn-Meidner model was the master plan for policy-making. It rested on governmental manipulation of fiscal and monetary policy to restrain aggregate demand below the full employment level in order to reduce wage pressures that might otherwise make themselves felt in the market. The unemployed could then be retrained and shifted from less to more productive labour. Wage compression provided the margin to cover costs; 'excess profits' were then taxed and sluiced back to the government. The policy made little economic sense – Sweden's per capita consumption dropped from fifth in the OECD league tables in 1970 to twelfth ten years later, the worst record of any nation. Repeated devaluations of the kroner were needed to keep the economy afloat. The entrenched interests of beneficiaries made it hard to challenge the existing system politically. Sweden was, for all practical purposes, a one-party state.

Change came suddenly in 1982, and was singularly the work of Finance Minister Kjell-Olof Feldt, a herald of the new market economy. An avalanche of reform legislation followed. The government cut spending, directed state enterprises to make profits, and even privatized some of them. It lifted restrictions on the movement of capital and consolidated the banking sector. In 1988 marginal tax rates were lowered from 85 per cent to 50 per cent, and corporate tax rates fell to the lowest in Europe. The economy boomed.

But all was not well. As the 1980s drew to a close a financial crisis broke that threatened to undo the reforms of a decade. The bursting of a housing bubble caused it. A bad combination of cheap money, excessive tax credits, and inflationary expectations fuelled over-investment in real estate, massive speculation, and household dissaving. The results were horrific – one-fifth of industrial jobs disappeared, unemployment shot up to 8 per cent, and Sweden found itself in the throes of the worst depression since the 1930s as well as in need of still another devaluation. Against such a background, in May 1991 Prime Minister Ingvar Carlsson announced his intention, which soon received backing from all quarters of the establishment, to break from Sweden's long-standing policy of neutrality and autonomy and to apply for membership in the European Community. It was by no means the first time that a country looked to Brussels to get it out of a mess. And not the first time either that – as the rejection of the euro in 2004 implied – its hopes would be deceived.[7]

Among the Nordics, Finland made the most remarkable and, arguably, successful transition from a state-controlled economy to competitive capitalism. The collapse of the Soviet Union may have been the most important date in Finnish national history since gaining independence from Russia in 1917, but it also resulted in a collapse of foreign trade. This only aggravated a dire pre-existing economic crisis, like the one in Sweden that resulted from the bursting of a housing bubble. The depression the country suffered was even worse than that in the neighbour to the west. By 1993 unemployment had reached nearly 20 per cent and output had declined by over 10 per cent.

At this point a new, and very young, prime minister named Esko Aho stepped in. He would set the course followed by subsequent Finnish governments during the decade. Aho announced at once an intention to seek membership in the European Union, which was ratified two years later. He also adopted a reform package similar to previous liberalizers in other nations. Included were tax cuts, tight budgets, deregulation, decentralization of wage bargaining, and privatization. The latter was of particular importance. Capital shortages, not ideology, are what had given rise to large public companies in Finland. In the 1990s, successive governments privatized them once they had become profit-making, and then encouraged foreign investment in them. The value of these companies was monetized, the Helsinki exchange grew and deepened, and the city fast developed into an important regional banking centre.

By 2007, the rise of Nokia exemplified what had become known as the 'Finnish miracle'. A former maker of rubber boots, within a few years of being transformed into a mobile phone manufacturer it became the largest company in Europe by market capitalization. The success of Nokia spilled over into the Nordic telecommunications industries, and Helsinki would develop into a European outpost of the new technology. By 2001, Finland was second on the list of the world's most competitive economies. No other European nation has transformed itself so rapidly from the old to the new economy.[8]

*Italy*
What was possible in Finland was all but impossible in Italy, in spite of extraordinary efforts by a politically virtuous

European-minded elite, which looked to Brussels as a lesser evil to Rome. Clientage – a system of mutual backscratching – reigned throughout the country. It was almost impossible to reform because most Italians, while victims of the rotten system, were also its beneficiaries. It is almost as if the entire country was caught between the horns of the prisoners' dilemma: no one could give way first, even in the common interest, because he could not trust the others.

Breaking out in 1992, the Tangentopolis (bribe city) scandal, was the biggest thing of its kind in postwar Europe. At one point, half the members of the Italian parliament were under indictment for corruption. The shameful affair discredited the entire political system, as well as most of the leading politicians in it, and led to a national mood of revulsion that gave wind to a reform movement led by technocrats, among whom bankers, professors, and leading industrialists were prominent. A determined effort then followed to draft a constitution for a 'Second Republic'. It made little progress, except in respect to a change in voting rules written to strengthen the powers of the president and prime minister, and, specifically, to extricate them from the political bosses in parliament.

In the 1990s presidentially appointed cabinets headed by technocrats alternated in power with those elected, which in 1992 and 2001 brought Silvio Berlusconi and his new 'post political' party, Forza Italia, into office. One need not waste many words on Berlusconi. A clown in politics, but also a media titan, he brought out the worst in the Italian system. Corruption was, at Greek levels, staggering. At least 30 per cent of all economic activity occurred off the books. Cheating, both large and small, paid better than ever before. The only real growth industry was, in its many guises, the mafia. The real tragedy of these years is the fate of the reform movement. What doomed it was the consequence of accepting the lead of Brussels – indeed fiercely insisting upon it.

Italy enjoyed a growth spurt as a result of having, along with Britain, been forced to drop out of the European Monetary System in 1992. But the gains were lost in the fiscal tightening in running up to the euro. Thanks to mighty exertions on the part of successive cabinets (as well as a certain amount of creative bookkeeping), the budget deficits decreased from over 10 per cent in 1992 to 2.5 per cent in 1998, enough to qualify for the currency union. Inflation came down to 1.5 per cent, but so, too, did growth, which in spite of a good start at the beginning of the decade was the most anaemic in Europe by the end of it. Unemployment averaged over 10 per cent. In 2001 Berlusconi swept back into office with a huge majority; he would remain prime minister for another five years. A final term, from 2008 to 2011, would make him the longest-serving head of the Italian government since 1945.

The reform governments made small improvements – significantly cutting public pensions and making (largely ineffective) bids to end lifetime employment and to water down wage indexing. They could otherwise book no signal accomplishments. The bloated national corporations dating from the Fascist era remained at the core of the economy and the patronage system. The financial structure remained archaic, and the Milan stock exchange all but invited insider trading. Privatization in key instances consolidated monopoly power. Regulations became more burdensome. There was also almost no sign of anything resembling 'the new economy'. Research and development outlays remained the lowest per capita of any large European country.[9]

## Spain

Felipe Gonzales served as prime minster of Spain from 1982 to 1996. The country he governed had been ruled by Generalissimo Francisco Franco, who died in 1975, for over forty years. Shaped in the mould of Mussolini's Italy, the Spanish economy was thoroughly corporatist, but in the last fifteen years of his life Franco set Spain on a course of modernization which, while gradually re-establishing contact with the world economy, also provided the working class with security, a form of union representation, and rising living standards. The nation was nonetheless still underdeveloped at the time of the *Caudillo*'s death. Industry was generally inefficient and finance in the thralls of the state; wages were comparatively modest and education levels substantially lower than those in most other parts of Western Europe.

Under Franco, a technocratic elite of economists and lawyers belonging to Opus Dei − a small, exclusive, conservative, Catholic, and highly secretive society − controlled the commanding heights in government and the economy. Gonzales tried to curb its influence, but managed to do so only in part. Success in this respect required substantial economic growth over a long period of time, a functional parliamentary system, and mass support. Each was in short supply.

Gonzales was politically a man of the left but economically became one of the right. The Socialist Party, which he headed, was a post-Franco assemblage of diverse factions claiming an anti-Franco pedigree, and held together more by mutual interests than ideology. Shocked by the failure of Mitterrand's first two years in office, Gonzales adopted the methods of Mrs Thatcher in the name of progress, yet without publicly identifying with them. Future membership in the EU provided a welcome public justification for policies that otherwise might have been hard to swallow. Spain was on the accession path from 1987 to 1994, over which period tariffs were to be reduced to the EU level.

The first of Gonzales' policies was to allow the Moncloa Pact of 1977 − a not-too-distant echo from the Franco years − to lapse. The Pact provided for a tripartite system of labour relations in theory similar to others in Northern Europe. The unions bolted, but rather than try to enforce terms, looked the other way in return for a measure of job protection and a government promise to step up spending in order to mop up unemployment – then sadly running at a near low for the decade, which at 16 per cent was still severe. Full-time employment dropped from 6.5 million in 1977 to 5.9 million in 1984, while those working on a temporary basis increased from 1.3 million to 6.1 million.

Bifurcation of the labour market and high unemployment became the rule from then on. The upside of the policy was economic growth. Following a rapid devaluation of the peseta, the socialist government cut the deficit and brought inflation down by raising rates and reducing the money supply. Wage increases trailed those in productivity. Capital gushed in from abroad, and Spain – then growing at an annual rate of 4 per cent – became an OECD darling for the rest of the decade. But all was not well. By 1990 the peseta had become seriously overpriced. Two years of economic turmoil ensued, followed by the inevitable devaluation.

Gonzales made only limited progress in modernizing the economy. A huge state-owned holding company Nacional de Industria (INI) dominated whole swathes of industry, including the railroads, electrical utilities, broadcast and television networks, gas distribution, toll road and highway concessions, tobacco, as well as oil refining and distribution. Foreign capital eventually shifted the balance of economic power. Inward investment flows increased from 67.6 billion pesetas in 1980 to 156.1 billion in 1984, and from there to 1,973.1 billion in 1990. There was plenty of room for 'catch up', ample opportunity to capture economies of scale and scope in the European Common Market, inexpensive labour, and large and growing demand for consumer goods. A new export-oriented automobile industry became a source of national pride.

Two other issues were harder for the government to deal with. One, a long-term problem, was public sector bloat, a consequence of both high unemployment and political patronage. Party control of office holdings skyrocketed from 67 per cent in

1991 to 74 per cent in 1994. The small administration of the austere Franco soon gave way to a diffuse 'associationalism' reaching down to the grassroots, in which the boundary between private and public spheres were difficult to detect. What brought down the Gonzales government was, however, a quite different problem: financial scandal.

In both Franco and post-Franco Spain the thinness of national capital markets limited government operations to direct dealing with the private banks. The clubby relationship that developed between the two hindered lending to growth sectors. The Spanish banking community objected to the introduction of 'Anglo-Saxon' methods, as proposed in the government's agenda. Protests from the European Union did little good. The opening up of the Madrid stock market, until then dominated by state-owned interests, echoed changes made earlier in London and Paris, but in Spain unleashed an orgy of speculation, pyramid building, and bank consolidation without, however, changing its essentially oligarchic character.

The scandals that eventually brought down Gonzales made great tabloid reading but resemble those of the same years in France, Italy, and elsewhere. They revealed abuse in high places, illegal party financing, and contempt for the public. Some have seen them as representing teething problems of a rejuvenating nation, others as the beginning of a process leading to its downfall. Doubtless there are lessons to be learned of interest to younger members of the EU as well as those nations still in the accession process, which also must make the transition not only from the old to the new economics but from dictatorship to democracy.

The Gonzales years began on a high note and ended on a low one. The two-tier labour system perpetuated social injustice. The concentration of power at the centre distorted policy-making, blurred the distinction between public welfare and personal interest, and invited corruption. Gonzales faced few easy choices. He could not have attacked the labour corporatism dating from the Franco years head on. He had to coddle his shaky party, even at risk of compromising it. There was no substitute for the technocrats inherited from the previous regime.

There also was no alternative to EU accession if only as a national goal. The phased-in tariff reductions were a welcome spur to economic modernization, the convergence course required by the European Monetary System (EMS) in balance was probably constructive, and the promise of a vast customs union attracted foreign investment to the low-wage nation. Yet political awakening and market-based structural reform of the economy are what contributed most to the emergence of the New Spain.[10]

## Germany and France

Those states which adapted least to the new economic trend were the ones who thought they had the most to lose, like wealthy and prosperous Germany and the Netherlands, even though they laboured under a false sense of security. For their part, the French governments of the era all moved forward whenever possible, not with the intention of creating a Thatcherite 'enterprise society', but of strengthening the power of traditional elites in order to become fit for a closer partnership with Germany as equals. These were years in which many enthusiastic words were spoken in Paris about the existence of an idealized 'Rhenish Model', that was supposed to combine the virtues of the two, it was insisted, basically similar economic systems.

The Germans listened with pleasure to the expression of such sentiments, but did little to accommodate them. They were basking in the glory and presumed perfection of their own much-admired *Modell Deutschland*, insufficiently aware that the methods that made them the envy of the 1950s and 1960s were slowly becoming obsolete. Absorbed in the momentous reunification process and, for what from the German perspective was its sequel, the negotiations for the Maastricht Treaty, Chancellor Helmut Kohl had little time or inclination to shift course economically, the result of which was to lower growth in the Federal Republic; transfer its outmoded approaches and institutions to the former East Germany; delay recovery there; inhibit enriching social and economic change in West Germany; and drag the rest of Europe into recession.

The structural weaknesses first felt in Germany during the 1980s worsened in the 1990s, chiefly due to the exogenous event of reunification and the policies adopted in connection with it. A fall in productivity was the chief index of decline and the source of it was a lack of innovation. The structure of German industry remained much the same, and so did its practice of adopting new technologies incrementally. None of the policies brought about anything resembling a breakthrough – were, in other words, what is now called 'disruptive'. High-tech remained underdeveloped. Investment in industry fell domestically, but increased abroad, as Germany became a large capital exporter. These were symptoms of economic fatigue.

The political scientist Wolfgang Streeck provides an excellent explanation as to why the German economy, so well-adapted to the third-quarter of the twentieth century, proved to be so ill-adapted to the fourth. German markets are, Streeck emphasizes, 'politically instituted, socially regulated, and regarded as creations of public policy deployed to serve public purposes'. German firms are, consequently, social institutions: 'Not just networks of private contracts or the property of shareholders, their internal order is a matter of public interest and . . . subject to extensive social regulation by law and industrial agreement'. Germany is best thought of as neither 'statist' nor 'laissez-faire', he adds, but *enabling;* its power to intervene is 'constitutionally hedged by . . . semi-public authorities'.[11]

Deeply conservative and reflective of consensual social values, the German form of organized capitalism is not an export product, but something that developed in a specific national context of interwoven public and private institutions and cannot be replicated elsewhere. The mobilization of public power for market-modifying and market-correcting interventions can in fact only occur in strong states, whereas globalization favours national systems like those in the United States and Britain that have historically relied less on public-political and more on private-contractual economic governance. In brief, it is unrealistic, as the French mistakenly attempted, to build a future European industry on the basis of a German, or Rhenish, design.

Chancellor Kohl's response to unification policy was consistent with German practice and calculated to protect the German social order from being modified by the event. Unification was executed as a giant exercise in 'institution transfer, a wholesale transplantation of the entire array of West German institutions to the former East Germany'. Business, labour, and the political opposition supported the policy. Government, employers, and unions alike committed without hesitation to phasing in wage equality, even though such a policy condemned the industry in much of the former Zone to extinction, deprived its citizens of jobs, and discouraged new investment. It was a formula for high unemployment and massive subsidization. In the first two years after reunification industrial output in the East fell by 65 per cent, and employment in industry by two-thirds, and in agriculture by three-quarters.

With wages pegged to 90 per cent of West German rates and productivity at only three-quarters of the West, for the next decade unemployment averaged 17 per cent, even though a million 'Ossis' (East Germans) migrated to the West. What little investment took place in the former Zone did not produce spill-overs into secondary industry. Institution transfer also involved the implantation, en masse, of West German cadres in the East and therefore internal colonization. There was, as a result, no national communion, but only, in the East, a sense of cultural capture from within and, in the West, a festering resentment of having to co-exist with ingrates spoiled by Communism into un-Germanness.

The costs of reunification would be horrific – 4.5 per cent of German GDP for ten years and declining only gradually thereafter.[12] In Germany, a reform process was not set in motion until the new millennium. It was the work of the last social democratic head of government in Western Europe to adopt crypto-Thatcherite policy, Gerhard Schroeder.

Having returned to the *franc fort* policy launched in 1976, the post-U-turn Mitterrand government, in France, and its successors, followed suit. The right-centre parties in office from 1986 to 1988 under President Jacques Chirac began the reform of the state by reducing its share of Gross Domestic Product by 10 per cent and lifting controls on prices, foreign exchange, hiring and firing, and pay, as well as with a promise to reduce the size of the civil service year by year. None of this quite unfolded as planned, but privatization, once begun, would continue. It followed a different course in France than in Britain. Its purpose – whether through amalgamation or by spin-offs and re-consolidation – was to build national champions able to complete with Anglo-American giants. The minister of finance made the big decisions in this process; industry leaders were seldom consulted, but instead compensated generously, with sweetheart packages of shares sold at giveaway prices. The main union, the Confederation General du Travail (CGT) fought the trend, and in the process lost a substantial part of its membership. Striking thus became more frequent.

Economic liberalism would nevertheless have trouble making its way down from the boardroom to the shop floor and spreading from the factory to the marketplace. Efforts made by Jacques Delors to introduce Rehn–Meidner labour policies, which combined forced savings and labour retraining, and were then actually being abandoned in Sweden, proved equally futile. Only in finance was headway made. The policy of selective lending to industry came to an end and the Banque de France was cut loose from finance ministry control, like counterparts elsewhere. New laws facilitated leveraged buyouts and created employee stock ownership plans, and the Paris stock exchange reformed itself along lines of the Big Bang in London. The only 'model' imported from Germany during the 1980s was that of the German-style universal bank with its close ties to industry. Ironically, at the same time the nation's leading Deutsche Bank launched a huge, long-term, and uphill campaign to restructure along Anglo-American lines.

French rates of growth were moderate during the years of 're-grouping', and enjoyed a spurt at the end of the decade that most experts attribute to employers having circumvented costly social legislation and, notably, the thirty-five-hour work week, which could not be enforced. Such so-called 'leakage' would become chronic. Unemployment, moreover, remained high through the 1990s. To blame was the convergence policy, which, in the EMS, overvalued the franc, tied the currency to the DM, and therefore also bound France to the decision-making of Bonn and Frankfurt, which, with devaluations or the threat of the same overhanging the currency, resulted in retreat or humiliation.

The only solution that occurred to French policy-makers was to create a new currency that would be independent of the Bundesbank: a euro. This, too, would be a misplaced hope. Dictating the policy of France was an emotional need for *la Gloire*, as felt by the nation's ruling elites. It was not, as things would turn out, a feeling shared by the French people themselves. They were quite thoroughly fed up.[13]

## The Netherlands
In the Netherlands, finally, a decade of good feelings anchored in the best-functioning social partnership of the era and a vigorous

reformed economy ended with a terrible crime. The nation had served both as pivot of the EU and lead indicator of contemporary European development. The unofficial leader of small nations in the European Community, the Dutch have favoured strengthening the Commission to offset the power of the big nations, but also mediated between Germany, France, and Britain. Membership in the EU has caused little pain and anguish. The economy of the Netherlands, trade-based and maritime in orientation, has traditionally been open. Even before the Marshall Plan, the Dutch government recognized and fully accepted the implications of the nation's dependence upon Germany. A national consensus developed from an early date on the need to maintain a competitive advantage on the powerful neighbour by keeping wage costs and the value of the gulden just slightly below levels prevailing in the Federal Republic.

A deeply inculcated, even hallowed, political tradition of national tolerance is the mainspring of Dutch national strength. It has, over the centuries, enabled disparate confessional and regional interests to arrive constructively at consensus on issues large and small without sacrificing distinct identities. This 'pillarization' has created a nation in which it may take six months to form a government but which seems to function equally well without one. The windfall discovery of vast resources of natural gas in the North Sea in the early 1970s was a curse in disguise for this placid society. It resulted in rabid inflation, large-scale failures of uncompetitive industry, and record unemployment – in short, the Dutch Disease.

The Wassenaar Agreement of 1982 cured it. Combining social partnership, democratic politics, and economic growth, it succeeded, where so many others failed, according to Pieter van der Hoek, because it 'has to do more with sociology than economics ... and especially with the key word consensus, [something] so rare that it cannot be replicated ... It is not a formula that can be copied elsewhere'. The agreement rested on wage restraint and decentralized collective bargaining as well as opened the process to the market. Medical benefits were reduced and health insurance privatized. The share of public expenditure in GDP dropped from 66 per cent in 1985 to 43 per cent in 2000, the number of jobs grew at four times the rates prevailing in the rest of Western Europe (thanks in part to increases in part-time work), and unemployment held steady at 4 per cent. By 2002 the Netherlands had outperformed nearly every country in Europe for over ten years, had a generous welfare state as well as a firm commitment to the EU, and seemed to be developing into a successful multicultural society at peace with itself.

No one predicted the rise of Pim Fortuyn. He was a complete unknown before 2002, when, campaigning under the slogan of 'Livable Rotterdam', he took first place in the elections for city council in something that can only be described as an anti-immigrant campaign. As in other Dutch cities, a large percentage of the population – in Rotterdam's case 40 per cent – was foreign born, something that in such a compact country could hardly have gone unnoticed. There was, however, little evidence of criminality or social conflict; the presence of so many non-Dutch was not of particular concern. What Fortuyn uncovered and exploited – in a place where such anxieties were thought to be absent – was a vast sense of public disenfranchisement, helplessness, vulnerability, and powerlessness.

Fortuyn was an unlikely political figure, especially on the right: an unapologetic homosexual, who flaunted his preferences in public. But he talked straight, in defence of openness, individualism, and a national tradition of public accountability that the politicians seemed to have forgotten. Fortuyn was not a racist per se; his appeal was rather to the many whom the influx of foreigners had made feel like strangers in their own neighbourhoods. He quite simply did not want any more of them entering the country.

Becoming an instant celebrity, Fortuyn improvised a party –
'Pim's List' – to contest the forthcoming national elections in
May. Forty per cent of those polled agreed that Fortuyn had
'won' the pre-election television debate with the other party
leaders. What might have happened at the polls will never be
known. Pim was fatally shot the day before the elections – not by
a foreigner, as it turns out, but by a mad vegan protesting about
cruelty to minks. The alarming appearance of Pim Fortuyn was
a wake-up call for all who would hear it, evidence of deep-seated
public unrest and mistrust of remote politicians, or of 'populism'
as it was stigmatized in the upper reaches of European governance. The Netherlands, as in so many other things, was a
bellwether.[14]

'Europe' was no panacea for nations faced with the prospect
of modernization in the final quarter of the twentieth century.
The Nordics faced painful problems with the high costs of the
welfare state but solved them nationally in similar ways. The
concerted effort of the Italians to shift the locus of politics from
Rome to Brussels misfired. The Spanish struggled with a legacy
that could not be shunted to a siding, but would take years to
overcome. The French attempt to copy the model of the federal
Republic proved to be unpromising. German methods, which
worked well enough in their own country, were not necessarily
good for the rest of Europe. The Dutch straightened out their
economy, but their embrace of multiculturalism was unrealistic.
The construction of 'Europe' would not be easy.

### M. Jacques Delors meets Europe

Jacques Delors took office as president of the European
Commission in 1985 and remained at that post for ten years. If it
can be said that the fate of Europe was in the hands of any one
person, he was that man. Like Jean Monnet, Delors was a master
manipulator with a powerful vision, in his case, of a Europe
organized like France but strong enough to hold its own with the

superpower across the Atlantic, about which he had highly ambiguous feelings. There is no sense ascribing any higher purpose to his ambitions; there was none. It is also a waste of time to try to identify Delors with any particular school or intellectual or moral tradition. His comments on such things were invariably woolly and tedious, as well as contradictory.

He was a man who should be judged, as he himself must wish, by actions and results. It is misleading to call him a technocrat. He did not attend one of France's *grandes écoles,* but rather applied his extraordinary political gifts to climbing up the slippery ladders of finance and public administration one rung at a time. He was, like Monnet, more effective from behind the scenes than in public and, being loathe to work through chains-of-command, sidestepped them and instead relied on a small circle of devoted supporters to get things done. Delors was anything but a gradualist. He always tried for the big hit – the legislative package, the *grand projet*, the daring forward leap.

He confronted an immense task: to fashion an imagined community into something real, and to perform the feat without benefit of an effective administration, in the face of countries with strong as well as very different national traditions and interests, and in the absence of mass support. It is amazing he got as far as he did: Delors breathed life into a moribund body. But that was all. The process he started got out of hand even before he left office, and far worse was yet to come.

One salient fact about pre-Delors official Brussels was that it was growing. The budget increased, from 1.2 to 2.8 per cent of GDP from 1972 to 1985, with personnel costs and numbers tripling over the same period. Who was this new Brussels civil servant? He was, as a *Wall Street Journal* reporter snidely remarked, 'a bureaucrat without a country [who] for the past twenty years has written rules that nobody had to follow. He has pronounced upon matters that no one particularly wanted him to pronounce upon. He has invented jargon nobody understood.

He has been well-paid, well fed, and universally mistrusted by the people who employed him. He was, and is, a Eurocrat.'[15]

More important, and more numerous than these office holders, however, were swarms of lobbyists, 1.3 for every Commission employee. More than a hundred large corporations, many of them American, set up offices in Brussels. They began to arrive in large numbers after the adoption of the Davignon Plan and soon formed networks of professional associations, law firms, public relations agencies, and ancillary services, the common purpose of which was to build an overall regulatory network in order to capture scale economies, particularly in 'sunrise' markets. Their immediate task was to influence the drafting of regulations and directives for setting product standards. They were influential in this role, if only because the Commission did not dispose of its own expertise, which as a rule it had either to engage from the outside or have provided gratis by professionals in the field.

The relationship between the business community and the Commission was symbiotic: Europe's business leaders helped the Brussels bureaucrats organize and manage programmes that put money in the pockets of their companies and, at the same time, leveraged Commission power. Agnostic concerning the competition principle, Delors was happy to work with big business interests – the necessary building blocks of future Euro-giants – confident that at the end of the day he could assert control over them, as had been done in contemporary France.[16]

Early on – even before the adoption of the Single European Act in 1986 – Delors applied himself to the task of creating a 'European technological community' as a first step towards something even grander, a 'European social and economic space' to complement a state-directed industrial economy. This was a quantum jump in the concept of industrial policy, but very much in keeping with it. It took thirty-five years to produce the first 315 technical directives and regulations. Another 1,136 would be published between 1992 and 1994 alone. Such instructions produced what one economist cited a 'substitution effect, in which member-states tried to cheat their way out of the single market'.

The field of research and development was the new focus of the Commission's de facto industrial policy. Promising future subsidies, Delors encouraged the leaders of Europe's high-tech firms, like Philips of Eindhoven, to set up R&D programmes in the Commission's name. This new 'competence' in scientific research would bear little fruit, but set a bad precedent. The attempt to compress this vital responsibility into the straitjacket of a bureaucratic industrial policy made a travesty of intellectual inquiry and the search for knowledge. It threatened to turn science into a pawn of Europe's politics.[17]

The Single European Act (SEA) of 1986 is rightly heralded as Delors' greatest achievement, but he should share credit for it with others. The proposal originated, and was developed by, industry commissioner Karl-Heinz Narjes between 1980 and 1984, but its inspiration and implementation were Thatcherite. A complicated enactment, the SEA has two main sections (and a minor third one granting co-legislative authority to the parliament). The first and most important part provided for liberalization, as enumerated in 279 proposals contained in a Commission White Paper drafted by Arthur Cockfield, a Thatcher protégé. It aimed at creating an area 'without internal frontiers in which the free movement of goods, people, services, and capital is assured' by 1992.

The elimination of non-tariff barriers called for a comprehensive opening of trade in services and the removal of domestic regulation that impeded competition; required reform of the state as well as the economy; and implied far-reaching changes in the relationship between the two. Included in the package were the elimination of customs procedures, harmonization and coordination of industrial standards and regulations, liberalization of trade and investment, abolition of discriminatory legislation, and the elimination of both preferential public procurement and provision of state aids. Many of the changes called for were concurrent and in line with reform measures taken by national governments.

The second section of SEA was political in character. It replaced the *liberum veto* of the 'Empty Chair' settlement with a new system of qualified majority voting in matters related to the proposed Single Market and, unsuspected by Mrs Thatcher, would serve less as a wedge for liberalization than for expanding the powers of the Commission, the courts, the parliament, and the Brussels bureaucracy, which, as a consequence of SEA, would assume new forms and acquire new functions. Delors used these provisions to turn the development of the EU (as it was now to be called) in a direction never imagined and vehemently opposed by the Iron Lady – towards a European superstate.[18]

Competition policy was, paradoxically, the means to this end. It was in this respect unique and represents the first truly supranational policy of the EU in so far as it is the Commission and not the Council of Ministers or the European Parliament that acts as the EU policy-maker. This policy actually carries 'federal' implications for the future administration and governmental structure of Europe. Consequently, the commissioner for competition policy, among the twenty then holding that rank, was the only one to have first-order responsibilities; the others, even as a whole, accounted for little in the overall picture. Mrs Thatcher dispatched two figures to Brussels to serve as competition commissioner, Peter Sutherland (1984–88), an Irishman who subsequently would head the World Trade Organization (WTO), and Leon Brittan (1988–94), a prominent lawyer and brother of a senior editor of the *Financial Times*. Both jousted frequently and vigorously with M. Delors – albeit with mixed results.[19]

It is impossible at this point to do more than generalize about the impact of an enactment as sweeping and complicated as the Single European Act. It can be stated without hesitation, however, that it has not had the comprehensive and long-range consequences intended by its advocates. Coordination of EU and national antitrust policies has never framed overall policy, and enforcement has been patchy. Practices still vary substantially from country to country, contrary to official claims that the 1992 programme is complete and that a Single European Market (SEM) exists. That is a bureaucratic fiction. In the judgement of the many economists who, from a variety of different perspectives, have studied the matter, the glass is, at best, only half-full. The long string of reverses suffered by would-be EU liberalizers, as well existing EU practice across the relevant policy sectors, confirms the impression. Put another way: the Single European Market is less a crowning glory than another ideology and institution-sustaining myth. It remains a work in progress.

Yet it represented movement in the right direction. The same holds true for the national politics of the member states. All of them, for different reasons, looked forward to 'more Europe' and made strenuous, though not always successful, efforts to work towards it. Together with the effective application of Thatcherite and crypto-Thatcherite methods as well as the liberalization of world trade they proved auspicious, in retrospect perhaps even optimal, conditions for the advancement of the European project.

# CHAPTER 4

# M. Delors' Europe

That Jacques Delors intended to create a federal union seems indisputable, but as to whether his approach to getting there was the right one can be questioned. Lionized at the time as a hero of integration, a second Monnet, his reputation has since declined, but still remains essentially unchallenged within Europhile circles. Yet his methods were devious. Sowing doubt and confusion about the integration process, they contributed to an atmosphere of jobbery, infighting, and grandstanding. Furthermore, he set the EU on a reckless course that would spread policy-making disaster across Europe like an oil slick.

Delors failed to recognize that, as the German political scientist Fritz Scharpf famously pointed out,

> There is not a single type of non-Anglo-Saxon 'welfare capitalism' or a single 'European social model', which could be adapted for the (EU) if only the votes were available in the Council of Ministers. Instead there are diverse, historically contingent and complex national solutions, [which are] deeply embedded in the institutions, values, and established practices of specific societies [and] are constantly evolving and changing only in path-dependent ways.

Any attempt to override such realities would be futile, and thus 'the only solution that could be uniformly imposed would be the Anglo-American form of deregulated and disembodied capitalism' and could only have followed the uncharted course presumed in the thinking of a Dahrendorf or a Shonfield.[1]

## M. Delors' Russian Dolls

It is hard to determine, short of the ultimate goal, precisely what Delors intended to accomplish and how he intended to do it, because he kept his strategy to himself and tactically advanced it in such a way as to keep potential opponents off-balance. His method was one of stealth and deception. He called it the 'Russian Dolls' approach, in which successive painted wooden figures might be opened one at a time to reveal ever smaller but different ones within – the various policy dimensions. The sequence in which this process unfolded was not, as the trope might suggest, pre-set, nor does it necessarily reflect either policy priorities or contingencies. The first Doll was the Single European Act; the second one a financial package; the third one, a monetary and political union; the next one a second financial package; and the final one, a plan for the future. Some 'Dolls' were clearly more important than others. Whether Delors meant that to be the case can only be conjectural.

The most important of the little wooden figures was the one that opened to monetary (and political union) as incorporated into the 1992 Maastricht Treaty (Treaty of European Union). If fully implemented, the treaty would have amounted to a re-founding of the EU and the creation of a European federal government. According to Diarmuid Rossa Phelan, it crossed the constitutional Rubicon to federalism by claiming that the *acquis communautaire* – the entire corpus of EU law and regulation – is permanent and inviolable. As a result, the ECJ has the right to fine any member state that fails to comply with an earlier ECJ judgment; EU citizenship overrides that of the individual state; and the 'movement to the third stage of Economic and Monetary Union' is irreversible.[2]

Whether such sweeping assertions of power could ever be enforced is another matter. The treaty was a bloated, shapeless, jury-rigged compilation, whose total was worth less than the sum of its individual parts, which could not conceivably have been synchronized. One finds it hard to imagine in retrospect that Delors' grandiose plans were ever taken seriously – and a high price is being exacted today for this having been the case. To begin with, the monetary and political sides of the treaty were not articulated, but separated from one another; beyond this, two-thirds of the political side of the treaty was essentially meaningless. One of them – Pillar III – made provision for an armed force, which did not exist or ever would; the other – Pillar II – envisaged (an equally imaginary) Euro-police and security arm. The third section of the political side of the treaty (Pillar I) concerned the development of the Single European Market, an ongoing project with promise. Attached as an appendix to it was a so-called social chapter containing the customary enunciation of lofty principles, but little more. As a blueprint for a federal Europe, the treaty was a non-starter.

By far the most important, and fateful, consequence of the Maastricht Treaty was to create the single currency, the euro, along with rules and institutions thought necessary to make it work. There was no need for such a thing, and many sound objections to the formation of the EMU. The reasons for actually doing so were purely political. The decision to move forward with the project was taken in full awareness of the economic risks involved, but in the absence of any consideration of possible contingencies or shortcomings, and in complete confidence that a new monetary authority, backed by governmental power, would have the will and the muscle to overcome them. The problem was, however, that no such government existed. The expectation that something of the like would soon materialize was unrealistic and attests to the power of the teleological Euro-myth.[3]

Though not reaching back to the Treaty of Rome, a long prehistory of monetary integration initiatives antedates the EMU. The first of them, the Werner Plan of 1970, was unrealistic because it required fiscal policy coordination and the strong Brussels institutions. The much ridiculed Snake of the early

1970s was bold in concept, but also premature; its collapse proved that economic convergence would have to precede monetary union. The European Monetary System (EMS), as regulated by the European Rate Mechanism (ERM), represented a significant advance on the previous endeavours. It maintained similar bandwidths, but provided for short-term lending and a new central bank currency, ECU – actually a basket of member-state currencies – to damper divergences in exchange rates. The system was mildly deflationary, did little to reduce unemployment, but did not significantly impede growth and was, above all, flexible. Its membership was fluid. Countries forced out of the band by payment problems could return to it with a stabilized currency.[4]

Largely as a result of sharp increases in the German interest rate due to the one-time costs of reunification, both Italy and the United Kingdom, their currencies plummeting, left the ERM in 1992. But the crisis was short-lived. The sense of national humiliation soon passed and growth stepped up smartly, especially in Britain. Devaluation turned out to be a blessing in disguise. The departure of Italy and the UK from the ERM put severe strains on the system, yet it had no serious adverse or long-term consequences; above all, the crisis was contained – it was national but not systemic. It neither spread across borders nor plunged Europe into misery. The sensible upshot of the events of 1992 would have been either to loosen the bands of the ERM, as recommended by Sir Alan Walters, Margaret Thatcher's top economic advisor, or to allow the ECU to circulate as a parallel currency as proposed by the British treasury and as advocated for at the time by Prime Minister John Major. Neither idea got a serious hearing in Brussels.[5]

The bankers and Eurocrats on the Delors Committee, who framed EU policy, were hell-bent on creating 'one immutable measure for the whole economy' that could be used like the dollar, a national currency. To discipline spendthrift governments, control of the currency was to be vested in a European Central Bank, which would be independent of Community institutions and of national authorities: '(It) will have as its overriding objectives price stability and, without prejudicing this aim, support for the general economic policy of the Community'. Ominous reservations like those of the University of California, Berkeley professor Maurice Obstfeld were turned aside. 'Tightly circumscribed by obscurely motivated provisions of EU law', he warned, 'the (EMU) inadvertently heightens the risk that political dissentions will be propagated into financial market turbulence . . . [It] is a gamble that can be won in the long run only if it overcomes the existing political stasis to force fundamental fiscal and market reform in the member-states. If Europe's leaders cannot do an end run around domestic opposition in the name of European integration, EMU could prove unstable.'[6]

Economic objections to the design of the currency zone were legion. They began with the straightforward observation that the Eurozone was, because of its diversity, a suboptimal single-currency area, and that the 'buffers' needed to make it work effectively as one – fiscal transfers and labour mobility – were absent. There was also no mechanism to coordinate fiscal and monetary policy but only unenforceable rules, imposed at the insistence of the Bundesbank, that limited budget deficits, the size of the national debt, and rates of inflation. Such constraints had a deflationary bias, a problem in a downturn. The lack of any political counterpart at the European level was an even greater shortcoming: a crisis requiring wealth transfers could break up the EU itself.[7]

All these vulnerabilities – now so painfully admitted, regretted, and grieved over – should have been apparent to anyone familiar with the histories of the EMU's predecessor organizations, in which times of crisis such as that experienced in 1992 brought to the fore very different and deeply ingrained national responses that made policy coordination difficult. The refusal of the Bundesbank to share the costs of economic clean-up from messes caused by irresponsible neighbours was, above all, a constant. These objections, qualifications, and expression of concerns were brushed aside, because the EMU was assumed to have a transcendent mission: it was conceived as a necessary step towards the future federal state.[8] The euro was a done deal before the Wall came down in Berlin.

The Delors Committee met thereafter, essentially to thrash out the timetable for the euro's introduction. In Stage I, capital controls would be lifted, inflation and interest rates were to converge, and exchange rates to be stabilized. In Stage II a new European Monetary Institute would coordinate monetary policy during the final transition, if by 1997 a majority of countries met the convergence criteria. At Stage III, exchange rates would be irrevocably fixed. The deadlines were met, the euro began circulating, and the new financial system based upon it would, contrary to pessimistic predictions, remain stable, and on the whole, popular, for almost a decade. Its apparent success was, however, soon overshadowed, politically, by the collapse of the Soviet Empire.[9]

The prospect of reunification rekindled European fears of German revival and significantly altered the context of the Maastricht negotiations. To allay the concerns of neighbouring nations, Chancellor Kohl loosened purse strings and backed Delors to the hilt. To assuage the French, furthermore, he accepted without quibble the government of France's framework proposal for updating EU institutions, as did Delors. The design of the French plan was based on three so-called pillars: one for the Single Market (I), another for internal security (II), and a third one for foreign and military policy (III).[10]

The treaty that emerged from the proceedings was a compromise document that read like a London bus schedule and was no easier to understand. Some provisions are simply ludicrous, others hopelessly vague. They did, however, grant Delors consequential new powers. The treaty would also serve as the foundation for subsequent negotiations aimed at completing his policy agenda. The gap between its sweeping claims and the feeble or non-existent means of implementing them would, however, have grave consequences in the future. It would be a time bomb.

Regarding Pillar III on foreign and military policy – it is hard to know whether to laugh or cry. It is, to be generous, not empty but *aspirational*. The first Gulf War divided the EU in 1991. The British and French backed the Americans while the Germans stood conspicuously aside. The breakdown of the Yugoslav state was for Europe a much more serious matter, and not only because of proximity; it was a symbolic issue and a test of strength. The Germans and French both came in behind traditional allies. The Germans backed the Croatian and Slovenian successions; the French tried to keep together what remained of the crumbling Serb-dominated state. The American president professed to having 'no dog in the fight'. Luxembourg's Foreign Minister Jacques Poos chortled on behalf of the EU, 'This is the hour of Europe, not of America!'[11]

Apart from noting a memorably asinine remark, nothing more need be said about the EU's defence and security policy in the Balkans. In fact, there was no such thing, and the US would go on to run policy there on behalf of Europe. Yet Pillar III did not collapse. Much strategizing – nearly all of it a waste of time – went into devising ways to escape from under the American security umbrella – a difficult move without an armed force at one's disposal. But who in Europe would pay for one?

The lesson of the Balkans was not learned. Years later others would pay dearly for Brussels' policy of words without deeds. After the Eastern Enlargement, the recovery of Russia under Putin, and the adoption of the so-called Neighborhood Policy, the EU held forth the prospect of accession to Ukraine, a nation of great strategic importance and over 40 million people. This proffer involved much hypocrisy. As with Turkey, Ukraine might be offered association, but never had a real chance for membership in the EU: for that it was too big, too poor, and too foreign. Yet hope dies hard. November and December 2004 witnessed the Orange Revolution in Kiev, resulting from peaceful demonstrations in brutal cold of hundreds of thousands on the Maidan, the vast Independence Square, for freedom, democracy, and alignment with the West. In November and December 2014, after nearly a decade of misgovernment, corruption, and political thuggery, the crowds returned in equal numbers to Independence Square, now dubbed the Euro-Maidan, many among them waving flags of the EU – memorable images of a misplaced faith that the EU would honour the values it purported to uphold and, in some unspecified way, embrace Ukraine.

Things had changed over the decade. Russia had recovered, and Vladimir Putin had consolidated his dictatorship and set his nation on a policy aimed at restoring national glory. The New Russia had little patience for the influence of the western democracies, a matter about which Putin left no doubt, as events would soon prove. Heedlessly – in a grandstanding gesture with a view to entering the history books – the outgoing president of the Commission, Manuel Barroso, offered Ukraine a trade pact which eliminated tariffs between it and the EU. Left unmentioned was the fact that the constructive-sounding proposal did not imply a step towards accession – a matter Brussels judiciously skirted. Unwilling, like most Russian nationalists, to admit the existence of a separate Ukrainian people, Putin warned in autumn 2013 that conclusion of the trade pact would result in military intervention and the possible destruction of the nation.

In late February 2014, with the pro-Russian prime minister of Ukraine, Victor Yanukovich, in flight and with the trade agreement still pending, Russian troops occupied, and would soon detach, Crimea, which Moscow thereupon annexed. Over the following months Russian irregulars, supporting local insurgents, then occupied Donbass. Separate governments were installed in Donetsk and Luhansk. And there things stand. Neither the EU nor NATO offered other than nominal assistance to Kiev. Ukraine lost 20 per cent of both its territory and population. The US and EU together imposed sanctions, which bit into the Russian economy, but failed to dislodge the occupation forces; the boots on the ground are Russian. Let down by the West, Ukraine is the scene of another 'frozen conflict' like those in the Caucuses. EU flags no longer fly over the Maidan.[12]

As for Pillar II, internal security, its first real test would not come until still later, September 2015, when the influx into Europe of over half a million desperate refugees mainly from war-torn Syria caught the EU completely unprepared. Europe soon found itself facing the greatest humanitarian disaster since World War II, as well as its greatest moral crisis and – in consequence as well of the 13 November suicide bombings in Paris – its greatest political challenge. The 1995 Schengen Agreement for passport-free travel within the EU – a major accomplishment, or so it seemed – became a dead letter and institutional unravelling began. The European Union would soon face a crisis of existence (*Existenzkrise*).

Pillar I of the treaty, the Single Market (SEM), was not – like Pillars II and III – hollow, but half-filled. The project formally ended in 1992, and thereafter progress was at best slow and beset by backsliding. The one big subsequent push for liberalization, the so-called Services Directive, which called for reciprocal national recognition of professional qualifications within the EU and thereby introduced competition into the services sector of the European economy, fell afoul of the French *Non!* in the referendum of 2005 on the European Constitution. Progress since then in opening up the economy has been only piecemeal.

The Maastricht Treaty did not, in the end, reflect Delors' own grandiose plans for Europe's future, but did include provisions that both strengthened the Commission and modified its modus operandi. German money was crucial in this respect; Kohl paid most of the bill. Thus the budget was raised from 1.2 per cent of GDP to 2 per cent to cover new spending, above all on a new Regional Policy, conceived as an equalization fund for the poorer member states, but which (after much horse-trading) included the richer ones as well. It became a huge slush fund.

Cuts in the Common Agricultural Policy (CAP) covered a portion of the outlays for the new project. At the same time CAP itself underwent a fundamental shift: from a price-support system to one of income maintenance, which over time would lower overall costs from three-quarters to about half of the Community budget, but shift benefits from producers to land-owners. The reduction of CAP also added to so-called discretionary funding that the Parliament could act upon, and over which it could exercise a measure of co-legislative authority. To reduce the Commission's dependence on the Council, Delors also gained a big concession, the multiyear budgeting cycle. It would no longer be necessary for the Commission to go cap-in-hand to the member states every year. It also shifted to them the onus of the always contentious budgetary haggling.[13]

As a codicil to the treaty, and appended at Delors' insistence, was a 'Social Charter'. The most recent of a long line of frustrated French proposals to equalize wage conditions nationally (and thereby undercut the competiveness of less advanced economies), it is widely regarded as non-enforceable, yet it has generated passionate partisan controversy, especially in the UK. John Major refused to sign it. Tony Blair eventually did in 1996. It is hard to understand the brouhaha. The 'Social Charter' is, like Pillar III of the Maastricht Treaty, aspirational in character. But it lacks substance. The Social Council, which it inaugurated, is a pure talking-shop and often considered the least effective of the many EU quangos. But Delors' proposal had an instrumental purpose that should not be overlooked: it served the cosmetic function of making credible the fictive notion of a 'European

Social Model (ESM)' as a singular EU achievement – as well as something often spoken of favourably in comparison to 'savage American capitalism'.[14]

The claim is unjustified. Europe has of course been social democratic or Christian democratic in complexion for over fifty years, as well as home to the mixed economy welfare state. The European Union has, however, contributed next to nothing to the result, and, if many recent critiques of the ESM are to be taken seriously, has actually undermined it. At every stage in the EU's development, policy-makers have favoured growth and competitiveness over social progress. This is not obvious at first blush.

A European Trade Union Confederation (ETUC) does exist, but has no weight in policy issues, is in reality only a shell, and serves largely as a convenient place to park early-retirees from the labour movement. Real power resides with the national unions of the EU, and attempts to organize across borders have met with rebuffs from Brussels. The decisive moment came in 1987, just after the adoption of the Single European Act, when the national trade unions for the first time made a concerted effort to lobby for a parallel act, which would compensate labour for the upper hand given organized business by the Single European Act.

Previously the two largest national unions, the British Trades Union Congress (TUC) and the Deutsche Gewerkschaftsbund (DGB) had refused to sacrifice their independence for the sake of cooperation with Brussels. Margaret Thatcher's no-holds-barred anti-labour policy galvanized them into action. A two-year campaign, in which the big unions invested much time and money, secured nothing from the Commission more than a Solemn Resolution – in plain English, a non-binding pledge – to support labour's cause. It had no sequel other than more promises. Delors' insistence on including the Social Charter had only one purpose, namely to keep alive the hope that broken promises had betrayed.

It is little wonder, then, that the labour movement, and its constituents, have been more sceptical of EU institutions than any other social class, and today are prominent in the many populist movements that have sprouted up across the union. It is hard to disagree with the judgement of a recent defector from Europeanism that the 'motivations for the European Social Model are orientated more to the realization of the EU and its survival as a system than the improvement of Europe's society' and that the Single European Market has 'now confirmed not just the subordinate position of workers in the EU, but also that welfare is subordinate to the market'. The sources of these changes, the author concludes, are both endogenous and reflect social democratic thinking since 2000, and exogenous 'in that growth in financial markets has contained the scope of welfare expenditure'.[15]

Political Maastricht – vague, unrealistic, contested, and fraught with perils – was only weakly linked to the monetary side of the TEU, the Single European Act (SEA), and the Treaty of Rome. This further complicated the structural problems of the European Union – a species of constitutional clutter that, over the remainder of the decade, would give rise to other and still less substantial treaties. The 'Consolidated Treaties of the European Union', as they came to be known, indeed fail virtually every test of clarity and brevity, and reveal shortcomings in the way the Union works. They should have been replaced by a single document that sets out the EU's mission in simple language and which carefully defines the role and responsibilities of the EU to Europe's befuddled voters. Instead, they would get the proposed European Constitution.

A funny thing happened on the way to the ratification of the Maastricht Treaty. It was considered a sure thing: only Denmark and France had laws requiring it to be put to a referendum; elsewhere legislatures could be expected to rubber stamp it, as they did. But the Danes baulked. It was difficult to explain why.

Denmark was prosperous, a model welfare state, and, according to the polls, the happiest country in Europe. Furthermore, the entire political establishment supported the EU.[16]

There was no organized opposition to ratification. What the well-paid skilled workers and the prosperous farmers of the country who voted in a majority against the treaty shared in common was a vague feeling of resentment at being pushed around by arrogant elites. And so they were. Brussels bullied the small nation into a second referendum that, sweetened with opt-outs and under the weight of heavy pressure, was ratified. It seemed to be of little concern to the Eurocrats that they had to break their own rules to achieve the desired results.[17]

France was too big to shove around. It was not easy, however, to persuade the French to like the Maastricht Treaty. The *Oui* camp presented the most united front mounted by the French establishment since World War II. Included in its ranks were not only the usual political figures, but senior administrators, bankers, businessmen, leading academics, public intellectuals, famous actors and artists, designers, musicians, athletes, several icons of pop culture, fashion designers, and the odd media priest. All of them warned that a *Non* would de-rail European integration, shame France, wreck the economy, revive German nationalism, and be a precursor to chaos. Worried by the polls, at the last minute the massive Chancellor Kohl appeared beside the diminutive President Mitterrand in a pre-recorded television discussion to drive home the point that the consequences of a negative vote would indeed be dire. A day later the French electorate made it fifty-one to forty-nine in favour – a *petite oui* – enough to save the treaty, but nothing more.[18]

## Democratic Deficit

During the decade or so after the haphazard and slipshod Maastricht Treaty was drafted, the Euro-establishment focused its energies on, as it was put, 'completing the European Project'

– in other words, finishing the work left undone by Jacques Delors. A succession of Intergovernmental Conferences (IGCs) then ensued, each of them dealing with treaty revision and together producing indifferent results. Until, that is, the ultimate such meeting, in 2000 at Nice, became so embarrassing a public debacle that the leaders of the EU decided to end the series by means of a constitutional convention intended to draft the framework for a future federal government. A massive build out of existing institutions would obviously be required for the envisaged superstate.

The campaign soon, however, faced a problem: the more that people got to know about the EU the less they liked what they saw, heard, read, and learned. In the thought-world of official Brussels such sentiments were considered simply wrong-minded and needing to be set right. Thus, a growing crisis of legitimacy came, in the jargon of the day, to be discussed as if it were a mere 'democratic deficit' that could be closed by a more effective application of familiar methods.[19] The term 'democratic deficit' is a misnomer. It implies taking something away that had been there before. Democracy has never had a prominent place in the integration process, but served mainly as window-dressing. Thus, for most of the EU's life, scholarly admirers have spoken of its 'output legitimacy' – its ability to produce good results – as opposed to 'input legitimacy', social scientific jargon for the missing piece of the puzzle: representative government.

With the credibility of the efficiency rationale badly tattered after Maastricht – and now in shreds – it behooves one to consider whether, at some point in the EU's history, it might have been possible to reverse course and, instead of building from the top down, to have done so from the bottom up – following, perhaps, the scenario of a Dahrendorf or a Shonfield. Such a battle would in any case have had to be fought uphill and in the face of a highly organized opposition, as well as waged prior to the neo-Monnetist surge associated with Jacques Delors.

Beginning in the late 1990s, public mistrust spread and the EU could do little to contain it. The campaign to transform the EU from a paper project into a political power and to shift it from the wings to centre stage in European affairs may have been doomed by the malfunctioning of the Brussels institutions. Yet the straws that broke the camel's back fell during the post-Delors years: blinkered policy-making, reckless ambition, intellectual impoverishment, demagogy, folly, and sleaze all did their part to discredit the European project.

Overlooked amid the confusion and all but forgotten in the official dialogue of these years was the obvious point that, in spite of the lofty ambitions of Europe's would-be political architects, the EU did very little beyond represent the EU in foreign trade negotiations. It made laws and wrote regulations that the people of Europe were supposed to respect and obey, but it delivered no public services. It taught in no schools, ran no hospitals, put out no fires, and protected nobody from malefactors. It supplied no gas, water, or electricity and maintained no roads, rails, airports, waterways, or harbours. These, and many other such tasks were the responsibility of state and local governments and the things that counted to citizens. What the EU did do, apart from give orders and make rules, was transfer money from one pocket to another – from consumer to farmer, from wealthy to less wealthy region, and from taxpayer to bureaucrat. It is no wonder that political loyalties remained local and national and that significant change in this respect could only be long term and earned by performance and not promise.

The attempt to put Europe on a forced march to unity in retrospect seems ludicrous, even pitiful, but there is more to the story than that: it put European democracy at risk. This need not have been so. Many circumstances worked in favour of the EU. The Uruguay Round unfolding at GATT (General Agreement on Tariffs and Trade), soon to be renamed the World Trade Organization (WTO), promised to achieve on a global scale what the SEA sought to accomplish regionally. The collapse of the Soviet Bloc opened wide vistas of opportunity for the EU, and Europe more broadly. Its basic flaws notwithstanding, the single-currency system worked satisfactorily for several years. The world prospered as never before. Finally, the EU could take pride in several solid accomplishments made in spite of its growing unpopularity, the most important but little appreciated of them being the Eastern Enlargement.

## The Uruguay Round

The Uruguay Round of tariff negotiations concluded in 1994 after eight years of protracted discussion. It came on the heels of previous such marathons, each of broadening scope, which served as both cause and effect of trade growth, and interacted with both the US and the EU as engines of liberalization. The Uruguay Round can be credited with several impressive achieve-ments: cutting industrial tariffs to insignificance; strengthening trade rules; eliminating subsidization and facilitating dispute settlement; and creating new rules applying to services, intellec-tual property, and investment. The trade negotiators also elimi-nated a broad array of non-tariff barriers in textiles, leather goods, and shipbuilding. In short, they undid much of the damage inflicted by the neo-mercantalism of the 1970s.[20]

The Uruguay Round set an agenda for the future, including a timetable for reducing levels of subsidies in agriculture and phas-ing in a shift from price supports to income replacement, a policy implemented by Delors in the EU. Included on the agenda were provisions for examining ongoing operations: expanding trade in services, and reducing abusive practices in government purchas-ing, health, product safety, environmental protection, and vari-ous other fields in which market-restricting practices were used.

These issues were to be taken up in the new Millennial Round, which aimed at the elimination of all remaining trade barriers between 2010 and 2020. Neither this hope, nor the new 'trans-governmentalism' that was to be part and parcel of it, have yet materialized. Not for over another decade would the most recent cycle of trade liberalization begin. This one would feature parallel negotiations for two new ocean-spanning trade blocs, the Trans-Pacific Partnership (TPAC) and the Trans-Atlantic Trade and Investment Treaty (TTIP). The future of the EU may well depend on their outcomes.

## Breakdown

Scholars have never managed to explain convincingly why the Brussels governance machinery broke down in the 1990s. This is not surprising given its bewildering complexity. One looks in vain for a route map of some kind to lead the uninitiated through the constitutional maze, not to mention the byzantine proce-dures, of the EU. Yet much policy-making has taken place outside these frameworks as well, sometimes on the basis of new administrative or judicial rules but at other times in the absence of them. Legality is a relative term when applied to Brussels: it amounts, in large part, to what the EU, or its courts, says it is. Rules are made but then violated with impunity; exceptions to them are frequent – or they are simply overlooked or enforced arbitrarily without the consent, or often even knowledge, of the governed. Procedures are opaque, transparency is a rare commodity, and accountability – both in the sense of bookkeep-ing and democratic responsibility – is missing. Honesty is often an early casualty of the situation.

Institutional deficiencies also play a role in undermining support for the EU. Policy gridlock, or something close to it, has often been the rule. Lack of coordination is another enduring trait. This was the case even with the community of the six founder members. Advances in the integration process have required either the ad hoc creation of institutions like the European Council; the assertion of novel powers by an existing one, as during the Delors years; or the application of new methods in conjunction with the discharge of new 'competences'. No EU institution has ever disappeared altogether, adding to the institutional snaggles.

The salient points that should be borne in mind in examining the peculiar operation of this unnecessarily complex system are the following. The Commission has, except during the Delors years, never provided effective leadership and lacks the necessary muscle to enforce its regulations and directives. Yet it retains sole authority to draft and initiate legislation. Final decision-making, as well as national-level implementation, rests with the member states either individually or collectively through the Council of Ministers and the European Council. Unanimity obviously being difficult to achieve with an enlarging membership, the veto rule has given way to qualified majority voting, which complicates the policy process.[21] Most issues can be resolved only in bargaining behind closed doors, with differences being aired later in public. The ineffectual 700-plus-member Parliament, finally, has limited co-legislative authority but much access to the media, a state of affairs conducive to cheap-shot demagogy. A system with such a convoluted division of powers is necessarily slow-moving, immobilized by numerous veto points, and divided as to roles and responsibilities. It is hard for it to act credibly at the best of times.

The EU also suffers from deep-seated administrative problems. Although the European Council has its own large staffs, the Commission is at the heart of the troubles – with 30,000 or so unionized civil servants, who cannot be moved, let alone fired, and who count on support from their home countries when things get a bit hot. Unlike national civil servants, they have no real masters but answer only to political appointees of a different nationality, many of them mediocrities, and most of them isolated from one another.

These officials earn upwards of $300,000 per year, pay taxes of only 16 per cent on their base salary, and net three times as much – and in poorer countries far more – than their national counterparts. Their emoluments include bonuses of 16 per cent for living abroad, monthly household and child allowances, free private school tuition, cash rewards for becoming a parent, and moving fees as well as settling in costs. Medical coverage is generous and pensions pay up to 70 per cent of salary. This almost embarrassing profusion of benefits produces what is known at the Commission as the 'wink-wink culture'. Friends, in other words, don't snitch on friends.[22]

The Commission is not a cohesive body. An inverse correlation exists between the sizes and strengths of its twenty-plus directorates – which are dished out on a *juste retour* (proportionality) basis – with some of them conveying the impression of providing unemployment relief for the educated middle class. Only a few directorates have policy-making authority. Adding to the confusion is the growing importance of quangos (quasi-governmental organizations) created to provide in-house expertise, lobby for special programmes, and give the impression of activity in policy areas when there is in fact little or nothing to do except to keep the European Dream alive and well.

A large part of the problem is a lack of financial controls.[23] It arises in part because the rigid multiyear budgeting cycle leaves deep pools of money unspent and unaccounted for. The Commission has consistently failed annual audits by the EU's own Court of Auditors for over twenty years. The few examples cited here can only hint at what these reviews have turned up. In 2003 only 10 per cent of payments made by the Commission 'faithfully reflect(ed) budgets and expenditures', the remaining 90 per cent could not be accounted for. Estimates of graft run from 7 per cent to 37 per cent of total expenditures. The EU's feeble anti-corruption squad (OLAF) uncovered over 10,000 cases of larceny in 2002, and little of the lost money could ever be recovered. Only 10 per cent of the CAP payment stolen by Italians from 1971 to 2002 was ever collected. The full extent of losses due to theft and poor bookkeeping will remain unknown,

not least of all because whistle-blowers have been regularly perse-
cuted and punished. Recurrent financial scandals have inevitably
resulted.[24]

In March 1999 a Committee of Wise Men set up to investigate
allegations of fraud made by an obscure Commission accountant made a surprise announcement: Edith Cresson, the French
commissioner for research and education, had, among other
derelictions, awarded a multimillion-euro contract for a study of
AIDS in Africa to her hometown dentist. Mme Cresson, a protégé
of President Mitterrand and, if press reports can be believed, his
long-time mistress, had a remarkable tenure as prime minister of
France: it lasted less than a year, with a resignation after her
popularity had plummeted to a new French low of 17 per cent.
Soon thereafter she was rusticated to Brussels.

The 'lowly bookkeeper' who made the charges, Paul van
Buitenen, had been collecting evidence on Cresson since 1998.
Attached to his thirty-four-page plea for action was 700 pages of
documentation exposing widespread graft in programmes of
foreign aid and the promotion of tourism, as well as hundreds of
instances of corruption and outright theft in Mme Cresson's
directorate. Driven to panic by his pursuers, Buitenen stuffed
several trunk-loads of additional material into his car and fled to
his native Netherlands after disclosing what he had found.
President of the Commission Jacques Santer, a Luxembourger,
then stonewalled, a fatal mistake. The material was too damning
to hide.

The Wise Mens' report to the Parliament was devastating.
They found 'a (veritable) catalogue of instances of fraudulently
altered tender specifications and disregard for lower tenders,
fictitious and double invoicing and inflated fees; unjustified and
illegal payments, simple fraud, clear cases of favouritism in
employment, and evasion of tax and social security obligations
as well as ghost personnel . . . a low level of overall competence
and a pervasive subculture of petty graft, favouritism, and

criminality'. Cresson would have to go, and yet, since the Parliament lacked the authority to sack individual commissioners but only the whole lot of them, Santer, though not implicated directly in the scandal, went with her, along with the rest of her peers, an incredible and completely unexpected turn of events. Van Buitenen was censured and eventually resigned. Others would not be so lucky.[25]

When chief accountant Marta Andreason reported that the EU budget 'was an open till waiting to be robbed', the newly appointed anti-corruption commissioner, Neil Kinnock, fired her. In July 2003, after another accountant, Dougal Watt, posted evidence of high-level corruption on his website, he soon found a pink slip in his box, even though, after a secret ballot, 40 per cent of his colleagues supported his claims. Yet another Scottish accountant, Robert McCoy, was shunned by his workmates after reporting on the basis of three years of research that most of the members of the moribund quango called the Committee of Regions charged first-class fares for bi-monthly meetings they did not bother to attend. He also found out that $500,000 worth of printing contracts had been submitted without tender, and was rebuked by the president of the quango for reporting it.

Dorte Schmidt-Brown, a Dane, was less fortunate. For reporting improprieties at Eurostat using evidence uncovered by a French investigation, she was smeared by Kinnock and suffered a nervous breakdown. An important agency, its statistics were used in allocating the EU budget. OLAF had investigated the outfit no less than six times, uncovering in the process shell companies, slush funds, and rake-offs. Several dummy companies each received between $3 million and $6 million, which could not be accounted for. The agency's director was the principal involved in the machinations, according to the reports. Eurostat also double-charged the Commission and billed for work lifted off the Internet. There was, according to a rare parliamentary critic, Jens-Peter Bonde (also a Dane), 'not one crook, two crooks, or five but a parallel system of financing' that continued until July 2003, when the whistle-blowing became ear-splitting.

After months of intense media pressure, Santer's successor Romano Prodi put an end to the public airing of dirty linen by performing a *mea culpa*, as well as promising to undertake a heroic sleaze abatement campaign – and in a closed-door session warned parliamentarians of the perils of pots calling kettles black. The unrepentant commissioner charged with the task of cleaning out the stables, Neil Kinnock, called the revelations 'the necessary price of doing business'. There would be, henceforth, according to policy expert Thomas Rupp, 'a kind of fraud which is tolerated because it is within the bounds of what is expected and therefore does not lead to any consequences'.[26]

The EU also had its share of spectacular political scandals, only one of which, however, had implications for the future. On 4 February 2000 a coalition took office in Vienna that included the Austrian Freedom Party headed by a disagreeable young firebrand named Joerg Haider. He owed his prominence to the dissatisfaction of a section of the electorate with the quasi-official parties of government – the reds and the blacks – as assisted by a swing group, the browns. Between them they controlled office holding and public contracting at all levels of government, as well as other perks conferred in the patronage system of proportional representation. But there is more to the story. The telegenic Haider won instant approval from disgruntled outsiders by refusing to disown the Nazis. He even praised the SS. Haider was not, however, in the cabinet, and the Austrian prime minister publicly rebuked him.

No matter. The Belgian foreign minister Louis Michel, with the support of the European Parliament, directed a campaign of scapegoating to disgrace the Alpine nation and, in effect, send it to Coventry by 'freezing all diplomatic contact' with it. To underscore the point, political spokespersons told Belgian taxi drivers and waiters to be rude to Austrians, discouraged Belgian firms from participating in Austrian trade shows, and encouraged schoolchildren to cancel student exchanges and traditional skiing holidays. Why did all of this happen? Neo fascists had previously participated in Italian governments, as had unreconstructed communists there and elsewhere – without consequences. Above all, the EU had no prior authority to interfere in the electoral processes of any nation for any reason whatsoever, least of all to impose standards of political correctness. The precedent was both disturbing and dangerous.

The origins of Michel's campaign, as he subsequently admitted, trace back to domestic problems in Belgium, most immediately the Dutroux affair. Marc Dutroux was a well-known convicted paedophile, who raped children for several years in the 1980s. After he had been rearrested in 1986 and later released, Belgians recoiled in horror at the discovery of the bodies of four little girls in houses Dutroux had once inhabited. Two others, aged twelve and fourteen, were found half-starved but still alive.

Dutroux was arrested only months later. The poorly conducted police investigation raised suspicions that there was more to the scandal than met the eye. These fears were confirmed after new evidence revealed that he was no lone predator but a pimp who had organized parties for wealthy patrons with a penchant for sadism and torture. An attempt to hush up a magistrate looking further into such unsavoury matters – who interviewed the surviving victims publicly – touched off the most extraordinary event in the history of Belgium since World War II – a demonstration of 400,000 women, all dressed in white, Flemish and francophone alike, against the corruption of the political system.[27]

The Dutroux affair was the most recent in a veritable stream of scandals which had rocked the unhappy and unstable bilingual kingdom over the previous ten years. They included: the murders of twenty people in Brabant supermarkets reputedly by a right-wing faction in the national gendarmerie; the unsolved killing of a Walloon politician on the doorstep of his mistress; the Agusta and Desault affairs, routine rake-offs implicating, among others, the Belgian former director general of NATO; the Inusop scandal, which caught the Free University of Brussels charging the government for work it did not perform; and the arrest of two homosexual ministers for having illicit sex with underage male prostitutes.

The Dutroux affair nearly toppled the recently elected coalition government. Thanks to the personal intervention of King Albert, and the diversionary campaign of Foreign Minister Michel, the cabinet weathered the crisis, only to fall months later over a scandal deemed only slightly less disgusting than paedophilia by food-conscious Belgians, the sale of toxic chickens in local grocers store. Yet the damage had been done. The Dutroux scandal was a warning, if ever there was one, of a festering mistrust of constituted authority swelling up from unexpected quarters beneath the surface of public life in a country which, if often at odds with itself, was prosperous and pampered. It was also evidence of a new demagogy at the summits of EU power and of a desperate search within the Parliament for relevance, even if that meant becoming the plaything of petty politics.

## Prodi in Wonderland

Romano Prodi was called to the presidency of the European Commission in the aftermath of the Santer resignation in 1999 as a White Knight with a mandate to restore the moral credibility of the EU and to invigorate the drive to federal union. He was in many ways an estimable man: honest, successful, highly intelligent, and committed to the task ahead. With him was an assemblage of the most impressive commissioners ever brought together in official Brussels: Pascal Lamy (later president of the IMF), Frits Bolkestein (a moral and intellectual force of great power), Mario Monti (trust-buster and subsequent prime minister of Italy), and Fritz Fischler (one of the two reform-minded chiefs in the history of the agriculture branch). With this team at his disposal, the new president might have done great things, but this was not to be. These figures made their marks, but as individuals, rather than as a team contributing to an overall policy. Prodi did little to lead or reorganize the Commission, and it remained what it had been when he entered office. When he left it, official Brussels heaved a sigh of relief.

Prodi was treated like a cypher. His maiden speech to the Parliament was a widely ridiculed disaster – a wearying string of clichés and vague promises which, if anything at all, revealed an absence of fresh ideas. Many editorialists advised him to step down in favour of someone with 'vision'. Buried somewhere beneath the blather in Prodi's windy address, it should be added, was a commitment he later honoured to progress with Enlargement. But no one paid much attention to that. Official Brussels was fixated on completing Delors' agenda. Every other priority was subordinated to it.[28]

Prodi was a victim of this obsession. He faced the same impossible task as Monnet and Delors: to build Europe without Europeans. Every step taken to discharge his mission only made things worse. By the time he left office in 2005, the Commission had ceased, except in name, to be the agenda-setter for the integration project. Only for the comparatively brief tenure of Delors had the Commission ever, in fact, discharged that function. How, precisely this *Apparat* should be described is hard to say. It was a technocratic organization dependent on outsiders for expertise, a vast patronage machine, but one at the European, not the local, level.

Yet it was more than a bureaucracy driven by slush-pump. The Commission was supposed to generate big ideas to advance the integration project, but only occasionally had a sound one. When the integration process progressed, it was usually because of a push from outside. What took place under Prodi was not just another episode in the perennial jousting between the executive of the Commission and the representative of the member states, the Council – it involved a definitive shift in decision-making power away from the Brussels institutions altogether. Prodi should not, however, be handed the proverbial bum rap. The Intergovernmental Conferences of the first years of his presidency are usually dismissed offhandedly as do-nothing events, and it cannot be denied that much *Zukunftsmusik* was heard at them, but a good idea or two were mooted as well.

The Lisbon Summit of June 2000, the so-called dot.com summit, announced a timetable for making the EU's economy the most advanced and productive in the world by 2020. Often cited as an example of policy-making foresight, it was soon buried under the bad publicity caused by the Austrian affair, shoved to the sidelines by the collapse of the tech bubble, moved off the agenda by the Nice debacle of December, and almost forgotten for years until revived for lip-service. The road from the IGCs led downhill from Lisbon.

The December 2000 Nice Intergovernmental Conference – a gala event planned to tie up the loose ends from previous IGCs – became the scene of a memorably angry member-state confrontation. It drove home to the European public as nothing had before that virulence and pettiness reigned at the summit of EU politics. It furthermore soured the personal relationships between key heads of state and government.

The breakdown was so complete, and expected to be so long-lasting, that, collectively, the member states in the European Council, now effectively in charge, decided to call a constitutional convention to get the European project rolling. Prodi was marginalized in this process, as was every other standing EU institution. Once again, in other words, a new mechanism had to be found to overcome obstructions met along the way. This time the baton passed, largely by default, to a former Great European born in 1926, Valéry Giscard d'Estaing. The result was a convention lasting some eighteen months, which he chaired, and from which issued a draft document even more grotesque and less viable than the Maastricht Treaty. For reasons the out-of-touch Brussels establishment could never quite fathom, it went down in flames. But that would come later.

To understand what happened at Nice in the meantime, it must be borne in mind that as of 2000 the decision to adopt the single currency was sealed, and remaining doubts concerning Europe's future were put to rest. To a man (there were no women involved) the heads of state and government in attendance at the Nice IGC expected the decisions made there to be permanent. The 'European finality' was thought to be at hand. Only the strength of such a conviction can account for the extreme tenacity with which the delegates fought over issues which, in retrospect, appear negotiable, and, as things now stand, even trivial – certainly not such as to move mind and spirit.

One might have expected, given the imagined immensity of the stakes involved, that the convocation would have elicited the expression of at least a few noble ideas or a theoretical insight or two, or anything else to justify a belief that what took place at Nice was more than a mere turf battle. Unfortunately, nothing said or done on that occasion would justify such a supposition. Statesmanship, to use an old-fashioned word, or even any semblance thereof, was absent from the proceedings. The future of Europe was, it seems, to have been settled by a dog fight.

The issue at hand was how to divide representation after Enlargement, a process by then under way and advancing as scheduled. It was a zero-sum battle waged with computers and batteries of lawyers and economists. It can be thought of as a game. The negotiating positions were as follows. The French opposed Enlargement but had to accept it; the Germans stood to gain the most by it; and the British favoured it by dint of the traditional preference for a wider as opposed to a deeper community. The Spanish, new to the game, wanted to assert an important role in it.

The negotiations proceeded accordingly. The Germans, who had most to lose, took a defensive posture, their purpose being to secure representation of the new entrants on the Council without sacrificing the 'French connection', while at the same time to make it difficult for a coalition to pass measures that they opposed. France wanted to maintain formal parity in the Council with the Germans, but to acquire increased representation for the Mediterranean nations to offset the Germans' eastern advantage. Chirac, who presided, as a Gaullist – and in the interest of France – preferred representation by nation rather than by population. The British opposed any 'deepening' of the community, wanted to retain the veto power in critical areas, and objected to the extension of competences other than those specified in the Single European Act. They wanted to participate only in issue-specific coalitions and to retain the wherewithal needed for trade-offs. Spain clung to a veto power over any cuts in regional aid and insisted on being treated as one of the 'Big Five', much to Poland's discomfiture.

A description of the agreements reached on voting rights makes for dull reading – it's institutional wallpaper – but provides essential background material. The Commission was a fairly simple matter. Each country could name one commissioner, but the 'Big Five' (Germany, France, Britain, Italy, and Spain) were entitled to two. It was agreed that each of the large nations relinquish one of the appointments until 2005, when Enlargement to twenty-eight nations would be completed. The number of commissioners would then be reduced to twenty and assigned on a rotating basis.

The weighting of votes in the Council was a more difficult and contentious matter. Under the existing system, the largest four countries (Germany, France, Britain, and Italy) had ten votes each. Luxembourg, the smallest country had two votes to prevent the big ones from dominating the small ones. After expansion, however, the small countries would be able to outvote Germany, which had more citizens than all of them combined. The compromise struck would have ceded more votes to the big nations, albeit with the proviso, conceded by Germany, that each member of the Rhenish duo had equal representation. In return Germany gained new seats in the Parliament. Qualified majority voting, finally, was extended to thirty new policy areas, with vetoes still applying to those of special interest to one or the other nations.

No one was happy with the Nice settlement. Blair left the meeting with a scowl on his face. The Portuguese delegate called the protocol a 'profoundly negative treaty'. The representative of the Parliament complained about being 'trampled under foot'. Chirac was universally condemned for his high-handed manner and for showing favouritism to France. The Commission was shoved aside and, Prodi conceded that he had 'lost the thread . . . the subtle protocols and more and more complex formulae cannot conceal our differences'. Although both parties officially denied the fact, the Franco-German partnership reached a 'notional turning point' at Nice. The badly fraying relationship would have to be re-woven. *The Nouvel Observateur* had the final word: 'The delegates all went to the Cote d'Azur not to make a baby but to despoil a corpse. Weakened by the departure of Jacques Delors . . . Europe has lost all sense of direction. The meetings of the Council increasingly resemble the haggling of rug merchants.'[29] This, surely, was a time to pause and reflect, but the juggernaut jolted on.

## M. Giscard's Constitution

There was more than one post-Nice effort to draft a constitution for the future Europe. M. Chirac produced one which, in Gaullist fashion, called for the creation of European boards to represent the states, but which over-weighted France. No one seems to have taken it seriously outside of metropolitan Paris. Several German proposals were in play, the most prominent among them penned by Foreign Minister Josef Fischer. All were similar and well intentioned in calling for an enhanced role for the Parliament and greater representation for the European public. The message to be taken away from the reception they received was that Europeans were not ready to be governed by Germans – even good Germans.

The Convention for the Future of Europe (2003–2004) was a parody of a constitutional conclave and what issued from it anything but a framework for a democratic federation of Europe. Its members were not elected either directly or indirectly by representatives of the public, but appointed from various quarters of the EU establishment, which should only have been expected, since the overriding purpose of the exercise was to strengthen the EU itself. Ninety per cent of the document's eventual content was the handiwork of M. Giscard d'Estaing. He controlled the conference procedures with a firm hand. The public remained in the dark over the year and a half in which the various treaty provisions were hammered out. The Convention's writ reached far beyond that of a mere post-Maastricht clean up job: it was meant to serve as a capstone of a new federal state equipped with a full-time president, a foreign minister, its own police, and armed forces – the internal and external attributes of a state. Political reality dictated the non-disclosure of such intentions, but they are there in the document for all to read – assuming that one can find them.

The 400-page treaty-document is so confusing that no two people can fully agree on what it's about. A few basic points nevertheless stand out. The European Constitution asserts its primacy over national constitutions; declares that the EU has a 'legal personality' and possesses the sole right to represent the member states internationally when it so chooses; binds member states by the principle of 'solidarity', requiring restitution for any acts detrimental to the EU; and includes a sweeping and detailed Charter of Fundamental Rights, whose interpretation rests exclusively with the ECJ. The Charter also includes a number of fields that do not customarily come under the rubric. They include medical, biomedical, and scientific ethics; workplace representation and job security; affirmative action; and social assistance (child care, housing, and other benefits). The document also confers a number of specific new responsibilities on European authorities, the most important of them being a common asylum and immigration policy and the 'mutual recognition' of legal judgments, meaning that one state must recognize another's court rulings, even if in violation of national law; the 'coordinating of economic policy', meaning interventionism; and control of intellectual property. It also centralizes the decision-making process. It is quite a wish list.

But one that goes on. To the 113 areas currently decided by majority voting, it adds forty-two new areas. Thirty-six additional ones fall under the 'co-decision procedure'. The Commission gained the right to propose legislation in several new spheres; and changes in voting procedure, furthermore, triple the odds of passing legislation and reduce the number of veto points. The document confers no new powers on the member states and includes nothing to strengthen the principles of subsidiarity and proportionality (which in practice were seldom respected), the purpose of which was to limit EU interventions to only those areas of responsibility that states cannot manage on their own.[30]

The sloppiness of the draft was a huge disappointment to a business community normally well disposed to the EU. *The Economist* recommended binning the entire document, which it ridiculed for having accomplished the incredible feat of making the EU's 'constitutional architecture harder to understand than it was before'. What was the public to make of such a thing? It met with apathy when introduced in 2003, except in Britain, where an aroused public opposed it by two to one. The decisive Swedish rejection of the euro in 2004, which occurred in the face of a campaign which spent five times as much as its opponents and had the support of the entire establishment, should have been regarded as a warning, but was overlooked as a Nordic anomaly. Incredibly, as every other EU government that could do so backed-peddled away from a constitutional referendum, the grandiloquent and pro-constitutional President Chirac, confident of his popularity, offered the French people a chance to vote. François Hollande, the socialist party chief, supported him. Among party leaders, only Jean-Marie Le Pen of the quasi-fascist National Front opposed the constitutional treaty.

During the pre-referendum campaign, the treaty itself – which hardly anyone had ever read – barely featured, overshadowed as it was by something altogether different, the so-called Services Directive (SD). Drafted by Frits Bolkestein, the commissioner for the internal market, the innocuous sounding measure would have opened up the service sector of the economy, some two-thirds of the total, as envisaged in the Single European Act, to wage competition by applying the 'mutual recognition principle'. A professional credential valid in one member state, in other words, would have to be recognized by another. The SD threatened every sheltered form of employment – from cab driver to architect. Mr Bolkestein unfortunately shared a final surname syllable with a mad Transylvanian scientist of fiction and was soon so pilloried. In little time another caricature also entered the political arena – the hapless Polish plumber as job-thief. The Constitution was roundly defeated and the project derailed. So, too, was the attempt to create a Single European Market. Faced with a resurgent populism, liberalization ended in Brussels.

The rejection of the Constitution in the Netherlands the following week was anti-climactic. The damage had already been done. It was nevertheless worrisome. The Dutch did not hate their politicians as did the French. Nor did they have a particular gripe with the idea of Europe, which as citizens of a small trading nation was regarded as necessary to the national welfare. And, as elsewhere, elites backed the Constitution as if by instinct.

It was turned down, almost sorrowfully, because a majority of the Dutch people had lost confidence in the European authorities. It was an intelligent decision and should have been heeded. It was not.[31]

At the subsequent Lisbon IGC, lured (one would surmise) by a cornucopia of glamorous new diplomatic posts, the European Council administratively adopted certain key features of the discarded treaty (while letting the sweeping claims lapse). How better might one demonstrate contempt for the public and widen a democratic deficit than by overriding the ratification process? The Lisbon Accord, as what issued came to be known, created a new diplomatic service and a foreign secretary to head it, as well as a new president of Europe. A regional Flemish politician, Herman van Rompuy, was raised to the high office, and at his side a new foreign secretary of sorts with a lifetime peerage, who was brought out of retirement. The one will be remembered for having managed to compose haiku poems while on the job as president, the other not even for that.

Lady Ashton can hardly be blamed for the blank record. No one knew what the organization she headed, the European External Action Service (EEAS) was actually supposed to do, or even how to describe it. Some scholars called it a 'quasi diplomatic corps', others an 'interstitial organization', or still others 'an embryonic version of a European diplomatic service'. Neither an independent agency like the ECB nor a Commission directorate, it was evident that its main activity was to fight turf battles, but rather than admit that the EEAS, yet another useless quango, should be dissolved, the author of a twenty-five-page article reviewing the literature theorizing on the subject, characteristically calls on the 'need for . . . better theorizing on the subject in the hope that more of the same will eventually lead to discovery of its purpose and mission'.[32] This would bring one close to cloud-cuckoo land.

## The White Paper on Governance

As disaster followed debacle, the importance of the single-currency project grew. It was the only remaining bridge to Europe's future. Any vestige of doubt concerning the euro was cast aside. The decision to adopt the single currency was sealed, and with it perhaps also the EU's fate. In the meantime, the Prodi Commission presented its reform agenda, the White Paper on Governance (2001) – in the event a meaningless exercise. Written to close the 'democratic deficit', it called for building a European superstate along the lines of the authoritarian governments of interwar Europe. Its officially stated purposes were to 'combat fraud and mismanagement' and to bring the EU 'more in tune with its citizens'. Yet, as a well-disposed political scientist regretfully commented, 'the White Paper is a very introspective document, containing much self-indulgent debate by the Commission on its successes and blaming others for failures, in particular member-states'. Put another way, the White Paper was conceived within the well-worn intellectual parameters of the so-called Community Method, meaning that the Commission sets the course for policy, then enlists the other EU authorities behind it. Yet it goes beyond this to new realms of activity and into advocacy of a 'visible and proactive presence in the daily lives of individuals', which entails 'the creation of some form of structured EU government . . . through increased activity at the domestic level'.[33] Here it was extending past work rather than initiating original ideas. The attempt to bolster Commission influence over the public was ongoing.

The German term *Gleichschaltung* (administrative coordination) comes closest to describing what the White Paper envisions. Jacques Delors first introduced the EU to the concept of 'organized civil society'. Conceived as all-embracing, it includes employee associations and trade unions ('social partners'), trade associations, professional associations, and non-governmental organizations that bring people together in a common cause. To these Prodi's Paper adds grassroots 'community-based organizations' that pursue 'member-oriented objectives – youth groups, family associations, and all others through which 'citizens participate in local and community life'. All of them should be encouraged to acquire a 'European dimension'. From 'chess competition between European towns, to mothers' knitting circles in village halls, everything is to be enlisted in the greater cause of European integration'.

'Network governance' is touted as a method to 'widen the unitary political space', and thus organize civil society. Future Euro-elites should be trained as 'force multipliers' to this end. Measures should include civil service courses in the management of European integration, and similar ones taught at the European Police College and the European University Institute. The Framework Programmes for research and development, and project funding in other fields, should also be put to the purpose of building loyalties. The same is true of up-and-coming non-governmental organizations in the field of ecology.

A new Framework Directive is proposed for the purpose at hand. In the manner of an enabling act, it conferred upon the EU authority to issue regulations that take effect automatically, which previously had required that laws be implemented. The White Paper further proposes creating new agencies to promote special Commission programmes as well as to enforce its writ. Neither in this or any other proposal is power assigned to or shared with member states. A final section of the Paper discusses making use of a manipulative foreign policy to build a sense of community.

The White Paper also takes on the challenge of what Delors called 'culture management'. In his maiden address Prodi bloviated that 'the culture industry will tomorrow be one of the biggest industries, a creator of wealth and jobs'. Regretting that he lacked the 'resources to implement a cultural policy', he promised 'to tackle the problem along economic lines'. Committees of bureaucrats and marketing professionals thereupon met to discover how to 'inject' unity into the masses, manufacture history as a 'genealogy of progress from Plato to NATO', and devise appropriately attractive symbols and rituals. This high-philistine endeavour presupposed an essentialist concept of culture as bounded, pure, and unproblematic.

There was nothing altogether new in this. The Commission-sponsored De Clercq report of 1993 called upon 'Mother Europe' to 'protect her children', to 'engrain Europe in people's minds', and stressed that 'newscasters and reporters must *themselves* be targeted to become agents of influence'. De Clercq also recommended the organization of a central office of communications ('so that the Community speaks with one voice'), the founding of a European Library and Museum, the institution of a European Order of Merit, and the issuing of birth certificates granting 'European citizenship'. De Clercq's report followed on the heels of the Adonnino committee, which recommended creating a Europe-wide audiovisual area, organizing a European Academy of Science ('to highlight the achievements of European science in its wealth and diversity'), forming European sports teams, setting up 'volunteer work camps', introducing a larger 'European dimension into the school curriculum, and setting up a Euro-lottery with prize money in ECUS' in order to 'make Europe come alive for Europeans'.

The campaign to create a 'Peoples' Europe' generated a spate of additional public relations gimmicks – by now some quite familiar. They included designing postage stamps with portraits of Monnet, Schuman, and other founding fathers; choosing an anthem (*Ode to Joy!*), encouraging team sporting competitions, funding a youth orchestra; nominating a European 'Woman of the Year'; and creating holidays to honour Jean Monnet, Robert Schuman, and Walter Hallstein. Then, too, there were the needs for a flag (the familiar clock-without-hands) and commissioned histories featuring the lives of the founding fathers. Finally, in the hope of creating a self-fulfilling prophecy, Eurostat fabricated a category of 'European public opinion'.

All the above loyalty-building devices are familiar to students of interwar authoritarianism. To mention this fact is not to suggest either that the Commission intended to build a similar sort of system at the European level or that such recent ideas have a disreputable lineage. Prodis White Paper does, however, betray intellectual sterility and provides a warning of what can happen when an executive authority is subject to neither public scrutiny nor democratic control. Fortunately, such a clumsy attempt to create a European demos cannot compete with the lures of the Internet, sexual and gender liberation, personal enfranchisement, improved health, and increased longevity – to mention only a few of the things that enhance human freedom and opportunity, and give contemporary life in Europe an intricate, rich, and endlessly fascinating flavour – as well as making a mockery of attempts to shape the human personality by cookie-cutter.

## Enlargement

Enlargement – the inclusion of the former Soviet Bloc states into the European Union – is the single great achievement of the Prodi Commission, but at the same time represents a missed opportunity of staggering proportions. The EU lost a chance to reform its own institutions as well as discover and fulfil a noble mission: to spread democracy, good government, and sound economics to nations held captive by authoritarianism. Instead, it remained trapped in parochialism. The Eastern Europeans were brought into the EU as second-class citizens – a status better than none at all but one far short of their hopes. Everyone suffered as a result. There would be no European renewal.

The intramural battle in Brussels pitted 'wideners' – the British – against 'deepeners' – Delors and the French. Delors viewed the accession of the Easterners narrowly through the prism of his European project; considered it an unwelcome distraction from the great cause; and, worse yet, feared that over the long term it could only weaken France within the EU, as well as strengthen Germany and the 'wideners'. His worries – shared by the Mitterrand and Chirac governments – were well founded on both counts.

The Commission may have grabbed the headlines, but the 'wideners', led by Britain, under Labour as well as the Conservatives, were already quietly winning the tug of war. Successive enlargements, all opposed and in some cases delayed by France, had already brought into the EU the Iberians (and Greece), the Nordics (except for Norway), and the neutrals (Austria and Ireland). Furthermore, the remaining 'EFTANS' had entered the customs union and, as a necessary admission price, accepted much of the existing body of EU law and regulation. Finally, conditions became inappropriate for the creation of the type of corporate capitalist system that might have supported the grand designs of the French; Stalinist economies were in ruins; corruption was everywhere rampant; and statism in disrepute. The economic reconstruction of Eastern Europe would have to be worked out, for better or worse, through the market.

The geo-political concerns of France were equally realistic. Eastern Europe was historically, of course, a German sphere of influence. The underlying purpose of Willy Brandt's *Ostpolitik* was to restore it by reviving political, commercial, and financial ties. The impact of Brandt's initiative cannot be overestimated. Brandt himself became the symbol of a new and better Germany, and the nation he represented a much-envied model. Willy Brandt had no intention of overthrowing the regimes in power; on the contrary, he tried to strike new partnerships with them, with an intent to reconcile the historic split on the political Left. The increased expectations he aroused, and the borrowing necessary to meet them, nonetheless produced a debt burden that the corrupt governments and the debauched economies of

Communist Poland, and the other captive nations, could not bear. The weight of it eventually set in motion the chain of events which brought them down.

Concurrently, and as part of the same overall development, the German economic penetration of Communist Eastern Europe was well under way before the system collapsed. The so-called 'Europe Agreements' of 1990, bilateral arrangements promoted by Chancellor Kohl, were an outgrowth of this situation. They called for free trade, closer economic cooperation, and an 'institutional- ized political relationship' between the EU and the 'more advanced' Eastern European countries. Although it would take years before the Europe agreements would be fully implemented, they aligned the Eastern European nations with EU rules regarding capital movement, competition, intellectual and industrial property rights, and public procurement. Yet they were also shot through with 'protectionist proclivities' inconsistent with the 'pervasive rhetoric of integration'. When it came to concrete market access measures, according to Desmond Dinan, 'the EC refused to make . . . concessions for agricultural products, textiles, and steel, [which are] highly important sectors economically for the [Eastern] countries'.[34] This was an ill-omen.

So, too, was the souring of public opinion in Western Europe that had torpedoed the Constitution: fear of labour competition and prejudice against foreigners. Although its impact varied country-by-country, its presence was undeniable, not least of all in Germany, which stood to lose the most by its spread. Except within the circles of the new populism, all concerned parties in both East and West agreed that such dangerous nativism should be, whenever possible, kept out of electoral politics. The Commission cooked up a pseudo-analysis to downplay the immi- gration issue, concluding that only 335,000 immigrants would enter the EU once barriers to labour mobility were lifted. The kind of public discussion that might have forced constructive change in Euro-politics never took place.

The accession process actually started out on a generally positive note, with the adoption in 1993 of the so-called Copenhagen
Criteria, three in number, as prerequisites for EU admission. The
first two called for open markets and democratic government
under law – unobjectionable principles. The third one was more
questionable. It required full acceptance of the so-called *acquis
communautaire*, the massive body of EU administrative and
regulatory law. The translation costs, borne by the applicants,
were substantial; more importantly, the *acquis* was non-negotia-
ble. This set a precedent for the new East–West relationship, one
more closely resembling that of master and serf than of equals.

After Copenhagen, the only recourse for opponents of
Enlargement was to throw up roadblocks to delay accession. A
new 'screening process' was introduced to this end. Yet after five
years of economic collapse, the lengthy process of rehabilitation
and reconstruction from Communism took hold in the East. It
involved a broad array of reforms: in law, finance, and business,
as well as privatizations, the modernization of agriculture and
industry, the clean-up of the environment, the overhaul of the
administration, the reform of the educational system, the re-tool-
ing of industry, and the upgrading of infrastructure. This took
place without the benefit of anything like a Marshall Plan; it
required large amounts of private investment and a willingness
to do much hard work. The peoples of Eastern Europe deserve
credit for meeting the challenge. They received little of it from
either the EU or Western Europeans generally. The rise of
populism in the nations of former Bloc nations should come as
no surprise. Why would they want to be treated as second-class
citizens?

Except for Romania and Bulgaria, the would-be newcomers
passed all the accession tests. Only one obstacle remained, albeit
a huge one, the Common Agricultural Policy. It still consumed
half of the EU budget. There were more farmers in Poland, as it
turns out, than in the rest of Europe put together. Admission to

the EU hinged on how to divide the subvention pool. After rounds of heated wrangling, Prime Minister Blair gave way to President Chirac, newly backed by the German Chancellor Gerhard Schroeder: the CAP would emerge unscathed, the EU remain unreformed, and the Eastern Europeans eventually raised from subsidization at one-eighth the prevailing rate to parity over a ten-year period. With this sordid bargain, the two halves of Europe, the fortunate and the unfortunate, would be reunited.[35] And Eastern Europeans would remain supplicants in the EU.

## The Delors Years

If the years between the Single European Act of 1986 and the rejection of the proposed Constitution in 2004 seem puzzling it is because, at the time, they were thought of as a fresh start in an integration process, as directed by Brussels. This was to have brought Europe to new heights of accomplishment. Instead, it marked its apex. Henceforth, the story would be one of decline, first gradual, then steep, and finally precipitous. The European Union would neither develop as the nucleus of a new superpower, nor outpace the growth of the rest of the industrial world, nor remain the beacon of hope for Europe's peoples. Its promises and claims were too often empty. There was no EU security policy worthy of the name, and the same is true of the 'social dimension' of policy. The Single European Market was only half-complete, and progress in opening it stalled. The governance machinery of the Community was unreformed, dilapidated, and decidedly inefficient.

The responsibility for the adverse turn of events rests primarily with the man at the helm for ten of these years, whose Napoleonic dreams drove policy forward and whose high-handed methods guided the process, Jacques Delors. His goal was unrealistic and his supercharged approach the wrong one. His elitism was unquestioned within a Brussels hothouse running short on new ideas and unchastened by democratic responsibility. At a time when the United States, Britain, and much of the rest of the world adopted market-conforming policies to capture the gains from huge increases in global productivity, Delors championed a traditional kind of state-building strategy on a European scale intended to operate from the top down by means of bureaucratic governance. He was indeed behind the curve, even in Europe. As problems mounted, so too did the collateral damage inflicted by the ill-considered defences thrown up against them. Under Delors the Commission set the EU agenda. His successors lost this power. Who gained it? Not the member states. The IGCs of the period accomplished little, and Nice was a scrum that no one came out of unbruised. The long-standing in-house controversy about the best way to advance the integration process – by means of the Commission-directed 'Community Method' or by means of the Council and the member states – no longer had much meaning. Neither worked.

Instead, power passed to extra-Community bodies, first to Giscard and his Convention, and later, above all, to the EMU. Even before the single currency circulated, the run-up to it dictated a tight monetary policy, which lowered growth in the late 1990s; the timetable set for entry into the currency union was, in other words, the major EU decision of the decade. Before anyone in Brussels quite realized the importance of the fact, the future of the European Union was at the mercy of the European Monetary Union.

Enlargement should have been the top policy priority of EU policy-makers, but was far from it. Surely no event in the postwar era would be of such lasting importance as the collapse of Communism. The fate of Eastern Europe hinged, however, on the outcome of a tug of war in Brussels between 'deepeners' and 'wideners' which, fortunately, the latter won. Otherwise, Enlargement would have been delayed indefinitely.

Two of the three ground rules set for accession (the third one being the *acquis*) offered assurances that the new entrants would be governed democratically, have open economies, and thus be in line with the changes transforming the world system. The new entrants would strengthen the EU, not weaken it; be a benefit, not a cost. Instead of being welcomed with open arms, however, they were ushered in through the back door. An opportunity to do the right thing – to become the conscience of a rejuvenated and united Europe – was missed. With the rise in 2015 with Putinesque authoritarianisms in Hungary, Poland and elsewhere in Eastern Europe, the chickens are coming hom to roost in the EU henhouse.

Even before the Euro-crisis began, the long-standing 'permissive consensus' had dissolved and been replaced by a new scepticism that veered into hostility towards Brussels and its works. None of this would have happened if, instead of acting like an end in itself, the Community had elicited active cooperation between well-disposed independent sovereign states and found practical means to promote growth and provide security without sacrificing democratic governance. If ever the time was ripe for a European construction it was the Delors years – of neo-liberalism, prosperity, and the collapse of Communism. This great achievement could have been accomplished within the framework of the Rome Treaty.

Europe might then have been knit together through a network of purpose-based, practical, and results-oriented bilateral and multilateral agreements consistent with the changes under way in the global the market economy. This need not have involved the machinations of a closed-door process but merely a revival of the way that international commerce and finance had traditionally been conducted. Post-1945 Europe was the scene of a gradual shift from state-centred economies – the products of the century's terrible wars – to more open market civilian economies, which drew strength from the most recent of three great waves in the long-term trend towards the increasing interdependence of nations and economies – that is, of an integrating world order. In the long term, the survival of the European Union will depend upon whether and how the European Union can adapt to progress occurring elsewhere.

# PART THREE

# LOST IN THE FUTURE

The new age that the world is now entering will place unprecedented strains on the European Union. It will be unlike the machine age that we associate with the industrial revolution. Its primary mechanisms are not physical, but virtual or cybernetic. The era now dawning is both familiar and mysterious: it is rapidly evolving but not yet well understood. The same thing is true of its relationship to politics and the economy. The age follows an economic logic of its own. Not one of scarcity but of bounty, not one of rival goods crowding the market but of non-rival goods, which, once the first in a series has been produced, are free. As one leading Silicon Valley innovator put the matter, 'Information is costly to produce but cheap to reproduce'.[1]

There is no simple relationship between markets and organizations in the new era, but many as mediated through multiple layers of causation. What makes things different this time are pace and amplitude. Moore's Law is still at work, and its exponential consequences are playing out. Change is accelerating as well as expanding and deepening at rates unknown in history. Information Technology (IT) is no longer just a breakthrough field: it is the core of, and pervades, the contemporary economy.[2]

For a European Union beset with a record of failure and already behind the curve, the catastrophic setbacks resulting from the still unfolding euro-caused disaster will make it exceptionally difficult to meet the challenges of the coming era. The end of the current miseries is not in sight, fresh ideas are rare, and bad practice persistent. The root cause of miseries is structural. The remedy, institutional reconfiguration, would require a degree of statesmanship seldom in evidence. Furthermore, the public does not trust those in power – politicians, central bankers, officials, and the so-called experts of the establishment – to mend the problem. Mass opinion, with unimportant exceptions, strongly opposes 'more Europe'.

The European Depression, to use the appropriate term for the several years of almost zero growth in the EU, has rekindled a dormant nationalism, bred new North–South hostility, aggravated pre-existing intranational divisions of language and tradition, created lasting generational inequities, widened the divide between incomes and classes, and added to a general public disgust with politics and politicians. The era of good feelings is over. The crisis has also debilitated European institutions, the Commission in particular: it is rudderless, operates in a legal limbo, and subverts the very principles upon which the EU was founded. It is also demonstrably incompetent and, along with the Parliament and Council, ineffective. In the absence of far-reaching reform – meaning democratization, replacement of the single currency system, and the renationalization of political institutions – no lasting recovery can take place.

Reform should not, however, be expected. Brussels is reeling from the compounding crises of autumn 2015 and is unable to contain them – it cannot sweep the Volkswagen scandal under the rug, turn the refugees away, or protect Europe from terrorists. It is also too disorganized to head off the threat of Brexit by compromise. The unravelling of the EU has begun. It will take more than muddling through to stop it.

# CHAPTER 5

# The European Depression and Institutional Debilitation

Europe's agonies have lasted far too long to be called a recession. Nor does the single word depression quite fit the circumstances. Europe's affliction is not global in scope but limited to a specific region. Nor is it a crisis of capitalism due to market failure, but political in character and due to institutional failure. The institution in question is the EU and its offshoot and now master, the EMU. It is, in fact, a *European Depression*, which can only be ended by overhauling, replacing, or eliminating its source.

This crisis, as the sociologist Ulrich Beck has pointed out, 'is not purely a matter of the economy, but of society and politics as well as of . . . prevailing ways of thinking about them'. The problems involved are serious. How should one, he asks, resolve disagreements between national democracies? Should 'Europe's builders exploit legal loopholes [as ECB President Draghi] has done in order to open the door to necessary changes ruled out by national constitutions and European treaties'? How does one, finally, 'assess the dangers of "uncoupling" politics from the law'? And might that not remove a 'landmark by which to orient political actions', and could that involve 'losing our compass for humane and intelligent organization of the twenty-first century'?[1] These grave questions overhang Europe's future.

There is a recent precedent for Europe's present economic miseries – Japan's lost decade. An exhaustive IMF-sponsored study authored by economists from Stanford and the University of Chicago uncovered distressing similarities between the two crises. The root causes of the European problem were bank undercapitalization aggravated by phony 'stress tests', which masked underlying problems; the complexity of decision-making; and the lack of a governmental backstop. Europe also faced structural problems like those of Japan: labour market protection; privileging of incumbents; and regressive tax systems as well as prevalent tax cheating. Beyond this, fear of triggering a panic has caused officialdom to deny the enormity of the problems facing the banks.[2]

The problems confronting Europe began on Wall Street in autumn 2008 with the threatened collapse of banks deemed 'too big to fail'. The still much-debated causes of the trouble includes the bursting of the American housing bubble and the shoddy lending practices that gave rise to it; the explosion of credit due to the overuse of new instruments – derivatives, credit default swaps (CDSs), and 'bundled' bonds, many of them guaranteed by the two big quasi-statal home mortgage banks; poor or non-existent regulation; and the 'irrational exuberance' that Fed Chairman Alan Greenspan first warned of, then fell victim to – by keeping interests rates too low for too long. The rest of the world, including the European Central Bank, followed suit.

Frightening though it was, the US crisis passed within six months. Acting together, first of all, the Fed and Treasury bailed out, temporarily took over, and administered 'haircuts' to ailing but system-critical financial and manufacturing companies; all of them went into receivership. The haircuts in question nearly wiped out shareholder equity as well as damaging the creditors of two out of the three giant automobile companies, two of the five largest banks and other key financials. The biggest and most crucial action was the rescue and takeover of the giant insurance conglomerate AIG. AIG was by far the world's largest issuer of credit default swaps, an operation run by a small autonomous group in London. A failure of the US government to support CDS prices and protect the value of what was, at bottom, an insurance product, could have destroyed the international financial system. Two of the five largest holders of the AIG-issued swaps were European, the Deutsche Bank and Société Génerale de Banque. The Fed and Treasury, in other words, bailed out Europe as well as the US, a well-known fact that neither party wanted to publicize for obvious reasons. The Europeans did not want to broadcast their vulnerability, but instead chortled that their 'sensible' banks were immune to the disease afflicting Wall Street. For its part, the US central bank could hardly have announced to the American public that it was rescuing Europeans with taxpayer money. So interdependent had the world of international banking become that the US action was a matter of dire necessity, not choice.[3]

There are three other basic explanations as to why the US economy turned the corner at an early date. Although the potential long-term adverse consequences of Quantitative Easing (QE) may yet have to be faced, QE – increasing the supply of new credit by issuing bills, notes, and bonds – pumped necessary liquidity into the system and prevented a breakdown in lending. Above and beyond that, the underlying economy was sufficiently buoyant to attract new investment to crucial growth areas, high tech (IT and biotech) and so-called 'fracking', a generic term for the use of efficient new petroleum and natural gas recovery methods. The expansion of the economy maintained business confidence in spite of the sharply rising national debt. Finally, the US had institutions in place, which operated under law, were democratically accountable, and considered legitimate by the public. The ECB had none of them.

As 2015 turned into 2016, the US and the EU were, according to Martin Wolf, in 'different places'. American unemployment, after the crisis running at 10 per cent, was at 5 per cent, inflation was just below 2 per cent and steady, and the economy was running almost full out at an annual rate of 3.5 per cent. In Europe, GDP was still 3.5 per cent below that of 2008, unemployment still stuck at about 11 per cent, and inflation at .1 per cent veered towards outright deflation. The two economies were at different stages in the recovery cycle, and the gap between them was likely to grow.[4]

## A Half-Built House

The European Union is at best a 'half-built house'. The European Central Bank (ECB) cannot guarantee 'full faith and credit' like the US government, because there is no European equivalent to it. The closest that the ECB can come to serving as a lender of last resort rests in a faith that the seventeen countries in the eurozone can reach collective and binding agreements on fundamental policy decisions, which involve substantial transfers of wealth. Even under the best of circumstances, unanimity would not be easy to arrive at, and under present ones is nearly impossible. Contrary to expectations, the single currency increased the divergence of member-state economies in rates of productivity and wage inflation; the so-called North–South divide widened ominously both before and during the crisis.[5]

The gist of the problem was the commitment backed by the EU that, regardless of the national issuer, euro-designated bonds would trade at par, thereby equalizing interest rates across the currency union. Such a notion is absurd. A bond is an instrument for spreading risk and its valuation must reflect that fact. Indirectly, bond pricing provides a means of disciplining borrowers. Stripped of these functions a debt instrument is just a piece of paper. And yet, for nearly a decade, the improbable fiction of equal value was sustained. Such suspension of disbelief among the thundering herds of the markets – especially on the part of lemming-like German and French banks which invested heavily in Greek sovereign paper – serves as resounding testimony to the credibility the European Project once inspired; it attests to the power of myth. This respect survived flagrant cheating by Berlin, Paris, and elsewhere on the 'stability and growth' rules – the supposed guarantor of fiscal probity – that restricted budget deficits to 3 per cent annually. When in 2010 it became public knowledge that Athens had cooked its books on a large scale and over a period of many years, the house of cards collapsed. The peripheral EMU members – which in addition to Greece, included Italy, Spain, Portugal, and Ireland – soon approached the ECB with outstretched hands.[6]

The very feature that had appealed strongly to these weak and vulnerable economies caused their downfall: subsidized credit made possible by riding German coat-tails – so long, that is, that one could cling to them. In Italy the easy money was sluiced into an already overstuffed and overstaffed bureaucracy, and the same was largely true of Portugal. In Spain and Ireland it produced housing bubbles even larger, relatively speaking, than in the American Sunbelt. In Greece, money was poured into the bureaucracy, pumped up the housing market, and lined many pockets. It is worth mentioning that both Ireland and Spain met the 'stability and growth' criteria built into the EMU treaty at German insistence as guarantees against fiscal imprudence; their economic problems arose from excesses in the private sphere. As disciplinary measures, in other words, the criteria proved to be largely irrelevant.[7] They made, in any case, as Prodi once described them, economic nonsense.

The background to the crisis of the Eurozone was excessive debt, a general world problem, but far above the 60 per cent of GDP allowed by the 'stability and growth' rules. It now approaches 90 per cent across the board. Structural flaws in the EMU compounded the economic problems of the weak states. They derived from the one-size-fits-all approach to policy-making, the purpose of which was the political one of advancing the European Project. Under the rules, devaluation was impossible. Two other characteristics of an optimum currency area were also missing and could not be supplied. One was fiscal transfers – the EU lacked the necessary resources for such a thing – and the other was labour mobility, historically very limited compared to the US.

After a brief period of fiscal loosening in the months after the threatened meltdown on Wall Street, and moved by fear of spiralling borrowing costs, governments across the eurozone, including in fiscally solid places like the Netherlands, turned to austerity by cutting budget deficits, reducing pension and other social benefits, and shrinking employment in the state sector. One unintended result was, by slowing growth, to raise the real costs of the European Depression and to spread political fallout. The problem, according to the economist Ashoka Modi, stemmed from an underestimate of the fiscal multiplier during a downturn. The contraction in incomes and demand resulting from budgetary cutbacks was, in other words, much sharper than expected. Wage reduction increased the real cost of debt, consumers spent less, and households saved more, which produced a deflationary spiral, thereby increasing the costs of servicing the debt. It also has bad long-term consequences: permanent unemployment and reduced investment.[8]

None of this bode well for policy-making. 'With limited options for dealing with the real problems', according to Modi, 'the tendency is to delay action while cloaking the delays with high-minded projections of progress and sentiments of European solidarity. And when the limits of rhetoric run out, ad-hoc technocratic solutions without political legitimacy are the outcome'. The costs of these delays to Greece, the other Club Med nations, and Europe generally, have been substantial.[9]

There were several alternatives to the scenario that have led to the present crisis. One hardly needs a nagging reminder that the single currency idea was structurally flawed and was not necessary. A eurozone could have been created around an improved version of the EMS. Storm signals went un-heeded, moreover, in the ten years after 1995, when the go-ahead was given for the single currency. Five years later, at the Deauville meeting of October 2010, Angela Merkel and Nicolas Sarkozy, then president of France, 'acknowledged the reality of unsustainable debts and agreed to a forward-looking debt restructuring' as well as made provision for distressed sovereigns to renegotiate with private creditors'. President of the ECB Jean-Claude Trichet accused the pair of wrecking the eurozone. The idea was dropped.[10]

So, too, it would have been easy to strike a timely bargain with Greece's private creditors. The 50 per cent haircut they eventually received in February 2012 made few ripples outside of Greece; bond spreads actually fell after it; and except in a few minor cases, the losses incurred had a negligible impact on quarterly bank earnings. Since nearly all Greek sovereign paper is now in the vaults of the IMF and the ECB, Greece could default without causing contagion to spread through the banking system. Political contagion is, admittedly, a more complicated and less predictable matter.[11] Greece is now entering its third bailout, albeit with doubts overhanging it. Rolling renegotiation is in prospect, not least of all because the IMF considers the terms of the deal too harsh.[12] Meaningful growth has not yet been restored in the EU, and the Greek economy has not yet begun to recover. The country faces endemic crisis.

The integrity of the currency union hinges on the willingness of creditor nations to provide necessary emergency funding to the debtors. Aware of this potential danger, the Germans had written into the Maastricht Treaty explicit prohibitions on the ECB's engagement in sovereign rescues. A move similar to the Treasury–Fed CDS guarantee, which saved the European banking structure in late 2008, was forbidden inside the eurozone by its own rules. Once push came to shove, Germany refused to be the lender of last resort to the hard-pressed nations of the periphery. That being the case, the only method for providing loans needed to keep the ailing countries from financial collapse was subterfuge. This began with a rhetorical flourish in June 2012 – a commitment of the new ECB chief Mario Draghi to do 'whatever it takes to rescue the Euro'. On its heels came two new financing vehicles, the European Stability Mechanism (ESM) in September 2012 and, a month earlier, the Outright Monetary Transaction (OMT) procedure. ESM enables borrowing from international markets backed by repayment guarantees of the member states; OMT enables the ECB to purchase sovereign paper in secondary markets in violation of the treaty.

Both amount to a disguised 'mutualization' – burden sharing – fiercely opposed by German taxpayers; albeit at their peril, the weak economies free-ride on Germany's high credit rating. The bond-buying supported prices but put much new bad paper (for accounting purposes assessed at face value) on ECB books. Lending to the threatened countries continues by means of a transfer facility known as Target-2, in which public money loaned to the Club Med nations substituted for private money outflows. This less than transparent procedure raised hackles in the world of German economists, but the public had little understanding of how it worked. Intended to be a stability union, the EMU had, by stealth, become a liability union.[13]

A tacit bargain underpinned the Troika – the ECB, the International Monetary Fund (IMF), and the European Commission – which collectively made lending decisions: bailouts would be provided when necessary, but in the form of loans requiring repayment; private creditors would be largely protected; and Germany would lend money within limits, but without incurring excessive political costs. This was a precarious juggling act, all the more so because growth stopped altogether in the borrowing nations and the real cost of debt-servicing increased correspondingly. Only reductions in spreads between the economically strong and weak member states provided a breathing space; at the same time, it risked moral hazard. The convergence of spreads also presupposed a relative absence of political and social unrest and the maintenance of ECB credibility. IMF warnings of such perils may indicate a future unwillingness to impose austerity.

Since 2008 the economy of the eurozone has been flat, while the GDP of the United States has increased by 27 per cent. The EU nations outside the EMU (which include the UK, Sweden, Denmark, Czech Republic and Poland) have also markedly outperformed the eurozone, even though dragged down by the lack of growth there. Unemployment is persistently over 10 per cent across the eurozone and youth unemployment hovers at well over twice that rate. Austerity-dictated cutbacks in 'social Europe' have, furthermore, fallen disproportionately on young people. All the major indexes indicate that while the East–West discrepancy has narrowed, the North–South divide has widened substantially. Hans-Werner Sinn estimates that to become competitive Greece and Portugal would need to a depreciate currencies 30 per cent or more relative to the euro in order to regain sufficient competitiveness to service outstanding debt. To achieve such cuts through further austerity, however, would, he speculates, push both nations beyond the breaking point.[14]

How can the European Depression be ended? One approach to solving the problem, adopted by the Commission, was to tighten regulation. Its three-point plan included a fiscal compact, a banking union, and a budget review process. The fiscal compact merely reiterated the two main points in the stability and growth criteria – budget deficits of no more than 3 per cent (sometimes unenforceable) and debt to GDP levels of no more than 60 per cent (never enforceable). 'Hedging' by France, Italy, and Spain on the budget numbers is tacitly being tolerated. Commission plans also call for a banking union to shift power from national authorities to the ECB. This, too, had long been discussed but never implemented. The third proposal, to assign budgetary review authority to the Commission, was 'a step too far', according to Martin Feldstein, 'even to get serious consideration by the Commission itself'. None of the proposals has had much of an impact.[15]

Mario Draghi and the ECB have adopted a policy of their own, to stimulate growth by reducing the value of the euro against the dollar. The effectiveness of underpricing the euro would seem evident in the superior European growth rates in the first five years of the new millennium, when it was pegged at 1.2 to the dollar, to which point it had nearly dropped by the beginning of 2015. So far this has had a positive effect, but success will depend on keeping ahead of other depreciating currencies – the yen, and yuan above all. With real interest rates now negative and dropping, Europe also risks falling into a deflation trap, which would add to the real cost of reducing the debt load. Draghi has also indicated, as has already happened in the cases of France and Spain, that the ECB will look the other way when the 3 per cent rule is breached. He will have to do likewise with Portugal, where an anti-austerity coalition took office in November 2015, and will have to do again to save the Renzi government in Italy from the insurgent Five Star Movement.[16]

The ECB president, like virtually all other commentators, places his ultimate hope on structural reform – something easy to advocate but hard to deliver. In the meantime, only three exit strategies exist, one of them worthless, according to H.-W. Sinn. As recommended by the president of the IMF, it would involve across-the-board wage increases – a reprise of the initial and disastrous policy of FDR's First New Deal. It would, quite simply, cause stagflation.[17] The other two strategies would have to operate in tandem. They involve stimulating inflation at the core as well as forcing devaluation at the periphery, and would require, as a preliminary, redrafting the Maastricht Treaty. The degree of pain that weak nations could bear remains an open question, but the downward pressure would be heavy. Sinn estimates that even France would have to reduce wage costs by 20 per cent to be competitive. The largest unresolved issue is, of course, whether the German electorate would accept a 50 per cent increase in the price level over a ten-year period as well as the reduction of 33 per cent of their wealth.

The ruminations of the Chichele Professor of Economic History at Oxford University are at this point worth pondering: 'The nature of modern economies, and of policies in the independent democracies that comprise the Eurozone, is such that Europe may not have the luxury of experimenting for 140 years (as did the United States) before finding workable arrangements (for monetary and fiscal institutions). Popular calls for public goods, social insurance, countercyclical macroeconomic policy, and financial stability cannot be brushed aside so easily as in the less-democratic era of the classical gold standard.'[18]

The adverse impacts of the European Depression, the end of which is years away, have discredited the European project. The European Union itself counts for little any more. The Franco-German duopoly is a thing of history. Europe's important decisions are made by the German chancellor, the president of the European Central Bank, and the director of the International Monetary Fund. A reading between the lines would suggest a grudging official recognition that to escape the Euro-trap the Maastricht Treaty will have to be junked, in spirit if not in name. The devaluation strategy of Draghi can provide a breathing space but not a solution. Banking reforms along Commission lines have little purchase – and are being quietly abandoned – not least of all because the crisis has already contributed to a process of financial re-nationalization. That is, however, the least of the problems facing would-be Euro-regulators. A much larger one is that of trust, something in very short supply.

'The present crisis', according to Ulrich Beck, has 'generated a new "precariat" of marginalized youths . . . in a fury about something that spends money on rescuing banks, while squandering the future of the young generation.' He adds that 'governments vote for austerity measures, while peoples vote against them', which reflects a 'structural divide between a European project devised and administered from above . . . and the resistance that swells up from below. Ordinary voters reject as highly unjust the demand that they should swallow medicine (which) may well prove lethal'.[19]

The governance machinery of the EU, while spinning wildly over the past several years, has contributed essentially nothing to the solution of the present financial crisis. The ECB and the IMF – both remote and unaccountable authorities – have taken up the slack, but in the South have become detested as an occupying power. In the North, the Germans, and their allies, understandably feel cheated. The eurozone holds together only through fear that getting rid of it would be the greater of two evils. Reform may still, however, have an outside chance.

## Failing Institutions

One might have hoped that the European Depression would bring about a searching review of policy at the EU. Yet nothing like that has happened; there has been no internal reform or even a housecleaning. The Lisbon Treaty (2007), the governing document, is so shot through with inconsistencies and ambiguities as to be worthless as a constitutional framework; it clears up none of the snarls, overlaps, and procedural oddities that makes a fool of one who speaks of a meaningful separation of powers in the European institutions. It is a grab bag from which can be drawn a policy rationale of choice. The verdict of recent research at the European Academy of Law is damning. The so-called 'New Governance' pronounced at the Lisbon conference in 2007, which was supposed to create a 'knowledge-based economy' and the 'European social model' failed, and its 2020 successor was 'even worse'. The latest policy formula, 'Post Euro-crisis economic governance', merely uses similar methods under a different rubric, is repeating previous mistakes, and the much-vaunted attempt to promote policy innovation and mutual learning between states is precisely what 'the new paradigm seems to have left behind'.[20]

The politics of Brussels turn, as always, on turf wars and elbowing for position. The Commission occupies centre stage in such struggles. It has more than doubled in size, to 45,000 full-time employees, over the past twenty-five years. Surrounding and intertwined with it is a barnacle-like encrustation of recently created quangos (quasi-governmental organizations), which employ another 10,000. Adding to the policy-making stew were between 15,000 and 30,000 lobbyists, representing 1,450 interest groups, 350 firms, and 260 public institutions.[21] More so than ever, policy-making is stealthy, opaque, and confused. Corruption continues to spread but is rarely admitted officially. Nobody is really in charge.

Words, however, there were – endless streams of them, the volume proportional to the loss of real influence and power to the ECB, Frau Merkel, and Mme. Lagarde of the IMF. This *de-politicization* has effectively deprived the Commission of its leadership role. Devotees of the so-called Community Method of Monnet and Delors now worry that excessive rhetoric is creating a 'credibility problem', meaning that Hallstein's platonic Guardians are becoming a public joke. When the European Depression eventually ends, it will find the Commission unfit for service. The young Juncker Commission is floundering. It has no programme worthy of the name and even subverts the principles upon which the EU is based. Only at the second echelon of policy-making does the executive authority still count for much. Trade policy might prove to be an exception, but this would require top-level leadership. The Commission itself, if not quite obsolete, is an artifact of the past. Power grabbing and mission creep nevertheless remain a threat to a state of law.

In August 2012, while Commission President Barroso was imploring the Greeks to 'Deliver, deliver, deliver!', he proposed raising the EU budget by 6.8 per cent to €138 billion. Included therein were substantial enhancements of pay and benefits, already far higher than enjoyed by counterparts in any member state, at the senior grade 18,000 euros above German levels. Benefits are even more generous. A supplement for living abroad equal to 16 per cent of salary heads the list. Next comes a tax-free 'Household Supplement' at a minimum of 201 euros per month, plus another bonus per child of 660 euros. School fees and supplies add up to another 880 euros. The EU also provides fourteen tuition-free 'European Schools'; students attending outside schools receive lump sums of 13,000 euros apiece.

For annual trips home each year, every official receives a first-class rail ticket or business-class air fare, in a lump sum, regardless of whether or not the beneficiary actually makes the trip. Included in the home leave package are up to six additional days off. In addition to regular vacation of fourteen to thirty days, additional time off is liberally provided. From Christmas to New Year's Day the EU shuts down the office. There are also special holidays like 'Green Thursday', and the Friday after Ascension Day. Officials can also take off ten days per year for advanced training, which does not have to be documented. While the age of early retirement is to be stepped up from fifty-five to fifty-eight and retirement from sixty-three to sixty-five, the increase is only to be phased over a twenty-five-year period, by which time pension obligations will have doubled. For the Commission alone, personnel costs run to 5.8 billion euros per year.[22]

The budget remains seriously misaligned. It is not designed to maximize economic returns across Europe, but to balance a range of interests between member states and cover the mounting costs of the Eurocracy. The benefits accrue to well-positioned insiders as opposed to disorganized and dispersed outsiders. It is extremely wasteful. More than a quarter of the trillion-euro EU budget supports the Common Agricultural Policy, which increasingly rewards landowners as opposed to cultivators, and farmers in rich as opposed to poor countries. Over 40 per cent of regional funding, a policy designed to transfer wealth from well off to less fortunate member states, is paid to the wealthy ones.

The now 750-member Parliament has operations in three different cities, and duplicate facilities in Brussels and Strasbourg, the latter of which stands empty for 317 days per year and costs 62.4 million euros to maintain. Outlays for quangos increased by a third between 2010 and 2013 and could be cut back by 30 per cent simply by eliminating those without any apparent purpose or function. And the new European External Action Service, the pseudo-diplomatic corps, which employs 3,611, spends about €500 million to little or no effect.[23]

The biggest challenge facing the EU is the most obvious one. The gap between the elitist approaches of the ruling Eurocrats and the democratic consensus needed for political legitimacy is huge. The problem starts with elitist thinking. Democracy, as the late Peter Mair pointed out, was much in vogue as a discussion topic among political theorists in the 1990s, but only in a very restricted sense. The focus of it was on making democracy compatible with technocratic governance, the preferred approach of the day. Traditional party democracy was, if anything, considered an encumbrance to the more efficient expert-run and stakeholder-based systems of the future – or so it was believed: representative government was thought to be ipso facto at the mercy of self-seeking politicians.

Technocratic bias at the European level mirrored certain trends at work in modern society, and to a degree furthered them as well. Suspicion of voter intelligence was particularly pronounced in Brussels. It is hardly surprising that democratic reform receives short shrift there. Or that no one from within the establishment has ever proposed a constitutional project based upon the consent of the governed. If some day there is to be such a thing, it will have to begin at the grassroots, will require detaching national politics from the EU, and reinvigorating political parties in the many countries where they no longer command citizen loyalty.[24]

The Single European Market (SEM) is a second challenge. Still regarded as the greatest of EU accomplishments, it was incomplete when it officially ended in 1992 and remains a work in progress. Services were still outside its scope, agriculture continues to be protected, state aids are, by and large, allowed, and public contracting remains unsupervised. The SEM has in fact been only a limited success. Barriers to trade exist in such network activities as energy telecommunications and transportation, as well as in capital markets, the digital economy, and energy. 'Creative destruction' has not been unleashed.

The SEM has had unexpected results. It did not, as promised, reduce unemployment. The trade effects were surprisingly unimportant compared to the financial ones. The level of intra-EU imports as a total of national imports scarcely varied, and export–import/GDP ratios remained largely the same in the core EU countries (other than Germany, because of reunification). Intra-EU exports as a percentage of total exports remained constant, at just over 60 per cent. Although extra-European exports have grown substantially worldwide, it is unclear as to whether this superior performance links in any way with SEM. Gross capital formation actually declined over the life of the programme, which may be attributed to the shrinkage of the public sector. The increase in foreign direct investment (FDI) has, by universal agreement, been the most important booster of growth, but it probably reflects a global trend. The EU's share of international inward FDI actually declined over the years in question. Best estimates of the contribution of the SEM to growth of operation vary from 1.1 to 1.5 per cent, far below the 4.5 to 6 per cent predicted in the EU's official Cecchini report.[25]

State aid policy is the divide between promise and performance, ideology and reality. Both the Lisbon Strategy of 2000 and the 'Europe 2020' programme call for it to be phased out. Yet this has not happened. State aid remains admissible under many conditions: *if* it is in the common interest, does not distort competition 'to an extent incompatible with the treaty', supplements entrepreneurial resources, is proportionate to the problem at hand, offers social advantages, is properly costed, and administratively transparent. It can take many forms: subsidies and grants; tax breaks, reduced social security contributions, subsidized loans; credit guarantees; purchase of state property at a discount; and tariff reductions. It can be offered in connection with climate change, research, company bailouts; small business loans, training and education, provision of risk capital, and services in the common interest. With so many exceptions it is difficult to speak of a rule. In the years 2000–2011 such aid amounted to about .7 per cent of GDP. The level of state aid did not decline during the decade in question. As for public procurement, now as ever, competition is absent.[26] According to the findings of an exhaustive study by the economist Patrick Messerlin, EU claims that such markets are more open in Europe than in those of their major competitors is wildly off the mark.[27] They are more restrictive than either those in the US or Japan.

The authors of a comprehensive report on the SEM process, while admitting to imperfect understanding, attribute its shortcomings in various measure to: poor implementation of directives; insufficient mutual recognition (of products and services); inability to influence public procurement; distortions in the service sector; and lack of labour mobility. Needed for the future, they report, are: fiscal harmonization; reduced environmental standards; infrastructural investment; and the elimination of 'cohesion' policies, which have 'exacted too high a toll in terms of growth'. 'Creative destruction', finally, should be encouraged to eliminate, among other obstacles, 'national regulations protecting undue rents, rigid labor market rules, industrial policy supporting national champions, prevailing public monopolies, [and] cumbersome procedures to set up new businesses' – none of which has happened during the present crisis.[28]

In spite of EU-optimists, who traditionally have viewed setback as veiled opportunity – 'beneficial crisis' being the relevant buzzword – little effort has been made by insiders to seize it. Frustration is rife. The defection of the Europeanists has begun.

The presenter of the 2014 annual review lecture of the influential but intramural *Journal of Common Market Studies* feared that,

> there seems little room left for the EU project to develop . . . no new frontier to bring into the Union and no new project to capture the imagination . . . Member states show little enthusiasm for revising the existing treaties or elaborating new frameworks for cooperation. Economically the Union has few new projects to offer and quite a number of challenges shoring up the single currency and the internal market. Politically, there is more concern with fending off the anti-European agendas of the new radical right than with fostering a common European identity.[29]

A senior, highly respected, but recently disenchanted Europeanist, Yves Mény, has a good explanation for the present frustration. Quite simply: 'There is not yet an obvious way out of [the] morass', if only because EU 'actors are in disarray . . . [and] caught between the necessity to act and the political reluctance to acknowledge fully the consequences of a multi-level governance system, notably democratic legitimacy and accountability'. Worse yet, he adds 'the EU system as such seems unable to address the challenges of the future, to suggest a program of action, to define its own fate in the global world of the twenty-first century'. The current crisis, he concludes, is not just monetary and financial in character, but political and institutional. Every major party in every member state is divided on the question of the EU and the public is, on the whole, strongly opposed to it. Although Mény hopes there is a way out of the present crisis, he cannot find it and fears that can-kicking will not suffice to save the EU. Change will have to be exogenous.[30]

Sensible reform plans were on hand but went nowhere. In 2002 the president of the European Commission, Romano Prodi, delegated to a distinguished EU-affiliated economist, Andre Sapir, the task of drafting a report with a strategy for delivering faster growth and for strengthening Community institutions in light of the impending Eastern Enlargement. The result was the single most rigorous critique produced in the history of the EU. Sapir's special concern was disappointing economic growth: decades-long declines that left Europe stagnating at 70 per cent of American per capita GDP. Attributing this poor performance to an inability to 'adapt an antiquated economic and social model to technological change and globalization', he saw a need for a greater mobility 'in and across firms', labour market flexibility, greater use of market finance, and increased investment in research and development.

Taking heart from the by then overshadowed Lisbon Agenda of 2000, Sapir devised a list of seven necessary structural reforms: strengthening the Single Market; raising investment in research and development and in education generally; introducing more flexibility and coordination into the European Monetary Union; focusing regional aid on poor countries rather than spreading it across the member states; improving implementation of regulations; slimming down and reorganizing the Commission as well as simplifying and introducing transparency into voting procedures; and restructuring the budget. The final point was of special importance. Terming the budget a 'historical relic', Sapir proposed targeting half of it to research and development and doing away with the principle of *juste retour* (proportionality). This would have entailed virtually eliminating the Common Agricultural Policy. Sapir's thoughtful plan went into the files, even though Prodi, who commissioned it, was an economist and, to all appearances, supported the recommended reforms. The lack of follow-up cannot be blamed on cumbersome bureaucratic machinery. It was due to an obvious fact: the Commission is in a deep funk.[31]

In the new millennium the focus there has shifted from fixing things to maintaining credibility. Bombast is now louder and more frequent. A painful search by a few conscientious insider-researchers for what went wrong has also begun. Professor Gerda Falkner of Vienna, a friendly critic, is the most serious academic student of the EU's failure to deliver. In early studies of what in EU jargon is called transposition – the incorporation of EU administrative directives into the laws of individual member states – to her surprise, she discovered not only serious discrepancies across the Community, but remarkably high levels of non-compliance. As to the actual implementation of policy, little statistical or other basic information was accessible to her. The frequency of scandals and the successive failure of audits led her to posit, however, the existence of a pervasive culture of corruption heretofore overlooked by the EU scholarly establishment.[32]

Falkner's recent studies have focused specifically on the credibility issue, which she calls 'compliance deficiency' and fears is destroying the public image of the EU. This is of critical importance, she argues, because the EU's 'landmark function' is 'integration though law'; if, in other words, the legal environment 'visibly degenerates' the EU will become a 'dead letter' and its survival will be at stake. She is warning, in other words, that its remaining legitimacy is at risk. The evidence suggests that it is already in big trouble: non-compliance is pervasive, growing, evident at every level of EU operations, and serious enough for the outgoing Commission president, Barroso, to address in a special speech to the European Parliament. In addition to his two basic concerns – non-compliance in summit-decisions and non-compliance in enforcing basic democratic values – Falkner found 'virulent' deficiencies in adherence to rules governing the EMU; failure to enforce laws in the member states; lack of respect for the rulings of the ECJ; and refusals to abide by previous agreements and commitments.

But the troubles run deeper, she fears. Beset by repeated scandals, Eurostat's statistics are suspect, as outside audits have consistently demonstrated. The Fiscal Compact of March 2012, the key policy by which the EU claims the authority to review and revise national budgets, cannot be enforced without stricter reporting standards. The Compact may also be illegal, according to her. Finally the 'no bailout' clause (Article 123) in the Treaty on the Functioning of the European Union (TFEU) has been seriously violated. The lack of legal enforcement has also facilitated political backsliding in both Hungary and Romania. Falkner's conclusion reaches far beyond the circumscribed scope of her inquiries. She says, in effect, that a state of law does not exist in the EU: 'Overall, there is no reason as yet to believe that EU law is actually obeyed in regular manner, particularly when the application and enforcement (not only the first step on transposition of directives) is concerned'. Adding that the Commission, except in rare cases, backs away from penalizing member-state violation of court orders, she calls for the creation of new enforcement machinery, but warns as well that one-size-fits-all policy-making invites cheating.[33]

The recent rise of quangos, the new feature on Brussels bureaucratic landscape, has added to the organizational confusion and lack of transparency found there. Prior to 1990 there were only three of them. This number doubled over the past decade. There are now fifty-two such quasi-governmental organizations. They employ 10,000 at the cost of about 3.5 billion euros per year. Most of these organizations, concludes the largest independent study made of them, 'add little or no value while duplicating the work of each other, or the core EU institutions as well as of the member-states' organizations and civil society'. Some, the study adds, like the Economic and Social Committee, 'have no impact on policy whatsoever. In existence since the 1950s the committee has never, within memory altered the outcome of an EU proposal.'

Once established, quangos are both hard to abolish and, according to an internal EU study, to keep in line; 'mission creep' is endemic. A sampling of characteristic quangos would include the European Foundation for the Improvement of Living and Working Conditions (EUROFOUND); European Centre for the Development of Vocational Training (CEDEFOP); Agency for the Operational Management of Large-scale IT systems in the Area of Freedom, Security and Justice; European Food Safety Authority (EFSA); European Insurance and Occupational Pensions Authority (EIOPA); European Joint Undertaking for ITER and the Development of Fusion Energy; and the European Defence Agency.

It is hard to specify what quangos do, as there are several different general types of them: advisory bodies, decentralized agencies focusing on a particular issue or field; financial supervisors; executive agencies tasked with executing particular programmes; public–private partnerships, many for research and development; and security and defence agencies. No overarching strategy has guided the rise of the quangos; rather, as an internal study concludes, the process has been driven by political interests. Twenty-two member states have at least one quango within their territory. While the relevance of many agencies has been questioned, 'the problem has usually been "resolved" by extending mandates instead of closing or merging them'. Due to their complexity and unclear remits, the quangos also suffer from lack of accountability.

Quangos inhabit a twilight zone of soft law. As a result, they are ungoverned by statutes. They can, however, exercise regulatory powers as technical actors. These powers are non-binding and growing in extent and numbers. They intervene in important policy areas like aviation, pharmaceuticals, and finance. This rule-making influence enables quangos to 'circumvent the properly competent legislative bodies in the decision-making process'. Their recommendations, while technically not binding, also show up in case law. It is unclear as to whether such enactments are consistent with the intentions of the statutory bodies. Nevertheless, the lack of formal procedures gives quangos a leg up in an otherwise time-consuming legislative process.

The result of such irregularities, according to an in-depth study, is a 'patchwork blanket' of policy-making. In fact quangos are out of step with 'institutional and legal reality'. This should be investigated in the financial field, in which the European Securities and Markets Authority has issued a whopping twenty-seven guidelines and recommendations in recent years. The irregularities in the soft law process undercut legitimacy, leave the legal status of enactments uncertain, and unnecessarily complicate the transposition of EU administrative law into national statutes.[34]

The way in which the Commission captured a 'competence' (administrative authority) to vet foreign direct investment illustrates, as an important study suggests, what the term 'integration by stealth' means in practice. It may, or may not, have consequences, or at least those intended. FDI is, as indicated above, crucial to economic growth. Yet no statutory provision had been made for it prior to the Lisbon Treaty (2007), which incorporated numerous articles from the rejected constitution. FDI did not enter the treaty as part of an overarching strategy. Nor did the member states necessarily want it; they were happy to compete for foreign investment by 'racing to the bottom' with tax incentives, subsidized loans, and so on. In fact, they had individually negotiated 148 bilateral investment treaties on their own. The European Commission often played an advisory role in such discussions and had repeatedly asserted a right, based upon the competition rules, to vet such bilateral arrangements.

At successive IGCs the member states had nevertheless repeatedly rebuffed Commission attempts to gain official recognition of such authority. Yet the Commission managed to slip the term 'foreign direct investment' into the verbiage of the Lisbon Treaty (Article 207) simply because the member states, tired of the wheedling negotiating process, fell asleep on the job. As further explained, 'the shift (in language) was not a political priority . . . [It] was one of thousands of amendments . . . and not prioritized'. While the Commission soon produced a slew of self-serving policy papers to consolidate its gain, the member states dragged their feet and continued to conduct business as usual. Stalemate resulted. The Commission informally agreed not to interfere with existing bilateral agreements but did not relinquish its claims. Its power to act in the future remains untested. The lawyers are having a field day. The article's author concludes that 'because of the absence of political debate . . . confusion still reigns. Member-states are not willing to let go of their sovereignty . . . the issue [may] ultimately [reach] the European Court of Justice'. Until such a time, the lack of clarity will impede FDI.[35]

Legal defences against integration by stealth are inadequate. The member states of the EU, although responsible to their citizens, have transferred powers to it with the expectation that precise limits would be placed on their exercise. However, this condition has not been met, as the relevant provisions in the Lisbon Treaty (2007) are elastic. The treaty distinguishes between exclusive and shared powers, those otherwise unspecified remaining under the subsidiarity principle reserved to the member states. Once, however, the Union regulates a shared power, it cannot be reassigned (pre-emption principle). As for subsidiarity, the Union itself determines whether 'an action can be sufficiently achieved by the member-states. In matters pertaining to the Single European Market, the standard is defined by the Commission.'[36]

'In a nutshell', according to the legal expert Emilie Ciclet, 'action depends upon what the Union wants for itself. The [application] of the subsidiary principle is deceptive and opaque.' Safeguards built into the treaty by the member states have proved to be wholly inadequate. In sum,

the unclear outer limits of EU action make possible not merely the expansion of power, but precisely the discretion to expand power that member-states in principle wish to deny. Deficient definitions of power may lead to EU policy-making à la carte, where the menu may not respect ... citizens' choices ... [and constitutes] a violation of the trust placed by the [member states] in the non-arbitrary of the exercise of the [EU's] function.[37]

## The Volkswagen Scandal

The Volkswagen diesel emissions scandal that broke in September 2015 placed the slipshod methods of the European Union in a glaring limelight. In that month, the American Environmental Protection Agency, with the assistance of clean air advocacy organizations, disclosed that by using so-called default devices – algorithms that gamed the testing system – the automobile manufacturer had systematically and massively violated the legal limits on nitrogen oxide. Some 600,000 American vehicles and up to 11 million European ones, including top-of-the-line Audis and Porsches as well as smaller VWs, were thus spewing out nine times the allowable amount of the deadly gas. Informed in 2013 of such findings, the European Commission refused to act, even though its own Joint Research Centre confirmed them, out of fear of the powerful automobile lobby.

Finger-pointing and recrimination began almost immediately. As reported in the *Financial Times*, 'Authorities across Europe have been passing the buck over who is responsible: The European Commission argues that it has no power to force the national authorities to look for default devices. But Germany has responded to a question about the cheating ... by citing the views of the Commission that there was no agreed method for preventing the use of illegal software.' 'We know', remarked a Swedish parliamentarian, 'that there are companies that don't give a damn about the rules ... the Commission is responsible for seeing we have a control framework that works.'[38]

The JRC had, in fact, discovered the discrepancies unearthed by US authorities as early as 2011, but in November 2012 the

Commission decided to postpone road testing until 2017, which prompted a complaint from the Danish environment minister, Ida Auken, that the delay was unacceptable and a dereliction of responsibility. In spite of warnings sounded by the EU environment commissioner, Janez Potocnik, that 'flaws in emissions testing meant that consumers were being grossly misled', no action was taken on the grounds that 'significant redesign of diesel vehicles would be required'. It was 'all about the financial crisis and saving the Euro', according to Ms Auken, 'the crisis had priority'.[39] She was only partly right. It was also about saving the Commission.

The collateral damage from the debacle continues to spread. The CEO of Volkswagen was sacked. The company's stock lost half its value overnight. A highly touted union-controlled business model was cast into disrepute. Millions of Volkswagen owners, the re-sale value of their cars plummeting, feel cheated. Plants are being partially shut down in Puebla, Mexico and Chattanooga, TN. The company town of Wolfsburg is bracing for hard times. Dividends will be skipped and the introduction of new models delayed, as Volkswagen faces falling sales, further investigation from national regulators in Europe, and liabilities, estimated at $30 billion. The head of Volkswagen of America got it right: 'Our company was dishonest with the EPA and the California Air Resources Board . . . We've totally screwed up!'

But he might have added that the company was bringing a lot down with it. All major European manufacturers, the innocent as well as the guilty, have huge stakes in diesel, and stand to be hurt. Would the scandal, as pundits suggest, mean the end of the diesel? Since both Germany and the EU had promoted diesel as environmentally friendly for over a decade, the infamous episode also badly tarnished their Green credentials. This did not augur well for the success of December's international clean air summit, or for the stalled TTIP negotiations still under way, which presupposed mutual trust. How, after such a debacle, could one count on the EU's reliability as a regulator?

The high rate of diesel market penetration, now at about 50 per cent, grew out of a 1998 compact between the European Commission and the car industry. This came in the aftermath of the Kyoto Protocol, a landmark in the fight against global warming, which provided a one-time opportunity for European automobile manufacturers to get a jump on the global competition. Under pressure to cut greenhouse gasses, the industry and member states then provided tax breaks to encourage the production of diesel engines. Although the fuel is efficient on $CO_2$ emissions, the nitrogen oxide it emits presents a substantially more serious health hazard than carbon. Two decades ago, in other words, Europe backed the wrong horse.[40]

Germans can seek consolation in sarcasm. As the scandal unfolded, a video aired on ZDF, a government-funded television channel, began with an announcement solemnly intoning, 'We interrupt this broadcast for an official threat to autoland Germany from the United States of America'. There follows a montage of oversized Ford, Chevy and Ram pickups, splattering through mud bogs, spewing out black smoke, followed by shots of bimbos in bikinis wildly firing guns – stereotypes of Americans at their worst. 'American cars', sneers the announcer, 'not manipulated. [Pause] For the good of the environment.' This kind of bad behavior, presumably, justifies VW cheating on emissions standards and official complicity with it.[41]

The public will pay the price for this colossal blunder in the future as in the past. In late October the EU struck 'a deal that has left [Europe] with a disappointingly weak testing framework. Manufactures will be allowed to exceed legal limits of [nitrogen oxide] by 110 per cent between September 2017 and the start of 2020. After that the motor industry will still be permitted to exceed the legal limit by 50 per cent – and indefinitely'. The EU has made a mockery of the existing emission limits framework, which explains in part why air quality in Europe has not improved over the past fifteen years. The EU entered the December environmental summit in Paris with halo aslant. In the meantime, the VW debacle continues to shred the credibility of Brussels.

## Corruption and Confusion

The most serious charge that can be levied against the Commission (and the Court) is the perversion of antitrust law, which not only distorts markets and reduces growth but undercuts the very legitimacy of, and rationale for, the customs union. Effective competition, as noted in a recent publication of Bruegel, a prominent Brussels think tank, 'constrains the exercise of market power: it effectively allocates goods and services to consumers, rewards productive firms that have lower costs of production and increases incentives to invest in new technologies'. The competition principle has, according to the paper, fallen victim to regulatory capture by powerful national interests in member states.[42]

The result is discrimination against foreign, mainly American, firms. The study adds that the problem of bias in enforcement, if unchecked, 'is bound to grow in importance in a world where economic activity is increasingly globalized, [as] mergers and acquisitions with a cross-border dimension have increased about 250–350 per cent since 1990'. It follows that such practices exact a high toll: 'In the long term, sub-optimal antitrust decisions allocating rents to domestic companies for reasons other than the promotion and protection of competition are likely to generate negative effects for everybody.'[43] The best defence against such misuse of antitrust law is to incorporate specific provisions into free trade agreements negotiated under the auspices of the World Trade Organization.

Coming on the heel of decisions to investigate Starbucks and Fiat Chrysler for violating EU rules on state aid, as well as anticipated actions against Amazon, Apple, and Qualcomm, the decision to prosecute McDonalds on similar grounds has raised eyebrows in Congress and set in motion countermeasures in the Treasury Department. The US federal authorities could no longer overlook the fact that only American firms have been the objects of such procedures. The legal grounds for them are dubious. The European Court of Justice, acting as the enforcement arm of the Commission, ruled that the tax breaks, given by Luxembourg and other EU member states, constitute state aid because comparable benefits had not been granted other firms – an unproven assertion. The agreements between American firms and European tax authorities rest on national laws, whose legality was not challenged at the time. They involve intra-firm transfers, in many cases of intellectual property, for which law tribunals have never established clear and binding rulings, and upon which European courts have never previously acted. The EU's case, should it succeed, would require the firms involved to pay back taxes to the countries with which they had reached agreement – thereby rewarding malefactors at the expense of US taxpayers!

Columbia University law professor Michael Graetz concludes from such bizarre legalism that 'European bureaucrats have found a new offense and imposed massive liability retroactively'. Attacking US multinationals is of course a political winner, but, asks Graetz, 'At what cost to the rule of law?' The matter will be fought out in the European and American courts for years to come. One might further ask, at what cost politically is the battle worth fighting at a time when a desperate Commission begs behind the scenes for the US Mediterranean fleet to aid in refugee repatriation and works overtime to enlist US tech giants into a cyber-campaign against Islamic terrorism.[44] The discriminatory anti-American business campaign, in which the state aid issue figures, may prove to be another case of overstretch.

Abetted by the un-rule of law, the pervasive culture of corruption in Europe not only impedes economic growth but undermines the integrity of the EU. Its importance is little recognized and denied whenever possible. Yet 76 per cent of Europeans think corruption is widespread and 56 per cent think it has increased in their own country. One trillion euros per year is lost to tax cheating. The size of the shadow economy, which varies substantially across the twenty-eight member states, averages 12.2 per cent. Old-fashioned income tax evasion is still the largest single contributor to the problem of tax cheating. The British Treasury estimates that it loses £15.3 billion to it, as opposed to £11.4 billion in VAT. The tax authorities in no other member country have published investigations of the subject.[45]

The leakiness of VAT collections, the main source of EU revenue, is a special problem. It is due to 'a protracted community decision-making process'; 'the absence of consensus on many issues'; and mistrust as well as absence of information exchange – all of which makes 'extorting taxes a profitable venture . . . and secure within the crime carousel from penalization'. Set up to deal with the problem, Eurofisc operates with 'twentieth- as opposed to twenty-first-century methods'. As with the case of state aid, there is 'an extensive catalogue of exclusions that allow refusals [to provide] information in practically every single case'.

The failure to collect the value-added tax (VAT) is the second largest contributor to the overall problem of tax cheating. The extent of such chiselling averages 18.5 per cent across the board and varies substantially from country to country. The virtuous Swedes, Finns, and Dutch come only 4–5 per cent short; the Germans, French, and British each divert about 10 per cent of the take from the EU treasury; the Romanians manage to hide no less than 41 per cent from the Brussels taxmen; and the Greeks and Italians each cream off between 35 and 40 per cent. For bulk amounts withheld – and for sheer chutzpah – wealthy Italy wears the crown with 47.5 billion euros stashed away from the fisc, as opposed to the runner-up, the much larger Germany, with a mere 27.8 billion euros. Such culture-specific discrepancies, which varied only a little in the individual countries between 2009 and 2013, are buried away in official reports and almost unknown to the public. It is hard to estimate the furore that would result if this ceased to be the case and the public became aware of the gross inequities that such numbers entail.[46] The Fiscalus programme adopted by the European Parliament to deal with the evasion problem has not produced any positive results. Characteristic in this respect 'is a duality of approach. On the one hand declarative statements about co-operation and community values and on the other hand legislation and provisions for actions which allow for protecting the national economy and even for unfair competition'. Plenty of talk, little action, and in the meantime, the EU's tax evasion problem, 88 billion euros annually, is . . . evaded.[47]

The recently elected president of the European Commission, Jean-Claude Juncker, can be depended upon not to reform official Brussels. He is very much at home there. Elected in June 2014 and installed in September, Juncker was a remarkable choice at a time when the angry public of austerity Europe demanded accountability and transparency, fresh ideas, and, perhaps, even a new sense of EU mission. He was the nearly unanimous choice of the right-centre-left coalition of the parties of state at the European Parliament, which united to deny a voice to the large bloc of newly elected populist Eurosceptics.[48] Juncker is the consummate Brussels *apparatchik*, an arch-insider who knows where the bodies are buried and the money is hidden. He was prime minister of Luxembourg from 1995 to 2013 (and therefore also a member of the European Council) and finance minister from 1989 to 2009. From 2005 to 2013 he doubled as permanent president of the shadowy Eurogroup of finance ministers. During the period of his ascendance in the politics of the Grand Duchy, the per capita income of his country outraced the leading six founder nations of the EU to the point that it is today twice that of neighbouring Germany.[49]

This extraordinary result was due solely to the expansion of the financial sector. Within days of Juncker's assumption of office, the International Consortium of Independent Investigative Journalists published a laundry list of big businesses, including leading American tech giants, which had received sweetheart tax deals from the government of his nation of 550,000 inhabitants, the size, President Erdoğan sneered, of a middling Turkish city. Juncker astonishingly professed to know nothing about such deals, even though the public record proves that, as he boasted at the time, he was instrumental in many of them. Juncker actually got away with this most bald-faced of lies and won a vote of confidence from the Parliament in November.[50] By agreement, the Parliament also promised not to raise the issue in the future, perhaps with an understanding that only miscreant Americans would be singled out for punishment.

Might this understanding also owe something to the culture of Wink-Wink! – and the likelihood that a certain number of the delegates held confidential bank accounts in Luxembourg? Only Juncker would know for sure. Pointing a finger, he claimed that Luxembourg was not the only offending country to offer giveaways to US big business interests. To underscore the threat of exposure, he directed his competition commissioner to launch a community-wide investigation of other member-state malefactors, one sure to drag on for many years, unearth much dirt, and divert attention from the Grand Duchy. Aware of his vulnerability, Juncker directed his slate of commissioners to make income declarations in preparation for the pre-nomination committee hearings conducted by the Parliament. Almost half of the twenty-seven nominees declared no financial assets, including those figures to be entrusted with the main financial and economic portfolios. Five nominees declared only their family homes. The average net assets of each nominee amounted to only 80,000 euros. Juncker himself made no disclosure. The declarations, a Commission mouthpiece sheepishly admitted, 'aren't supposed to be a comprehensive list of every single asset', but only those which, in the minds of the candidate, 'might create a conflict of interests'. 'The degree of transparency', commented the *Wall Street Journal's* sceptical reporter, 'appeared to vary widely'.[51]

Ever an opportunist, Juncker stands for everything and nothing. In November 2014 he set five priorities for his presidency: to create a single digital market, develop an energy union, negotiate a trans-Atlantic trade agreement with the United States, reform the economic and monetary union, and negotiate a new deal with Britain. It is, of course too early to judge outcomes, but during his first year in office it can be said that he has made no apparent progress in any of his designated goals. The same applies to two other fields reputedly of special interest to him: the European social model and defence. Wobbling along on in uncertain relationship to the larger events surrounding it, the weak Juncker presidency is hard to take seriously.

To date, his most significant initiative has been to strip the competition commissioner of his independence, and more specifically, to merge the office with that of industrial policy. Instead of protecting the consumer, as intended by the Treaty of Rome, Juncker would move the EU towards the Chinese model in which antitrust policy serves programmatic economic goals. Earlier in the year, Juncker indicated, with regard to the proposed coupling of the German operator E-Plus with Telefonica SA, that 'antitrust policy should be used to foster consolidation in the EU's telecoms market'. Antitrust experts concerned with such Orwellian policy-making still look, perhaps over-optimistically, to the European Court of Justice to block such an evident departure from what the EU purports to stand for.[52]

How Juncker plans to advance his agenda is shrouded in mystery, not least because of his misleading budget proposal, the central feature of his growth strategy. It included a new European Fund for Strategic Investment (EFSI) of 315 billion euros in infrastructure, education, and research and development in order to offer hope to 'millions of Europeans disillusioned after years of stagnation'. Yet only 21 billion euros of this money is actually public, and none of it is new. Sixteen billion of it will be drawn from existing EU funds; the other five from the European Investment Bank. The balance is supposed to be raised through voluntary contributions from the member states and private financial interests. To encourage state contributions, the EU will exclude amounts invested from the budget deficit figure used in monitoring compliance with fiscal rules, making a mockery of them.[53] Even with the projected outside contributions, M. Juncker's package will amount to only 0.8 per cent of EU output over its three-year course. One wonders what is to be gained from such inflated promises. According to a business intelligence service, 'Juncker's tactics', in short, 'raise broader questions over . . . the reality of his infrastructure plan, what impact it might have on Europe's economy and whether some of it is "smoke and mirrors" political posturing'.[54]

Similar doubts surround Juncker's promise to elevate 'Social Europe' as a priority. According to two recently disillusioned Europeanists, it has been hopelessly debased. Delors' claim that market integration would spill over into political and social integration has had, in their view, little purchase; the iron laws of functionalism apparently did not apply. His successors, the Third Way social democrats, geared policy to the market mechanism and neo-liberal assumptions; they were, the two complain, little more than neo-Thatcherites. The two Barroso Commissions, both dominated by centre-right conservatives, all but abandoned Social Europe. The much-touted Open Method of Coordination as proposed in the 2001 White Paper also made little difference in this respect. The Eastern Enlargement has further pushed the social agenda to the margin. The austerity policy of the crisis years has shredded what is left of Social Europe.[55]

One must also give a second thought to the new Commission president's commitment – something unexpected from a citizen of a country with only a 500-man army to defend Europe's borders – to build a military force. This curious priority, which he insisted upon during the selection process for the presidency, confirms the wisdom of the bestowal of the Louis XVI Prize conferred upon him by *The Economist* in 2005 for being the European most out of touch with reality. Overlooking the EU's ruinous policy towards Ukraine, Juncker proposes to grow an armed force strong enough to command the respect of Mr Putin. This will be a stretch. The EU spends less than a third as much on defence as the US, and there is no desire, even in France, to increase outlays for it. The twenty-eight member states of the EU have twenty-eight separate military establishments and, as a rule, operate only under one joint command, NATO. Even when occasionally acting independently of NATO, as in the small-scale Libyan operation, the French and British required logistical and intelligence support from the United States.

The European defence industry, apart from EADS, is national in character, and 'locked in a downward spiral of high costs, chronic over-capacity and declining military budgets', which raises the cost of military equipment by 30 to 40 per cent and makes it difficult to compete in export markets. Further budget cutbacks are in view for the next decade. The largest EU arms producer, BAE, does half of its business in the US. Its merger attempt with the Franco-German dominated EADS failed, and will not be renewed. US technological leadership, it hardly need be emphasized, extends across the board in the field of weaponry.[56]

One wonders, finally, where research and technology fit into Juncker's scheme. He inherited the Horizon 2020 programme dating from 2010, the purpose of which is to 'turn on the innovation growth machine in Europe', in other words, to catch up with the American high-tech industry. A successor to seven successive EU Framework Programmes for research and development, none of them notably successful, Horizon 2020 is an only slightly updated version of its predecessors and differs from them chiefly in being better funded by 15 per cent. At least such was the case until the President of the Commission Juncker raided it to the tune of 2.7 billion euros. Amid howls of protest from the Royal Society and other august scientific bodies, he agreed to sin no more. In the midst of the uproar Juncker also sacked the Commission's chief scientific advisor for disputing the case against genetically modified organisms (GMOs). These were, however, preliminary skirmishes in the high-stakes campaign to overcome the technology gap. The looming question is whether the Commission is competent to make the leap.[57]

As a first step, it must clean up its act. Administrative efficiency must be increased, salaries and benefits cut, tenure for officials ended, and superfluous quangos eliminated. Transparency should be improved by requiring documentation of provenance, that is, where policy papers originate; important information – for instance, meetings of the Commission – should no longer be classified; and the financing of lobbies and think tanks should be disclosed. To improve democratic legitimation, member-state legislature should be allowed to challenge Commission directives. The budget must be trimmed and waste reduced, above all in regional funding and in agriculture. Bureaucracy must be cut back by eliminating some of the twenty-eight commissioners. A new one should, however, be appointed to enforce the subsidiarity principle. A regulation should be enacted only if and when an old one can be struck from the books; sunset clauses incorporated into new laws and directives; incentives given to shrink administrative costs; and cost–benefit analyses required in all subsequent legislation.

The European Commission, if it is to survive, must become, as befits its purpose, 'the protector of the treaties'. The Commission must also strengthen its credibility by achievements rather than by crafty bureaucratic manoeuvring and windy proclamation. Finally, it must be fitted into a framework of representative institutions operating under law.[58] The reform agenda is lengthy, runs against the grain, and is unlikely to be realized piecemeal. It would face long odds in normal times. No one has a clue as to how all, or any, of this can be accomplished in face of the crises of Autumn 2015 or the demands of the new era.

# CHAPTER 6

# Threat of a Promising Future – or Endgame?

The European Union, or its successor, must adapt to a rapidly transforming world in which technology is changing the operations of the economy and requiring updates of law, governance, and administration. Techno-geopolitics, as the phenomenon is known, places new leverage in private hands and requires states to reshape laws and regulations in order to protect human rights. Power is being redistributed internationally and borders are losing their value as barriers. That such global influences are largely benign does not eliminate threats to independence, tradition, and freedom itself. Technology can be a two-edged sword. The strength of the forces in play raises the stakes. International shifts in power, moreover, increase the unknowns in Europe's future. The new China could either liberate spirits in the West or become a world model of state-capitalist authoritarianism.

Brussels lacks both the competence and the authority for the tasks facing it. Policymaking flounders in the critical fields of energy, finance, and IT – especially the latter. The advance of technology requires a new ecosystem, which cannot be created by administrative fiat, but must evolve endogenously through the economy. A protracted learning process will be needed to meet the challenges it poses. The time necessary for such a thing is no longer at hand. The problems confronting the EU are far greater than anything purely administrative. Future change, as perceived in Europe, will result from heavy economic and political pressure from abroad. It will be disruptive – upset pleasant lifestyles, challenge cherished values, create new social divisions, increase inequality, as well as generate as yet unforeseen political problems – and it is also certain to meet with heavy public resistance. Europeans face hard choices between economic growth and political preferences, and they must be made democratically. This is impossible in the present institutional setting. Any attempt by Brussels at this late date to restore growth by means of a Schumpeterian wave of creative destruction, however economically desirable, could be politically ruinous in the absence of public consensus. But no such thing is in the offing.

The very survival of the EU is now at stake. The refugee crisis of autumn 2015 caught the already demoralized, overstretched, dysfunctional and nearly immobilized institution off guard and unprepared. Like no prior event, its brutal accompaniment, the 13 November suicide bombings in Paris, dramatized the perils to which an alarmed and angry European public is now exposed. Even Brussels belatedly recognizes that retrenchment is inevitable, in particular that the Schengen agreement for passport-free travel within the EU must come to an end. Thus the process of deconstructing the European project has already begun. Brexit – British withdrawal from the EU – is likely to advance it. The retreat of Brussels can either be orderly, a rout, or some combination of the two. In any case, the history of the EU has run its course, and in times to come its role in Europe will at best be greatly diminished. Successful adjustment to future economic challenges will require as a first step political devolution and the revival of national power. There is no real choice in the matter if the future Europe is to thrive.

## The Interconnected Economy

The commanding economic importance of information technology is evident in the comparison of US–EU productivity data. American per hour productivity fell behind Europe in the 1970s, but has accelerated thereafter, from 1.3 per cent from 1980 to 1995 to 2.2 per cent in the following decade, whereas Europe witnessed declines of 2.3 per cent to 1.4 per cent between 1995 and 2005. The United States continues to outstrip Europe. While the IT-producing sector of the European economy has not slipped in relation to its larger American counterpart, in the IT-using sectors the story is a different one.

According to economists Nicholas Bloom, Raffaella Sadun, and John van Reenen, the gap has widened because of poorer internal management of IT resources, a point underscored by same-sector comparisons of European firms with US-owned foreign affiliates. Their general conclusion is that Europe's future economic welfare will depend heavily on the adoption of state-of-the-art American business methods.[1]

Some 2.3 billion people today have access to the Internet and by 2020 some five billion will be connected. Three-quarters of human beings now have mobile phones. Mobile data traffic increased eighteen times between 2011 and 2016, and a similar rate of increase is projected for the next five years. The McKinsey Global Institute estimates that flows of goods, services, and finance, chiefly driven by digital technology, have increased one-and-a-half times since 1990 to 36 per cent of global GDP. These flows add 15 to 25 per cent annually to it. The 'digital divide' is narrowing, with the fastest growth now occurring in the developing economies and in South–South trade, which has tripled its share in overall international commerce since 1990 and now equals 38 per cent of the total. This expansion is increasingly concentrating in high-tech and capital-intensive branches of production. For every job lost to the internet, 2.6 have been created.[2]

The global digital network fosters 'recombinant combination', according to the authors of *The Second Machine Age*, by which they mean that 'each development becomes a building block for future innovations. Progress does not run out, it accumulates.' There are, they add, 'infinite numbers of possible recombinations . . . The constraint on the economy's growth [is] the ability to go through all . . . possible [ones] to find the truly valuable [exception].' This places a premium on 'sustained exponential improvements in most aspects of computing, extraordinarily large amounts of digitalized information, and . . . innovation'.[3] It favours the big numbers, the nimble, the risk-taker, and, more often than not, the odd man out. It places at a disadvantage the deliberate, the incumbent, the routine, the established, and the bureaucratic, and presents a threat as well as a challenge.

Organizational innovation is necessary to capture the potential benefits of the new era. It will feature countless interactions of machine intelligence with millions of interconnected brains. It is difficult to predict what might come next, but it is worth bearing in mind that within ten years of the launching of the world wide web entrepreneurs were finding ways to use it to reinvent publishing and retailing. The larger enterprise-wide IT systems of the 1990s made possible a wave of business process redesign. Huge productivity gains resulted, which disproportionately benefited small firms. The first five years of the new millennium brought a welter of new applications as well as breakthroughs in process innovation, as evident in aerospace, biotech, oil and gas exploration, agriculture, medical care, precision manufacturing, banking and finance, retailing, distribution, and logistics.[4] IT is changing how we think, work, and socialize. The keywords now are peer-to-peer, the Cloud, the Internet of Things, and crypto-currencies.

There is reason to believe that the future impacts of the changes now under way are underestimated. Five to seven years are normally needed for improvements in IT process and design to show up in productivity gains. The impacts of technological progress, increased interconnectedness, economies of time and place, quality enhancement, and speed and ease of operation, are not necessarily reflected in estimates of GDP. The acceleration of change is, and probably will be, faster than yet realized.[5] It is almost impossible, first of all, to capture the value created by the

Internet of Things. The McKinsey business consultancy estimates it at between $3.9 and $11.1 trillion per year, based on an analysis of nine 'settings': home, office, factories, retail environments, worksites, human health and fitness, logistics and navigation, cities, and vehicles. Seventy per cent of the value created is in business-to-business settings and depends upon the interoperability of systems. A single example of what this involves will have to suffice. Operations at a mine site can benefit from condition-based maintenance (through continuous monitoring); operations management (both centrally and remotely); health and safety (by tracking real-time condition of workers and equipment); diagnosis-related R&D (to avoid component failure); and pre-sales enablement (by providing usage data to optimize costs and maintenance).[6]

Interoperability creates 40 per cent of value and will generate new business models.

> For example with the ability to monitor machines that are in use at customer sites, makers of industrial equipment can shift from selling capital goods to selling their products as services. Sensor data will inform the manufacturer about wear and tear on machinery, enabling the manufacturer to charge by usage. Service and maintenance can then be bundled into the hourly rate or all services be provided under an annual contract. Machine performance can inform the design of new models.

It follows that '[such] an approach will give the supplier a more intimate tie with customers'.[7] What the Internet of Things potentially offers, in other words, is a better management system that will reduce costs, waste, and capital requirements, as well as have positive spill-over effects.

To meet the economic challenges of the new era, the EU must break with anti-growth practices, the first of which is an anti-scientific bias. It grew out of a campaign orchestrated by the

European Parliament, in a desperate bid for relevance, to exploit public fears of so-called Mad Cow Disease, which afflicted British herds in the mid-1990s. The success of this exercise in fear-mongering gave rise to a larger one against so-called Frankenfoods, produced, ironically, thanks to the most recent of agricultural scientific breakthroughs, genetically modified organisms (GMOs). Apart from the fact that they are chemically identical to the natural product, cheaper to raise, environmentally friendly, and medically harmless, public fears, easily fanned, of ingesting an unfamiliar product resulted in a ban. The demagogic European Parliament campaign was surely also related politically to the fact that an American seed company, Monsanto, controlled the relevant patents.

The GMO ban retarded the development of the European biotech industry generally, which, after promising beginnings, soon fell hopelessly behind its US counterpart. With a single 'grandfathered' exception, no GMOs have been planted in Europe, nor will they soon be. A decade of testing – none of which can yet be undertaken there – is required to develop strains able to thrive in specific climes. In the absence of domestic GMOs, Europe has become the world's largest importer of Brazilian and Argentinian animal feed stocks, which are grown (don't tell anyone!) with Monsanto seed. Europe has lost the chance to supply the market itself. The Commission, belatedly aware of the adverse consequences of its policy, is now directing a hapless campaign to reintroduce plantings of the modified seedlings locally under the otherwise traduced subsidiary principle.[8]

GMO policy set an important precedent. Out of it grew the Precautionary Principle, by which, according to consumer economist Karl Purnhagen, 'EU institutions pretend to have answers to citizens' fears'.[9] It gives the Commission the authority to ban any product or process relating to the environment. This is God's own gift to the regulators, who can act in areas which member states would prefer to preserve the right to intervene. It also saddles producer with coils of red tape. It takes three times longer and costs ten times as much to bring a chemical product to market in Europe than in the United States. In this formerly German-dominated field, industry is in retreat.[10] It is troubling, according to Giandmenico Majone, that the EU is 'presently promoting the (precautionary) principle to the status of a "central plank" of Community policy . . . and to a general principle of economic and environmental law.'[11]

To overcome the subpar performance of European science, the Commission has adopted successive Framework Programmes, beginning in 1986, each varying somewhat in emphasis, but all combining elements of research and product development, along with the mission of building a European scientific community. That is, to qualify for funding projects, grant applicants have had to build in a 'European component'. Awards are on the basis of proportionality and, instead of being peer-reviewed, are vetted by bureaucrats. 'All of this', according to one critic, 'produces little of scientific distinction and few of the commercial break-throughs that were its main motivation . . . Knowing how the Commission's scientific patronage system works becomes more important than your research product', resulting in 'wasted billions of EU taxpayers' money'. Then, too, there is the paper-work: 'the Commission maintains a system of 200-page propos-als with up to 13 revisions of an accepted proposal needed before the funds flow, followed by hundreds of pages every quarter and many more at the end, plus detailed and usually fictitious "exploi-tation plans" and audits'.

The most recent R&D funding scheme, Horizon 2020, differs from the Framework Programmes in only one particular – allo-cating a larger portion of the programme 'without any consid-eration of geographical distribution', in other words, on merit.[12] It features prominently, however, in Commission rhetoric, as the core of EU 'smart growth' or innovation strategy. It is being thwarted, however, 'by the consequences of comprehensive de-leveraging by states, banks, and households, and the associated evaporation of demand from within the region, (which) is further aggravated by the weakening of member-states fiscal resources and tax avoidance'.[13] Only Finland and Sweden devote more than the EU-targeted 3 per cent to R&D.

The results of Horizon 2020 have been less than impressive. Europe has remained a leader only in terms of public money spent on research and development. In all important growth sectors, however, it continues to fall further behind. The general explanation for this situation is that 'New firms fail to play a role in the innovation dynamics of European industry, especially in the high tech sectors'. Would-be innovators complain, specifically, of lack of financial resources (68 per cent), domination by established competitors (64 per cent), red tape (62 per cent), weak demand (68 per cent), and poor distribution (50 per cent). How well-founded such gripes are is difficult to determine. It is evident, however, that – due to the advent of Cloud computing, the Internet of Things, and the increased virtualization of the value chain – innovation will occur in so many ways that, to be effective, government programmes should do no more than focus on a few critical roles and monitor their development, but otherwise generally keep hands off.[14]

The rapidly progressing complexity of the innovation economy is outracing policy-making everywhere, but especially in Europe. Some tentative lessons follow that can be drawn from recent experience. Innovation is, first of all, increasingly less closely related to spending on research and development than previously. New products are being brought to market with low capital costs. A second point is that, even more than before, innovation results from team efforts by persons located throughout the globe and operating outside legal and patent structures (like open sourcing). There has been, thirdly, a shift from supply-side innovation to co-innovation to user-innovation – in other words, to self-generation of product and process.

Finally, innovation requires the existence of an ecosystem of businesses large and small; universities and research institutes; venture capitalists, angel financing, crowd-sourcing; and state support. The implication of this fact is that investment in research and development will not, in the absence of these additional agents and actors, result in innovation. As for the state, its role in this process should be limited to maintaining the flow of information in the marketplace, without which development will be stunted.[15] This consideration is all the more important now that Cloud computing is lowering the costs of market entry. At the same time, competition between platforms (Google, Microsoft, et al.) is leading to the emergence of competing, semi-open architectures, each of which aims at maximizing the number of applications available to their customers.

The Internet of Things, the latest stage in the evolution of IT, entails the use of cyber-physical goods and services to optimize production of increasingly personalized products, thereby enabling a consumer to tailor the use of objects and processes to individual preferences. 3-D printing is a further development along this line, which points to the end of scale economies and a new era of mass product and service customization. Finally and above all, sectoral distinctions are disappearing and synergies proliferating. The development of biotech requires that of information technology; the modernization of sensoring supplies immense amounts of new data; and the mining of metadata has applications throughout the economy.[16]

The interrelatedness of these processes requires a sharp cutback on EU regulation, according to Britain's minister of life sciences and technology, George Freemen, lest current excesses lead to a 'new Dark Age' in bioscience by 'strangling the revolution in big data and digital health at birth'. In connection with the ongoing negotiations over Brexit, UK officials are resisting attempts to broaden the range of medical products that must be screened by a 'premarket security panel'; fighting a proposal that genetic testing must be carried out by qualified medical personnel, arguing against allowing member states to ban GMO products unilaterally as damaging to the Single Market; and heading off attempts restricting the use of animals in research.) The Luddites, Freeman concluded, 'threatened to hold back discovery in the nineteenth century (and) we face a similar challenge today'.[17]

## Information Technology Policy

The European Union's Information Technology Policy purports to be about protecting citizens from misuse of personal information by the giant American platform companies. This is a mere fig leaf for old- fashioned protectionism. The policy itself is futile, and can only raise costs of IT service in Europe and discourage new entrants. It is also in headlong retreat from a public which demands taking full advantage of the web to prevent terrorism. The result is much sound and fury, signifying almost nothing, The European Union's IT regulatory policy betrays a characteristic imprint of industrial policy, but in an odd turn, the EU is twisting antitrust activism in order to shelter incumbent businesses. The approach, according to the former head of research at Microsoft, cannot work, as controlling the data is ultimately self-defeating. Put differently, it is pointless to retrofit a governance structure which was derived from geographic borders in a borderless world. The impending provision of global wifi, for instance, will threaten existing telecommunications companies.[18]

The European Union's state-centred approach to internet regulation, the core of its misconceived innovation policy, grew out of the deregulation of the telephone companies (telecoms) in the late 1970s, and is archaic in today's world, according to Harvard Business School professor Shane Greenstein. Whereas in the United States trustbusters had broken up 'Ma Bell' (AT&T) in the 1980's, making possible 'innovation from the edges', in ways unforeseen by any planner, elsewhere the control over internet access was most often handed over to incumbent monopolies for the capture of rents.[19] EU telecommunications policy represents one such case. It has rested on a compromise, in which national incumbents retained control over network infrastructure and telephony as well as of a theoretical power of great subsequent importance 'to control new operators concerning abuse of dominating position'. The settlement that was reached set the standards for networks and services, rules for access and interconnection, telecom equipment, and separation of regulation and operation. It also set the stage for a wave of policy papers regarding satellite communications, mobile, infrastructure, and convergence. The initial hope that the sector-specific regulations for telecoms would give way to a more competitive market has not been realized at the wholesale level. Absent the liberalization pressures of the 1980s and 1990s, 'it has never become politically acceptable to abandon the national character of telecom provision'.[20]

Multinational corporations have lobbied hard to internationalize network services, to weaken the telecommunications monopolies, and to increase service provision, but with little success: 'The incumbent operators – the former monopolies – still dominate most of the telecom markets in most European countries . . . Even in retail markets, incumbent operators still dominate'. Technology nonetheless advances. While circuit-switched services (telephony) remain overwhelmingly national, 'packet switched service (the internet) is international', and demand for them continues to increase. Thus, talk about the need for a Single Digital Market has not been accompanied by much action. Roaming charges remain painfully high. The political will to do something is lacking, according to the IT expert and EU consultant Anders Henten.[21]

At the same time, 'new players have become the organizers of the eco-systems . . . Apple and Google, and . . . other platforms in the communication area'. This has hurt the telecoms, particularly in their stronghold and cash-cow of voice communications. The only way out, Henten sheepishly suggests, is to put pressure on the newcomers:

> The struggle for dominance . . . has a European dimension . . . The US has now forcefully entered the scene because of its domination of the IT industry. Practically all the global service providers are US-based. These kinds of regional dominance relations are not always explicitly on the policy agenda. It is a bit embarrassing if it becomes too explicit . . . But the challenge is there . . . and does play a role in EU policy-making.[22]

In the view of the chief of the European association of IT users there can thus, 'Never be a single digital market at either the retail or wholesale level'. He adds that a growing variation in national regulatory systems and the weakness or absence of liberalization pressure is aggravating the situation.[23]

Cloud computing occupies centre stage in EU IT policy. The term is, first of all, a misnomer, as the 'Cloud' in question is not something somewhere way up in the stratosphere, but very much earthbound and made possible, in fact, by very large, immensely powerful, and low-cost data centres (server farms) coupled to improved apps. Together they enable users to rent services as needed rather than to purchase capital equipment, which involves large upfront expense and may lead to excess capacity. The savings are considerable, a one-quarter decrease in storage costs over the past three years. The industry, now estimated at about $180 billion, is growing at 50 per cent annually. Costs are expected to drop further.[24]

Protectionism is the driver of EU Cloud policy, the underlying idea being 'to encourage domestic . . . providers and develop domestic infrastructure'. In view is the creation of a single European digital IT market. Lobbying actively, the big German and French telecoms have enlisted Chancellor Merkel and President Hollande behind their position. Embodied in a confidential February 2015 paper penned by EU Digital Commissioner Guenther Oettinger, and hysterical in tone, it calls for the creation of a powerful new regulator to oversee a vast array of US-based Internet companies and is more far-reaching in scope than anything publicly announced. The paper warns that online websites 'are transforming into super-nodes that can be of systemic importance for the rest of the econ-omy, only a limited part [of which] will not depend upon them in the near future . . . putting the whole economy at risk'.[25] As correc-tives, it proposes the creative application of competition policy (meaning the organization of Euro-champions), tight rules of data protection, restrictions on the transmittal of information, and the storage of data only within Europe. Combined with parliamentary grandstanding – the passage, for instance, of a resolution calling for the break-up of Google – it amounts to little more than a campaign of harassment.[26]

To lend heft and credibility to his programme, Herr Oettinger might consider learning from the Chinese, whose thinking along similar lines is far more advanced than his own. The Cyberspace Administration of China is now in charge there. It will operate on the principle of internet-sovereignty, as expressed in a recent nine-point manifesto claiming that countries should have the right to govern Internet traffic within their borders, effectively giving their governments a veto power over technical protocols interlinking the global net, and fracturing the international system that makes it essentially the same everywhere. To this end, the Chinese government is providing financial and policy to support to giant domestic firms like Alibaba, Tencent, and Sina (an information aggregator) that are developing semiconductors, servers, search engines, social media pages, and e-commerce sites far larger than any in Europe.[27]

Facebook, Twitter, and Google have faced outright bans in China. Other well-known American providers like LinkedIn,

Hewlett-Packard, and Yahoo have caved in and are collaborating with the government. China has gained allies in Russia, Turkey, and the Central Asian dictatorships. The European Union might someday also be eligible for membership in the group. It cannot, however, thrill to the notion, expressed by the director of the China Labs think tank that 'China in the next two decades will become the center of cyberspace'. Europe is, in any case, too far behind the curve to cherish similar dreams, and the EU is utterly lacking in the tools necessary to make any such effort.[28]

EU high-tech policy bristles with problems, beginning with the fact that as a result of the emerging internet phenomenon vast swathes of telco producer surplus have 'benefited the ... consumer ... and deserve celebration, not hand-wringing'.[29] Europeans like and use the new consumer services stored on the Cloud no less than Asians or Americans, and businesses of all sizes need the economies it provides. A restrictive policy must therefore confront daunting, and arguably insurmountable, practical problems. One is the conflation of physical location with access and legal jurisdiction. Should location be defined as the state where a firm is headquartered or those where it conducts operations? How far down the supply chain must one look? Do the restrictions extend to foreign-owned European companies? What if multiple physical locations are involved in transmittal and storage of information? What about data that is accessible remotely? Additional issues arise from the conflict between the proposed EU regulations and existing WTO rules. What, finally, is a 'European Cloud'? Does it include non-EU members and non-Schengen states? And should member-state laws simply be overridden? In any case, the Cloud thrives on metadata, and metadata requires the Cloud. Interference with this truism will exact a high cost.[30]

The attempt to use restrictions on the Cloud as a catapult to a single digital market is absurd in light of the European Union's inability to overcome the legacy of national telecoms influence. Neither can the IT economy function properly without American hardware. Yet the EU policy is more than an annoyance to Silicon Valley. The last thing the big tech companies fear is, to be sure, European competition. After all, the market capitalization of Google increased by $65 billion on a single day in July 2015, while Apple held $200 billion in cash on the same day.[31]

The threat facing the tech giants is, as with China, that restrictive legislation will end the party for everyone. Even so, the danger would seem to be slight. The demonization of the American IT industry will likely continue, but at little actual cost. The platform companies still pour three times more money into lobbying Washington than Brussels. In any case, a Europe in depression would be ill-advised to lame the most advanced and dynamic sector of its economy, which over a fifteen-year period has generated over 700,000 new jobs.[32] If and when recovery comes, it is certain to attract large amounts of American venture capital and invite buy-outs of many kinds.

For the EU, a sensible IT policy would, according to Bruno Macaes, Portugal's secretary of state for European affairs, bring together 'the slowly accumulated results of the industrial revolution with the . . . explosive innovations in computing, information, and communications systems'. By 2030 it would increase the size of the European economy by a quarter. The critical step is the move from 4G to 5G, which provides the necessary bandwidth for the Internet of Things. The fragmented structure of the EU electronic communications market stands in the way of such a step forward. In addition, a single set of rules must govern the future transfer and storage of data, equally binding on European and foreign firms. Public sector tenders must also be opened across borders, and globally integrated production chains fostered, following the principle of 'No transfer, no Production'. The Trans-Atlantic Trade and Investment Partnership (TTIP) and its tran-Pacific counterpart (TPP), as Macaes concludes, 'represent a critical opportunity to advance the . . . modernization effort'. He does not discuss what will happen if TTIP fails.[33]

The prospects that an approach similar to that outlined by the Portuguese expert will be adopted are not great. On 6 October 2015, the European Court of Justice, upholding Commission policy, struck down the fifteen-year-old 'Safe Harbour' pact used by 4,500 American companies, including the platform giants, to transfer European data wholesale to the United States, on the grounds that it violates European privacy laws. Billions of dollars in advertising revenue are at stake, as is, far more importantly, the principle of internet seamlessness. The ruling would require Europeans, or Americans, to create a separate storage system and, more seriously, accelerate cyber-Balkanization. Europe would end up with a patchwork of national systems – and an internet regime with harmful implications for the economy.[34]

None of this upset Microsoft, which in November reached an agreement with the Commission to allow EU citizens to choose between storing their data domestically or allowing it to be transferred to American servers. Additional costs could, the company concluded, be passed on to European customers. The other US mega-techs are expected to follow suit. The effect of the European court's decision, in brief, will simply be to stifle new market entrants forced to confront the higher costs of data storage in Europe. Worries about market fragmentation, state-dictation, and the seamlessness principle seem to have been put to rest at Microsoft in recognition of the fact that ill-conceived regulation will, in this case as in so many others, merely reinforce oligarchic power.[35] The machinations of the Commission's IT policy are, however, a mere prelude: the intensification of the European war on terror will reinforce the power of the US techno giants by tightening the bonds between them and national intelligence agencies.

## Finance and Recovery

While it may be true that the only way to salvage the European Union is to transform the EMU into a system of parallel currencies, in the absence of catastrophic failure an organized dismantlement of the eurozone will almost certainly be incremental and involve years of slow-grow, no-grow, or worse. The European Depression has done serious damage to the financial structure. The debt load has increased substantially, private banking has been de-Europeanized, the Basel III regulatory requirements will require de-leveraging, important 'too big to fail' financials remain at risk, and rates of investment are low. As of December 2015, even after a perceptible upturn, European banks carried bad loans of 10 per cent (excluding financials) and 7.3 per cent overall, over twice the American rate and equal in amount to the GDP of Spain. Such overhanging legacy problems derive from the 'unpardonably belated recapitalization of the banks' as well as the 'old habits of making taxpayers foot the bill'. The unfortunate proclivity was still evident in the belated but timely December 2015 proposal of the Italian prime minister Matteo Renzi to split off a 'bad bank' from four bankrupt financials before the 'no bailout provisions' of a recent reform set to take effect on 1 January 2016.[36] The move is expected to be a predecessor to a larger 'bad bank' deal, which will violate rules limiting state aid. Italy has also not signed on to Single Resolution Mechanism (SRM) for the orderly shutdown of failing financials.[37]

Official EU finance policy represents a reiteration of the familiar, is overly defensive, and anchored in a commitment to saving the euro as a single currency rather than to Europe's economic welfare. It includes a spate of disciplinary procedures to enforce fiscal probity, and mechanisms for insolvency resolution, as well as for deposit insurance – all of them iterations on the discredited 'stability and growth criteria' and none of them yet put to the test. Financial realities nonetheless are inconsistent with the official line, creating the uncertainty disliked in financial markets.

Official policy has barely got off the ground. The compliance system is 'so baroque it's incapable of delivering results. Finance

ministers are groaning under the burden of the system's complicated procedures. Many of the recommendations to national
capitals are not being followed.' EU officials can poke and prod
national economic policy according to 100 indicators. It is, in the
view of one of them, 'gradually bordering on the insane'.[38] A
deposit guarantee fund exists only on the drawing boards;
national financial authorities ignore the 'bail in' rule, which
would require bondholders to take haircuts, and refuse to adopt
a European standard for bank resolution, that is, for the shutdown of bankrupt financials – to mention only three of the loopholes and exemptions that are standing in the way of a level playing field.[39]

EU financial policy also includes heavy doses of rhetoric
attaching to the phantom of a Single Financial Market. The
latter is nowhere in sight, not least of all because the City will not
take orders from Continental Europeans, and cannot be forced
to do so. Any pooling of interests will be on its terms. Meanwhile,
quantitative easing will undervalue the euro, stave off sovereign
default, and keep the eurozone on life support. In the longer-
term, repair of the financial system will require a new openness
to change. In practice this will mean dropping ambitious EU
reform plans in favor of American banking practices and accepting increased influence for US investors and financial methods.

A *Capital* Markets Union, a much more ambitious endeavour,
will be necessary for recovery, in the view of Nicholas Veron and
Guntrum Wolff, senior researchers at an EU think tank. This
standpoint marks a break with the still unenforced Commission
policy of disciplining national fiscal policy by means of compulsory reviews to assure compliance with budgetary rules – a
warmed over version of the unworkable stability and growth
criteria. Although, at the onset of the crisis in 2007–2008, exotic
new forms of Wall Street funding – above all securitization,
derivatives, and shadow banking – received blame for the near-
collapse of the financial system, it has since become apparent,

according to the authors, that American non-bank lending was a source of strength. President Draghi of the ECB observed as much in stating that 'the crisis has shown the drawbacks of over-reliance on a bank-centered lending model. ... We need to develop reliable sources of non-bank lending, such as equity and bond markets, securitization, lending from insurance companies, and asset managers, venture capital, and crowd funding'.[40]

Such a reliance on financial markets (as opposed to banks) will require a revolution in European finance as well as in EU policy. It must rest on the leadership by the City, the only world-class financial centre in Europe, that is, with capital and credit markets on a par with those of Wall Street. European companies rely 90 per cent on bank financing; American ones about three-quarters on capital and credit markets. European retail banking has remained largely national in character, and wholesale banking has, in the course of the Depression, lost its cross-border importance. The same home bias is evident in equity holdings, 61 per cent of which is domestic in origin. US-type capital markets, in contrast, spread risk across regions and smooth the impact of deep recessions on consumption and investment. Such EU–US distinctions carry over into households. Europeans save in deposits, Americans in shares. Americans have nearly three times as much per capita wealth in stocks and bonds as Europeans, albeit less wealth in the form of state pensions and home equity. Incentives should be provided for shareholdings in order to deepen and broaden the capital pool, according to Veron and Wolff.

The financing of small and medium-size firms, including start-ups, is a matter of special concern: they, and not large incumbents, are the main generator of new jobs. Securitization is the best available source of funding for them in most cases. Venture Capital (VC) is critical for high-tech start-ups. Public funding is no substitute for it, since, as Veron and Wolff conclude, the control mechanisms that are inherent in any use of public funding easily enter into conflict with the high-risk high-return logic of VC investment . . . and [lead] to market and price distortions which have ended up penalizing rather than helping the most innovation-oriented VC's. The EU should refrain from throwing public money at the VC market.[41]

Even in the banking sector of the financial world, the US has taken a commanding lead. Several things have delayed bank recovery in Europe. Lack of strong leadership was one of them; there was no equivalent to TARP. European banks also had bloated balance sheets and lower capital ratios than their US rivals going into the Depression, and they faced more complicated regulations. Finally, they were mired in a zero growth economy. As of December 2015 European banks carried a trillion euros in bad loans. Not surprisingly they badly trailed their US counterparts in return on equity – 3.95 per cent as opposed to 8.54 per cent. Thus the market capitalization of the six biggest US players increased by over $250 billion since 2010, that of their European competitors by only $9.5 billion. They have the scale 'that we no longer have', according to the chairman of Barclays PLC, 'to go global'.[42]

US banks also have the wherewithal to go digital, the defining characteristic of the present age in finance. The conclusion, according to a McKinsey analysis, is that 'revenues and profits will migrate in scale toward banks that successfully use digital technologies to automate processes, create new products, improve regulatory compliance, transform the experiences of their customers, and disrupt key components of the value chain'.[43] It will take three to five years to fully digitize, and a failure to execute will invite new international competitors like Alibaba (which in addition to retail banking has now entered the field of wealth management) as well as other new entrants from high tech. 'The most significant impact, according to an expert study, will be in price erosion, as technology companies allow delivery of financial services at a fraction of the cost, and this will be transferred to the customer in lower prices'.[44] Within the near future, the digital revolution could wipe out two thirds of bank earnings.

Survival in the financial field, including retail, will require substantial investment, but still more importantly, flexibility. Top-down regulatory methods must be adapted to the dictates of worldwide change and may require repatriation of regulatory authority to member states, some of whom (and the Nordics in particular) are at the forefront of the digitalization process. New banking models could well usher in a disruptive era like that of the 'American Challenge' of the 1960s, in which fresh ideas and new money trigger changes from within the European economy. No such developments will be forthcoming, however, until the questions overhanging the EMU are settled. Europe will most likely remain a laggard in the near future.

At the same time, real reform – or is it restoration? – is finally in the works, and may foreshadow the kind of arrangement that Prime Minister Cameron will strike in order to head off Brexit. Recent policy shifts may well give the City the autonomy it has long sought. In September 2015 the European commissioner for financial stability, Lord Jonathan Hill, proposed to break with doctrinaire schemes of financial regulation followed since the financial collapse of 2009 and to update banking along American lines. He vows to deepen European venture capital markets, at present only one-fifth as large as those in the United States, to raise securitization similarly in order to reduce the dependence of small businesses on bank financing, and to improve retail banking. Rather than advancing 'grand schemes or swashbuckling reforms', Hill vaunts a 'proudly workmanlike agenda', in which 'the UK needs to be shaping the system—not looking on while others make the rules'.[45]

Hill's pronouncement marks a departure from the official stance of the Juncker Commission, but also from that of the champions of an EU Capital Markets Union. Decrying Hill's proposal as 'underwhelming, a designer of the far-reaching capital markets proposal of 2012 criticized Hill's approach as unlikely to 'trigger a qualitative change in the structure of European capital markets'.[46] He also concludes that Britain's apparent lack of ambition may betoken cautiousness born of the refugee crisis. Yet the financial commissioner's plans have been backed by both the European Central Bank and the Bank of England. As a first step towards spurring new investment, the new finance commissioner is proposing to lower capital requirements by 25 per cent on bundled auto leases, mortgages, and credit cards. In view is the restoration of securitization to pre-2009 levels.[47] As 2015 drew to a close, Lord Hill provided an offhand estimate that fifteen to twenty years would be needed to create a capital markets union. For its part, the Commission is considering postponing its 'Mifid II' reform plan, now scheduled to start in January 2017, for still another year.[48]

Meanwhile, and far removed from Europe's capital, a striking innovation with far-reaching implications has occurred in the financial field that may make present policy discussions irrelevant. At the epicentre of financial innovation is the cryptocurrency known as Bitcoin. The term refers to a technology as well as a virtual monetary unit. The unit is not physical but computer-generated. It is in fact no more than an entry on an encrypted ledger known as a blockchain. Transfers can be made all but costless as well as instantly to and from other such accounts. Transactions are immediately recorded on the respective blockchains and, within a few minutes, verified.

Powerful algorithms or 'hashes' are what makes the blockchain system work. They derive from what amounts to a race between powerful computers ('miners') to generate a sixty-four-character alphanumeric code which captures the change in the account balance ('wallet'), for which the 'winner' receives a small reward *if* a certain number of other competing machines verify the correctness of the transaction, for which they receive a slightly more than nominal payment. It should be added that both buyer and seller, as well as the nature of the transaction, are anonymous, and also noted that millions upon millions of such transactions can be conducted simultaneously.

The technology is a completely closed digital system that does not rely on trust or require intermediaries. The value of the 'currency' depends upon the volume of transactions for which it is used. The operation of the system presupposes control of the Bitcoin supply, which is scheduled to increase at progressively lower fixed rates over a thirty-year period. The value of the crypto-currency reflects projected future demand in relation to the money supply. Cost and, ultimately, security are the keys to its appeal. Merchants using Bitcoin, to take an obvious example, can save the 4 per cent fee attached to credit card use. The potential for cost reduction in business-to-business transactions is immense. The technology is especially suited to cross-border settings and to the unbanked majority of the world's population. It can also potentially break the link between governments and the money supply; libertarians thus love the idea.

The technology can, however, also be adapted for internal exchanges within existing fiat money systems. More than likely, Bitcoin will be folded into, but also modify the operations of, existing financial institutions. Or it may generate powerful competitors, other crypto-currencies, thereby mimicking a theoretical Hayekian world of competitive public and private monies. Finally, the technology has ramifications extending far beyond the realms of finance and commerce. An automatic self-enclosed system, it does not require laws or even ethics to function.[49]

Although Bitcoin technology is new, it is at the same time the most recent chapter in the rise of electronic money. The path to its adoption has been paved by the credit card, the ATM, and so on. Bitcoin is only six years old and still beset with teething problems – both fraud and malfunctions – but the technology is here to stay if properly regulated, buttressed with insurance products, protected from hackers, and made easily convertible into physical currencies. Interest in the use of Bitcoin is expanding rapidly, and in a digital age with exponential rates of change, can be counted on to mount in the future. Venture capital is on the hunt for investment opportunities, Wall Street financials are investigating possible usages, and governments, central banks, and treasuries are studying the financial and strategic implications of the new technology. No one can predict how or when a break-out might occur, but it is reasonable to conclude along with the authors of *The Age of Cryptocurrency* that,

> if applied globally to the inner workings of the economy, the model could save trillions in financial fees; computerize much of the work done by payments processors, government title offices, lawyers and accountants; and create opportunities for hundreds of millions people who do not currently have bank accounts, but who do own smart phones.[50]

Bitcoin can now no longer be dismissed as a gimmick. In the 'first significant commitment by the banks to collaboratively evaluate and apply the emerging technology to the global financial system', nine of the largest investment banks, led by Goldman Sachs, JP Morgan, and Credit Suisse and including many others as affiliates, 'are planning to develop common standards for blockchain technology to upgrade back-office systems and save perhaps billions of dollars in costs to automatic execution of contracts'.[51] Only accredited users will be granted access to the system. Other similar consortia are also in the works. Conceived by its developers as a way to circumvent the global banking system, blockchain technology is now heralded by the big financials as 'the ultimate back office makeover'.[52] Bitcoin is a challenge, and perhaps opportunity, whose implications are only beginning to unfold. It should be taken seriously in Brussels and Frankfurt.

In the meantime, bank lending remains a weak link in the European economy. The Commission lacks the power and the know-how to redress the situation. The best that can be hoped for in the near term is that the adoption of American financial methods and the encouragement of American capital investment will restore conditions like those antedating 2009.

## Energy and Recovery

Recovery will also require shifts in policy towards energy. Up to now, it has been a mess. According to the researcher Georg Zachmann,

> the European internal energy market is drifting apart . . . Europe's security of supply is not assured and energy prices are substantially higher than in the USA . . . Europe's pioneering role in climate change has failed to produce an international agreement . . . The targets adopted in 2008 (20 per cent renewables, 20 per cent increase in energy efficiency, and 20 per cent reduction in greenhouse gases) and the third internal market energy package have not [improved] sustainability, security, or the competitiveness of European energy supply.[53]

Rather, EU emissions trading and cross-border energy exchanges have declined in recent years, national considerations drive investment decisions, and financing has been unavailable for the expensive transformation from a carbon-based economy to one of renewables. The Green agenda has driven up costs and not improved energy security. The proclamation by Council President Donald Tusk of the Commission President Juncker's intention to create an Energy Union has met with inter-state squabbling and complete inaction. A combination of the Volkswagen crisis, international unrest, and high costs, if anything, betoken a turn away from the primacy of environmental considerations in energy policy.

There are few certainties and many unknowns in the energy field. It is subject to the vagaries of geo-politics, market forces, technological change, and scientific discovery. Long-term planning can at best be indicative and must be subject to continuous review. Energy policy should grow out of informed public consent; it requires strict adherence to the canons of scientific evidence and should not resort to scare tactics. Only belated have these lessons been learned by Brussels. Energy policy must confront a 'trilemma', and somehow serve three not necessarily compatible ends: supplies must be secure, affordable, and minimize greenhouse emissions. The latter gets priority in official EU policy, which Germany leads. At the same time, security has been a recurrent concern, but not one in which, notwithstanding extended policy discussion, the EU has had much influence. Cost has taken a back seat in Brussels, but can no longer be overlooked, as it is seriously reducing competitiveness. Security is a constant concern, and subject always to political circumstance. To speak of overall EU energy policy implies coherence, where there is none.[54]

The Kyoto Protocol of 1997 culminated in the first major foray in the long-standing EU-led campaign to assert international leadership in the immense field of climate control. It was at the time heralded as both a great diplomatic triumph and the forerunner of future grand projects. Signed by thirty-seven industrial nations plus the EU, the protocol focused on designing a single global market for trading carbon permits as a panacea for addressing global warming.[55] The approach never worked as planned, in part because the EU's purportedly pathbreaking Emissions Trading Scheme soon broke down, as evident in the price fluctuations per pound of $CO_2$. Set at 8 euros in 2005, they jumped to 30 euros by early 2006, only to fall by half in April, then return to 8 euros, until collapsing to zero in 2007. The malfunctioning system led to speculation, price increases, and windfall profits – wretched results quite unrepresentative of cap-and-trade policies in place elsewhere.[56]

At the same time, the various subscribing parties developed their own methods for coping with the carbon problem. Thus, at the Copenhagen Conference of 2009 the EU failed in a daring bid to secure full-scale international commitments for targeted emissions reductions. Ambitions have since been tempered, in practice if not in theory. The 2014 purported upgrade of the 20-20-20 plan adopted in 2007 (calling for an equal percentage of cuts in emissions, increases in efficiency and in consumption of renewables) was, in fact, nothing of the kind. According to the Oxford Analytica Daily Brief Service, the targets set for 2030 were actually quite modest; the EU was 'strong on commitments [and] weak on instruments. Energy efficiency requirements have been debilitated, while carbon pricing and harmonization of energy policies have made almost no progress . . . Environmental considerations are taking a back seat to economic and social concerns in Europe'.[57] Targets were henceforth non-binding.

The Paris Conference of February 2014, called to renew Kyoto, was, except in official public statements, a complete bust. Although the gap between promise and real-world performance should not necessarily be equated with failure, it would characterize EU energy policy generally. As in many other fields, the member states managed to safeguard their national energy systems – be they in the area of fossil fuels or electrical power generation.[58] The quango set up to monitor compliance, the Agency for Cooperation of Energy Regulators, lacks not only enforcement machinery but the necessary statistics for the job.

The December 2015 climate summit in Paris, COP21, which was attended by no less than 40,000 delegates, set lofty goals but, once again, failed to reach an agreement with teeth and resulted only in can-kicking; implementation would remain at the national level and be up for review only every five years.[59] For the EU this result was anti-climax, but hardly unexpected. The big deal was the bilateral agreement previously reached between China and the United States on reduction timetables running to 2030, which were written into the draft agreement. The two mega-emitters had agreed in advance to reject a binding international treaty, as insisted upon by the European Union, which thereby ceased to be the central player in climate control diplomacy. Its importance in overall energy policy will, correspondingly, be reduced.

The lockdown of Paris in the aftermath of the suicide bombings was a grim reminder of more pressing problems than an eventual warming of 2 to 5 degrees by the end of the century. The shocking terrorist act will create rich opportunities to critics for whom climate change is dogma rather than scientific fact, and who argue that global warming does not merit the high importance assigned to it in Euro-American public policy and as a humanitarian issue. China, India and most other emerging nations agree.[60] The new uncertainty surrounding climate policy is of serious concern to the CEO of the Norwegian national energy company. Norway is Europe's most reliable gas supplier, with a 30 per cent market share equal to Russia's, but over a quarter of the nation's reserves are in the Barents Sea above the Arctic Circle. To deliver gas from there to Europe at current levels and prices will require hundreds of miles of pipeline and therefore also a twenty-year supply contract not subject to the unpredictability of environmental policy, the lobbying of coal producers, and or Russian strong-arming; in the absence of such a commitment, Barents natural gas will – to Europe's detriment – have to be liquefied and sold overseas.

The new uncertainty surrounding an EU reset in policy towards Russia will change the cards, according to the commentator, Nick Butler. Neither France nor Germany wants to fight for Ukraine, and a Russian commitment to battling ISIS in Syria will make it possible to return to business-as-usual, in which in return for a long-term delivery contract, the EU will agree to lift sanctions, ditch plans for a European Energy Union, and drop any objections to proceeding with the Nord Stream II pipeline (across the Baltic). How these plans fit in with the current eco-agenda remains to be seen.[61] Their significance for Ukraine is, however, clear. What had previously been a frozen conflict, subject to melting, would now go into permafrost. The EU declared itself unable to 'block a project that abides by the region's laws', and as such had to terminate its opposition to Nord Stream II. Russia would, in other words, no longer have to depend on Ukraine to deliver half of the Russian gas supply to Europe. The truncated, beleaguered and economically struggling nation was left without its only big cash cow and hung out to dry.[62]

It is hard in a few words to describe adequately the diversity of factor endowments, strategic vulnerabilities, cost structures, and so on across the energy economies of the twenty-eight member states of the EU – or do anything more than hint at the problems they raise for overall policy-making in the energy field. Suffice it to say that, for instance, France generates most of its power in nuclear plants, and Poland with subsidized coal, while the Baltic nations are almost totally dependent on Russian gas, and Finland is building nuclear power plants to export electricity to Russia. Only three European nations – the UK, the Netherlands, and Norway – have domestic sources of natural gas, and only one, non-EU Norway, is a major exporter. Only Germany, apart from Poland, mines a significant amount of coal. The Federal Republic and its North Sea neighbours do, however, have good facilities for handling overseas shipments of the fossil fuel. Malta has no domestic sources of energy whatsoever. Nothing can come of President Tusk's European Energy Community.

Cost is certainly a factor in the unofficial loosening of environmental policy. Renewables (solar and wind) require heavy subsidization, and the targets now set for it – 25 per cent by 2013,

35 per cent by 3030, and 50 per cent by 2050 – will probably prove unsustainable. In the meantime, 'feed-in tariffs', which require utilities to buy costly energy from solar and wind producers but allow them to then pass the increases on to both household and commercial consumers, have raised prices by 17 per cent for the one and 21 per cent for the other. At the same time, they have resulted in shutdowns of old-fashioned coal-burning plants, even though their 'base load power' is needed at times of peak demand, when, because of darkness or fair weather, solar and wind producers cannot operate.[63]

As a result, the German government has subsequently restricted mine closures, and the coal industry, facing huge losses, has demanded compensation for having to maintain idle plant. Aggravating the situation facing renewables has been consistent underestimates of transmission costs, especially for wind power, which must be conveyed from the North Sea to Bavaria. Making the situation still worse has been Angela Merkel's refusal to budge from the *Energiewende* (energy transformation), a policy adopted with much fanfare and little cost-analysis in the aftermath of the Fukushima meltdown, which steps up the pace of planned nuclear plant shutdowns. In consequence of the new power shortages, Germany imported record amounts of American coal in 2013 and 2014 and missed the 20-20-20 targets.

The big utilities have taken a hard knock as a result of Green policy. Europe-wide they lost 55 per cent of their market capitalization in the five years between 2008 and 2013. Although the high costs of environmental policy have had adverse impacts across the EU, the German case is of particular importance. The Federal Republic's two giant utilities, RWE AG and E.ON SE are now drastically down-sizing, and the latter actually splitting into a 'clean' company and a 'dirty' one. Mounting expenses for power – currently twice those of the United States – undermine the competitiveness of whole swathes of German industry and lower industrial investment. The availability, thanks to fracking, of a reliable long-term supply of cheap American oil and gas has lured German money from the chemical, fertilizer, paper, and manufacturing industries into the American South, thereby further reducing a long-standing decline in the rate of domestic industrial investment. This bodes ill for the future.

Even a brief discussion of European energy policy must at least make reference to the security issue. The EU has not played a strong hand: it could not finance the planned Nabucco pipeline, which was to have supplied the Mediterranean countries with central Asian gas; did nothing to prevent Putin from diverting the South Stream line from the Balkans to Turkey; and flapped arms impotently as he annexed the Crimea and, through proxies, occupied eastern Ukraine. Surely the US–EU-imposed sanctions did not please Mr Putin, but, they did, if anything, add to his popularity with the Russian public. The desirability of a new EU–Turkey strategic gas partnership has thus far generated only hot air and has been overshadowed by Russian military intervention in Syria and Turkey's relationship to the current refugee crisis.[64]

The good news is that Putin did not reduce gas deliveries last or this winter. Indeed he cannot afford to, given the collapse in carbon prices. The fracking boom, which environmentalists decry, has substantially weakened his position. In 2014 Russia actually increased oil and gas production, and will continue to do so as long as technically possible, even in the face of OPEC opposition. It is Russia's only major source of foreign exchange. The current US–EU sanctions, it should be noted, do not apply to either the oil and gas industry (Exxon and BP) or the giant exploration companies (Schlumberger) – each of which has recently cut big deals in Moscow. The European Union will remain by far Putin's largest customer even if the large-scale joint enterprises with China develop as planned.[65]

Changes in world supply may well determine the EU's energy future. For Europe, fracking is no more than a beneficial might-have-been. Vast reserves in Argentina, Russia, and China, where significant exploration has now begun, will be on tap long before any domestic source is available. It is remotely possible that Prime Minister Cameron's decision to open twenty-seven gas blocks of Britain's vast reserves to drilling will eventually change the picture, but they will not produce for an estimated five to ten years.[66] Fracking may well prove to be a case similar to that of GMOs, in which the boat was missed. One cannot, of course, rule out the chance of a disruptive technological breakthrough in the energy field – for instance, in battery storage capacity – but the incubation process will likely occur elsewhere, given the unfavourable European innovation environment. Significant reductions in carbon consumption – by substituting natural gas for coal – can nevertheless be expected, even without benefit of EU intervention. The introduction of renewables could, however, face delays as a result of the collapse in carbon prices.[67]

In the energy field, as elsewhere, the priority assigned to strengthening the EU politically has produced inefficiencies and exacted high costs. A recent paper from scholars at the University of London concluded that 'past experience demonstrates that a regional, bottom-up dynamic seems to be more suitable to tackle issues encountered by the actors involved in the internal energy market as the latter prefer to work with the neighbours with whom they share common interests and hardships, rather than at the EU level, where it is often difficult to reach a common concern'.[68]

Rather than as a means of vaunting the European Union's leadership in the fight against global warming, policy should be made with a view to reconciling the need for economic growth, clean air, and security of supply; to balancing the costs and benefits of cleaning up the environment; and to re-examining the most economical way to do the job. This will entail dropping unrealistic targets, eliminating costly regulation, replacing wasteful cross-subsidization with a flat carbon tax, reviewing the cost-effectiveness of different approaches to energy-saving, and revising policy in light of new scientific evidence. The public stands to gain from the relinquishment of the EU's claim to 'owning' environmental policy, something favoured by majorities across the nations of the industrial world and recognized as necessary by the leaders of China, India, and Brazil.

In each of the three critical economic fields – IT, finance, and energy – policy-making had broken down even before the events of Autumn 2015 stunned, paralyzed, and left the Commission clueless. The result was long in coming, the consequence of excessive ambitions, intellectual rigidity, inept execution, and tone deafness. In each case, initial plans had to be abandoned and in disorderly retreat measures be taken, which would have the effect of a return to the status quo of 2009, except for one fact. Before that point could be reached, the deterioration of Europe had to be staunched.

*Trade: A Last Chance*

Negotiations are now underway for two international agreements – the Trans-Pacific Trade Pact (TPP) and the Trans-Atlantic Trade and Investment Partnership (TTIP) – each of which is of unsuspected potential importance globally and in Europe. In line with international trends, though unsynchronized with official EU policy, each, or both, could be a game-changer for Europe. Nothing as ambitious as these mega-discussion-rounds has ever been undertaken on a world scale in the commercial realm. They not only cover trade practices; if successfully concluded, they will set common ground rules for the general conduct of business internationally and provide the framework of a global economic constitution. For its part, TTIP could spur recovery in Europe, strengthen the Single Market, increase national interdependence, advance the integration process, revive the EU, and improve Europe's global standing.

Yet the chance that such things will come to pass is slight. The institutional machinery in Brussels is in disarray. The Commission has lost its role, the Parliament has not yet found one, and the Council is badly divided – and each of them represents a veto point in the treaty ratification process. Neither together nor separately have they presented the TTIP issue to the public or tried to create a popular constituency in favour of it. To be sure, the elites in every member state strongly support the trade agreement. Yet the same was true of recent referenda – over the proposed Constitution, Swedish EMU membership, the Danish ratification of the Maastricht Treaty, and the Irish one on the Nice Treaty – and each of which they lost to populism.

A mirror of political dissatisfaction, this grassroots movement has been on the rise across the EU for years. The unmanageable refugee crisis can only fan the flames of discontent. The public mood now runs from angry and sullen to the merely defensive. Mistrust of the technocrats who purport to run Europe from Brussels is widespread. No one wants 'more Europe' or speaks of a 'European Dream'. Few imagine any longer that the European authorities can protect customary ways of life or uphold standards of living. A general lack of public trust will likely cause the TTIP negotiations to collapse before they are concluded and ratification begins. A last chance for the survival of the EU as a viable institution will thereby have been missed.

International trade, although relatively flat in 2015 (estimates vary from growth of 2.8 to 3.1 per cent), is set for a prolonged boom and a marked transformation. Oxford Economics expects world trade to quadruple to $68 trillion by 2050, and a think tank of Citicorp, the huge Wall Street universal bank, projects growth of 6.1 per cent annually between 2010 and 2030, as compared to a growth rate of 5.4 per cent between 1990 and 2010. Internationalization, and the emergence of new supply hubs will play an increased role in future growth in the impending 'third phase of globalization'. The most striking new change will be the emergence of Asia, which will soon overtake Europe as the world's largest trading area. As previously, the value of internationally traded goods will double the rate of GDP growth once unreported gains in the high-tech field are taken into account. A new trade agreement is overdue. The last major one is over twenty years old.[69]

Exogenous forces can once again be a catalyst to European reform. Together – and perhaps even without the latter – TPP and TTIP can create a new international context and can set in motion a process that would open markets, restore growth, trigger a reconfiguration of the eurozone, revive national political institutions, and bring the ailing continent abreast of fast-unfolding and dynamic trends that are driving development in the geotechnical age and shifting global power to the revived civilizations of Asia. If only by dint of sheer numbers, China, India, and the nations in their region will, in the near future, assume co-governance authority worldwide with a still technologically more advanced Europe and United States.

If within the framework of TTIP the European Union can accommodate such an epochal change, it may survive as an institution – not, however, as an embryonic federal government but as a stepping stone to a new global order in which the role of the state is overshadowed by that of the giant companies that shape the global economy. In the absence of such a development, the EU risks becoming a relic, or disappearing altogether. If TTIP should fail, and, as likely, TPP be adopted, Europe will miss its place at the banquet table. Adherence to the Pacific Basin alliance-dominated global trading bloc will then be piecemeal and occur without EU intervention. Individual nations would either sign on to TPP or face de facto discrimination outside it.[70]

TPP and TTIP are more comprehensive than traditional trade agreements, which are chiefly concerned with tariffs, and also broader than the updated version of recent bilateral free trade agreements, which have proliferated in the years since the failure of the Seattle meeting of the World Trade Organization. The mega deals also include provisions for eliminating non-tariff barriers, as well as so-called 'behind border tariffs' or administrative regulations which impede the free movement of goods and services.[71] They thus inevitably impact policy areas normally subject to legislative regulation in the fields of labor relations, environmental policy, and public health.

The most critical concerns of both sets of the trans-oceanic negotiations are intellectual property rights, rule-making, and the regulation of product and process markets. These matters are of special importance in high-tech growth fields, as well as in those in which economies of scale and scope are critical, of which automobile manufacturing offers one prominent traditional example, and any of the fast-breaking IT sectors several others. The impetus to agreements concerning such matters derives from the unprecedented border-bursting dynamism of technological change and the unleashing of creative energy in the non-European world which, together, strengthen market power in relation to that held by governments. It is a force which the latter, barring catastrophe, can at times restrain, but not, over the long-run, contain.[72]

The two sets of negotiations are often seen as running in parallel, but the Pacific Basin track began earlier and, as is by now evident, will be concluded sooner than the stumbling trans-Atlantic counterpart. TPP will also set important precedents for TTIP, if the latter is eventually enacted. The United States stands to be the main beneficiary from the current trade diplomacy, regardless of whether either one or both agreements are eventually concluded. This judgement is based less on the commercial benefits of the new arrangements than on the additional power that would accrue to the leader of one of the two new trade blocs or the only member of both of them.

Washington cannot take credit for having developed a grand strategy with this result in mind. President Obama paid little attention to trade issues during his first term. Only after his famous 'pivot to Asia' in 2011 – a purely strategic decision – did the Pacific Basin gain priority in regional policy-making. Until then, negotiations for free trade agreements between the United States and its NAFTA partners (Mexico and Canada), on the one hand, and Pacific Basin nations on the other – New Zealand, Malaysia, Singapore, Vietnam, Brunei, and Chile – had proceeded without urgency, their general purpose being to contain Chinese economic influence. Their commercial importance was something of an afterthought.

This, in retrospect, seems surprising. According to Alan Deardorff,

> as a free trade agreement (FTA), TPP will overlap numerous other FTAs, so that its economic effects . . . go beyond simple trade creation and trade diversion. It will also include a host of other issues, such as trade in services, technical barriers to trade and intellectual property.

Though less important in terms of trade than TTIP, it will, he concludes, nevertheless 'transform the domestic economies of the many member countries'. The potential significance of this fact should be seen, according to Razeen Sally, in light of the fact that 'Technological innovation has enabled the modernizaton of [developing Asia], but the crucial enabler has been liberalization of internal and external trade, of domestic and foreign investment, of product and factor markets'.[73]

The appearance on the scene of Japan's Prime Minister Shinzo Abe, a man with a sense of historic mission, transformed a secondary concern of US policy into something of international importance. After his landslide victory in December 2012, Abe – breaking with a generation of failed economic policy-making by his ruling Liberal Democratic Party – pressed for radical reform of the Japanese economy, by means of the so-called 'three arrows' policy of monetary easing, increases in public spending, and (the most difficult) structural reform. The two main stumbling blocks to the latter were guaranteed lifetime employment in industry and subsidized rice cultivation – both costly sacred cows of Japanese politics. Along with the main business association, the rice farmers cartel (JA Zenchu) is the main pillar of the Liberal Democratic Party, but Abe's overwhelming political strength, according to Professor Nakano of Sophia University, has 'eliminated any credible threat of switching votes to another party', and thus enabled him 'to push through critical agricultural reforms [and] sign up to a TPP deal without a damaging backlash in the rural ballot boxes'.[74]

Comparing his policies to those of his Meiji predecessors, from the very outset Abe committed Japan to joining the trade pact. 'Future historians will no doubt see', he ventured, 'that [it] was the opening of the Asia-Pacific Century. Participation in the negotiations ... will be a provident masterstroke.'[75] Abe's persistence and showmanship were rewarded once Washington belatedly recognized that Tokyo had handed it a golden opportunity to head what could potentially become the world's largest and most powerful trading bloc, some 40 per cent of the total volume. It was not, however, until June 2015 that Congress managed to pass so-called Fast-Track authority, vesting the American president with an in–out vote instead of the impossible task of negotiating each line separately. Almost unnoticed during the months of Congressional bickering over TPP was the fact that the new presidential authority could be used in connection with the TTIP, which had, to Europe's great good fortune, passed quietly under the political radar.[76]

Once, however, the Obama administration picked up the ball, it ran. The advantages of TPP were obvious. It would tie Japan into US Pacific Basin FTAs, thereby doubling the value of the treaty network. Even more significantly, it could provide a forum – as the WTO could not – for addressing the chief American trade concern, rule-making. According to the trade expert Bryan Mercurio,

> it is clear that that the USA entered the TPP [negotiations] with a view to . . . creating a new standard for the twenty-first century, which can be spread not only as a template for subsequent FTAs but also be multi-lateralized back to the WTO and (also provide) a new template for global trade relations.[77]

Other Asian and Pacific nations are in the process of joining the Trans-Pacific Trade Pact. They include Korea, Thailand, the Philippines, Taiwan, and Costa Rica. The evidence would suggest that the US is seeking to use the deal to 'direct the future economic order in the region for decades to come'. Finally, Japan's announcement that it would join the TPP, resulted in a Chinese decision to speed up negotiations for trilateral trade agreement to include Korea as well; ASEAN (the South East Asian customs union) dropped objections to a Japanese affiliation; and the EU announced its intention to proceed with 'FTA negotiations with Japan after years of delays'.[78]

TPP was concluded on 5 October 2015 after a marathon negotiating session. The deal must now be ratified, by no means an automatic process. If and when it comes into force it will be the biggest breakthrough in international trade in the past two decades and could end up being President Obama's most important economic legacy project.[79] The agreement bans the obstruction of the free flow of data across borders. It puts pressure on India and China to conclude their own deals, as well as on Europe to get on with TTIP. It might even herald the beginning of a new round of global trade talks under the auspices of the World Trade Organization (WTO).

TPP is a serious threat to the EU, according to Matthias Bauer of the ECIPE international trade think tank. The tipping of the global balance towards Asia favours American exporters, 'a natural presence in the region', the destination of one-half of US exports. TPP thus harmonizes and lends coherence to existing FTA relationships. The strengthening of regionalization will undermine the authority of the World Trade Organization, Bauer adds, and the WTO is calling for an EU–US counterpart. Under the rubric of Neighbourhood Policy, European FTAs have traditionally been strategic rather than commercial in purpose, to the detriment of Europe's trade relationships with Asia, he notes.

Trade diversion by the Pacific Basin arrangement will thus be substantial and will also inevitably reduce investment in Europe. The fact must furthermore be faced that '(TPP) will . . . discipline corporate governance, investment competition, and state-owned enterprises, substantially improving the business environment by strengthening competition and innovation'.[80] Finally, the proposed agreement 'could make the first and best claim of being the new (international) agenda-setting pillar', covering, as it now will, some 60 per cent of world trade.

The Trans-Atlantic Trade and Investment Pact (TTIP) would be advantageous for both sides. The EU–US bilateral trade amounts to about one trillion dollars each year. The mutual investment is three to four times that amount, and, in the American case, thrice that of Asia. The EU invests eight times as much in the US as in China and India combined. The Commission estimates that it would raise European GDP by half a point annually and American GDP only a tenth of a point less, with most of the gains deriving from the simplification and harmonization of regulatory regimes.[81]

The elimination of non-tariff barriers in regulatory procedures, product standards, and registration expenses would reduce American product prices by an estimated 8 per cent in Germany. Since the differences in such technical measures are mostly only minor, bilateral trade should increase by 30 per cent, which amounts to an addition in European annual disposable household income of €545. More important still, at least from the

European standpoint, TTIP will provide the Trans-Atlantic partners a one-time opportunity to draft common rules and standards that later can be fitted into international agreements through the WTO.[82]

Negotiations for TTIP have been actively under way since July 2013, but have not made substantial progress. The reasons for this are less surprising than they might initially appear. A couple of them are historical. The EU's authority to represent Europe in foreign trade negotiations was, of course, vested in the Rome Treaty and soon recognized by the General Agreement on Tariffs and Trade (GATT). Yet this step forward occurred in the context of the state-centred Bretton Woods system. While it is true that the US and EU acted as partners in successive negotiating rounds leading up to the Uruguay Round, from the standpoint of the EU, the international aspect is less important than the intra-European one.

Monnet was no free-trader. The European Coal and Steel Community was not set up to introduce competition into West European heavy industry in the sense of American antitrust doctrine, but to enable a state-like authority to administer a cartelized industry. Delors was even more strongly opposed than Monnet to *laissez faire,* which he viewed as a threat to industrial policy; to him export success was important as merely a prerequisite for the formation of Euro-champions. His economic priority, and that of his successors, was to strengthen trading relationships within the European market. In any case, the foreign trade directorate at the Commission had for years been something of a stepchild in Brussels. Not until 2006 did the EU, at the behest of Trade Commissioner Peter Mandelson, adopt a 'Global Policy' of trade promotion based upon the market potential, as opposed to geo-political importance, of trade partners.[83]

Since the Congressional passage in June 2015 of the Fast-Track Bill, which enabled the US president to submit a trade agreement to an in–out vote, the ball has been in the EU's court.

The talks are now entering the eighth round. The Commission has received a mandate from the Council to proceed. It can do so with the backing of every member state and the blessings of trade and industry associations across the union. There has been little disagreement between the two negotiating parties in principle concerning the mutual recognition of process and product regulations, but no meeting of minds as to whether and how to include agriculture and public contracting into the talks, even though progress on such points is anticipated in the future.[84]

It was stalled, however, in early 2015, by a campaign of orchestrated public protests launched in Germany, backed by left-leaning unions and environmentalists, and amplified by Members of the European Parliament, which, as part of the institutional competition game with the Commission and Council, demands a voice in framing policy. It must ratify trade treaties and thus can block TTIP. Whether this will actually happen is another question. The campaign was not substantive, instead reflecting a general malaise rather than reasoned opposition. The object of the public outcry was a purported US threat to product standards centring on 'chlorinated chicken', which refers to a chemical rinse required by the US Food and Drug Administration to kill bacteria. It does not affect taste and has no adverse consequences for health. It is, in other words a non-issue raised in behalf of a scare campaign, something all the sillier, as it was not clear whether agriculture would even be included in the negotiations; the fuss may, however, have succeeded, if only as a European bargaining chip, to exclude the sector from the negotiations.

A second, less trivial spat concerned a proposed investor-state dispute settlement (ISDS) mechanism. The treaty would create an independent panel to mediate disagreements between the two parties; similar language has been included in nearly all German bilateral trade agreements. The clauses in question have rarely been invoked and are relevant only to asset seizures in emerging nations with weak legal traditions. Joanna Diane Caytas of Columbia Law School argues, however, that ISDS could be used to compensate investors for damages resulting from legislation in areas like environmental protection, data protection, privacy, financial markets, food standards, health, labour, social security, energy, and media and that such issues should be made subject to judicial review rather than an arbitral court. She adds that courts of this nature protect incumbent interests and therefore constitute a drag on innovation. Complicated issues like this one, she concludes, call for public diplomacy rather than closed-door settlements. The ISDS procedure may not be necessary to TTIP, and the matter can be dropped if need be in order to silence the clamour. The nub of the issue is, however, that matters of such importance require airing in a public forum – and the treaty's advocates are wont not to take such risks.[85]

The protests could well serve as harbingers of things to come. A European Citizens' Initiative to revoke the Commission's TTIP negotiating mandate garnered over a million signatures and secured enough supporters in seventeen states to demand a public discussion under the auspices of the Parliament. But the powers-that-be seem determined to quash such talk. The Commission simply refused to register the complaint – hardly the first time it has overridden democratic procedures.[86] One is reminded of the Danish refusal to endorse the Maastricht Treaty, the Irish rejection of the Nice Treaty, and the French and Dutch non-ratification of the proposed Constitution – each of which was reversed by *force majeure* or administrative fiat. In early October 2015 demonstrations in several countries, in Berlin above all, brought out hundreds of thousands of anti-TTIP protestors.

Although a TTIP may not be on the cards, there is a fallback position for Europe in trade matters: it involves the dense network of FTAs between the EU and individual member states on the one hand and foreign nations on the other. Some 400 in number and precursors to the mega-negotiations, they have advanced trade liberalization quietly and in the absence of both top-level encouragement and lobbying by powerful business interests. Their spreading influence can be attributed to several things: progress made towards the as yet only partial Single Market, increases in foreign demand, spillovers due to most-favoured nation provisions, as well as through the 'generalized system of preference'. Following in the footsteps of a similar American effort, and both cause and effect of global economic interdependence, the expansion of the EU's thickening web of these agreements could provide a welcome accompaniment to political devolution, and even complement a Brexit. A vestigial EU could then, ironically, serve as custodian or trustee of the very treaties that, ironically, liberate the energies of economic interdependence that make the Brussels institutions increasingly irrelevant.[87] An optimal outcome might involve connecting the bilateral FTAs to TPP. Although, perhaps slow and cumbersome, such a procedure would serve the greater good of restoring democratic accountability to the liberalization process.[88] It would allow Europe to participate wholeheartedly in the coming expansion of world trade.

## The Refugee Crisis
To conclude, TTIP against the background of the present refugee crisis would exact prohibitive political cost, shift EU decision-making still further from governmental control, and crystallize public opposition. Yet this will likely not come to pass. The refugee crisis of autumn 2015 caught the European Union completely unprepared, an inexcusable oversight in a continent that has been facing the threat of rising terrorism from the Middle East for over a decade; a preposterous shortcoming in light of the EU's pretensions (as exemplified in Pillar II of the Maastricht Treaty) to a 'competence' for maintaining public security across the union; and a humiliating blunder, as it exposed

the powerlessness of the Brussels leadership, not to mention the lack of everything needed to manage the inflow of the more than a million displaced persons expected to arrive in 2015. The debacle represents the worst case to date of EU overreach.

More serious yet, the attitude of European policy-makers is morally contemptible. From the outset, Brussels discouraged any mention of a 'humanitarian crisis'. Perhaps as a form of denial, not until weeks after the human avalanche had cascaded out of control did official Brussels first use the term 'refugees' in reference to the hundreds of thousands of sufferers; up to then they were not treated as victims of war, but stigmatized as 'migrants' seeking higher wages and better working conditions at the expense of European taxpayers. Brussels' response to this human tragedy has been pitiful. A coordinated, Europe-wide attempt to manage the continuous inflow of the hundreds of thousands and eventually millions of displaced persons from the war-wracked regions of the Islamic world can no longer be expected. Frau Merkel's naive hopes of opening the doors to refugees have been shattered, not least of all because the human, financial, and physical resources needed to care for them are absent.

The Community is hamstrung by internal strife. The only common denominator of nationhood in Europe at the moment, it seems, is hostility to foreigners, especially Muslims. In such a situation, responsibility for doing something – anything – will revert to the individual states and localities, or groups of them, that are able to find some basis for cooperation. The political and financial costs involved in such efforts will be huge, even prohibitive, the potential for conflict is obviously great, and the need for statesmanship is nothing less than extraordinary. Although the human pressure on Europe's borders may be temporarily reduced by cold weather, the pool of perhaps seven million persons from the Middle East and Africa deprived of home, livelihood, and a sense of community leaves little doubt that the crisis is only beginning. An estimated 1.5 million refugees will be at Europe's gates in 2016. Heavy costs, public disorder, and inter-group conflict, will drive home, as not even the European Depression yet has, the emotional toll that has been taken by Brussels' empty promises.

The 13 November 2015 ISIS-inspired suicide bombings in Paris have eliminated whatever sympathy the European public may have had for Muslim refugees and shifted the political centre of gravity sharply to the right. The new mood is tangibly weakening the EU as an institution. Having lost the trust of the public, the Schengen agreement for passport-free travel, which includes twenty-two EU states is, for all practical purposes, dead. The revelations concerning the plotters removed any remaining doubt on the matter. They lived and worked in a single street in the majority-Muslim commune of Molenbeek in Europe's *soi-disant* capital city, Brussels. The perpetrators, some of whom had done jail time together, hung out in a low bar owned by one of them, which was infamous locally for brawling and drug-dealing, that is, when they were not otherwise loitering in a nearby store-front mosque known to police as an Islamist hotbed. The young delinquents shuttled with impunity between the all but imperceptible Belgo-French border over a period of months. Both before and after the Paris tragedy, the Belgian security authorities acted with fecklessness reminiscent of the Marc Dutroux affair.

The erection of border posts will hardly suffice to regulate the hundreds of thousands of displaced Muslims. National security services will have to be bolstered, even in cases built up from scratch – expensive undertakings. Whether, as a prominent commentator suggests, the expenses involved will undermine the fiscal rules governing the EMU remains to be seen.[89] Unless the refugee population is to be expelled, it will have to be housed, fed, and eventually integrated into the labour forces and societies of Europe, an explosive proposition at the best of times. A storm season of politics can be expected. It will bring to an end the era of grand European plans and inaugurate a new and bitter one of retrenchment and consolidation.

## Brexit

Speaking at the London offices of Bloomberg business services in January 2013, Prime Minister David Cameron promised to hold a referendum by the end of 2017 for a vote to determine whether or not Britain would remain in the European Union, the time lapse being thought necessary to give the EU a chance to reform itself on the basis of five principles. It should, Cameron insisted, first of all remain competitive by completing the Single Market and concluding trade deals with the United States, India, and Japan and also both be flexible and respect the diversity of its twenty-eight member states. The Single Market must further, he added, be its common core in the future, and the aim of political union be dropped from the treaties. Additionally, in recognition of member-state diversity the prime minister stipulated that Brussels must allow power to flow to them, and democratic accountability must be enforced by national parliaments.[90] Finally, he insisted that non-EMU members of the union must be treated fairly. Not mentioned in the speech, but of great subsequent importance in the UK's stipulations, labour migration within the EU will have to be limited. The vast majority of Brits would surely ascribe to such views, at least in theory.

Cameron admitted in his speech, however, that support for the EU was only 'wafer thin', and that the tide was turning against it. Nothing has changed in this respect over the past three years. Yet the prime minister expressed confidence that, if given enough time, he could get a better deal for the people of Britain. The prime minister recognized having to face hurdles, as Brussels continued to lay claim to new powers in the attempt to overcome the economic crisis, but also offered reassurances that structural reform could turn the tide of public opinion in favor of the EU and that the electorate could be persuaded of the economic value of EU membership.[91]

Cameron's personal views on the issue at hand are well-concealed. He has flip-flopped in the past and was fence-sitting until the conclusion of the EU summit on 19 February. His primary concern is, in any case, to break the fiercely anti-EU United Kingdom Independence Party (Ukip), silence the one third of his own similarly inclined backbenchers, and set the stage for sweeping the next election. He could do it either by wresting huge concessions from the EU or, if that fails, by assuming leadership in the break away from Brussels with the argument that he is the best man for the exit negotiations. At a stroke, he would kill off Ukip and bring right-wing Tories back into the fold. Only Jeremy Corbyn would stand between him and a sweep.

Cameron's policy was put to an initial test in the November–December 2015 EU summit, but he came away with nothing more than a bit of administrative tinkering, vague promises, and an empty threat to get moving or else – a paltry harvest and far less than necessary to placate wary voters. As for the tight timetable, the truth is that the EU is no position to act: "During the talks several members expressed irritation at having to devote time to the British question amid the political hiatus in Europe over the migration crisis and the Paris terror attacks.'[92] Such concerns may overshadow the 'British question' until it is too late to do anything about it. The matter will come before another summit in February 2016.

But the current disorganization on the EU side is only one obstacle confronting the prime minister. There are larger issues. The better life promised Europeans has not materialized and will not in the near future; the economic appeal to the British voter of the European Union is minimal. It is, moreover, hard to imagine that the unanimous assent required for treaty revision could be forged from twenty-eight squabbling member states of the EU (some of which are obliged by law to hold referenda) – not least of all because the proposed limits on freedom of movement are a red line for Eastern European governments.[93]

Whatever the outcome of the Brexit referendum    and even a near-majority would keep the anti-EU movement alive in the UK – the European Union will emerge seriously weakened from it. The changes Cameron promised the British electorate would result in an organization more closely resembling the free trade area proposed in the late 1950s than the present Brussels institutions, albeit with one important difference: the eurozone would remain. That would be, for the EU, an optimal outcome. If, as appears increasingly likely, the Leave campaign succeeds, member-state defections could follow. Britain might then lead a new economic and political coalition of like-minded countries, or be one among several new members in an expanded (and renamed) TPP.

Outcomes will depend on the policies as well as the economic and political conditions in effect if and when the British decide to get out.[94] The outlook for the EU is not propitious. The European Depression grinds on, its end not in sight. Europe's share in the world economy continues to shrink. The EU is ill-prepared for the challenges of Asia and Silicon Valley. And while the Pacific Basin pact (TPP) shows promise of developing into a single mega-market, negotiations for the Trans-Atlantic Trade and Investment Partnership (TTIP) are stalled. The EU looks more and more like a sinking ship. The future will not, in any case, be shaped by Europe, the US, and Asia separately, but, in varying measure, by all of them together, as the 'third phase of globalization' advances and borders become more porous.

The refugee crisis intensifies and the Volkswagen scandal continues to spill over. The centrist parties of state remain in retreat as the anti-austerity and neo-nationalistic movements of both the right and left advance across Europe. The decisive Danish rejection of further EU integration in the December 2015 referendum 'stands as an example of how voters can turn against the establishment even when a pro-EU vote was predicted before the campaigning began'.[95] Brussels is running scared. It cannot take decisive action on any front. The outcome of Brexit will be determined in large part by its weakness. No one can lead, let alone reform, it. The real threat from Brussels is collapse.

## The Iron Cage

Who could have imagined in 1950 that Europe's fate might be determined by a trade pact or that the institution designed to liberate the human spirit from the nightmare of past wars would, over decades, paint Europe into a corner? For that is exactly where things now stand. Europe is governed today neither by its peoples nor by its ideals but by a bank board. This outcome was hardly intentional: it was the result of a long history of poor decision-making, bureaucratic empire-building, intolerance, and anti-democratic sentiment. Together they have exacted a crushing price in the goodwill born of hope and expectation and strengthened over years of enhanced prosperity and security. The so-called European Dream is dead.

At this point one must ask: Was this vision a mere phantom? Or was there real substance to it? In a profound sense, there was: the increase and intensification of economic and political interdependence has been a formative influence in Europe and the world since the eighteenth century. It will be no different in the future. This integration process was never, however, the property of the set of institutions indicated by the catch-all term, 'Brussels'.

Their role in securing the peace and prosperity of Europe was only secondary, if that. Until the 1980s, the political and economic influence of the so-called European institutions was in fact marginal. Yet even in this early period, there were troubling portents. The notion, implicit in Monnet's governance methods and dogmatized by Walter Hallstein, that Europe's fate was best placed in the hands of a cadre of Platonic Guardians – was an empty conceit. The lack of a democratic component was the fatal structural flaw in the EU as an institution.

The relationships between the central authorities and the member states were, at an early date, in practice conflictual, in principle unresolved, and otherwise non-transparent. New ways were repeatedly found either to short circuit or circumvent the gridlock in 'Europe's capital city'. Amid the institutional shuffling, the design foreseen in the Treaty of Rome tended to blur. No one could have predicted that Europe's fate would, for decades, be at the mercy of a price-support system for farm crops. Nor that the competition principle, by which so much store had been set in the Rome Treaty, would be brushed aside in favour of organized capitalist policies familiar to interwar Europe. Nor, for that matter, that the collapse of the Bretton Woods system would open up vast new vistas of opportunity to those nations and peoples who would seize it. The US and China, followed by others, have adapted successfully to the new conditions of a neo-liberal global economy. Europe has not: command and control methods have remained a constant in a world of dynamic change.

The misbegotten relaunch driven forward by Jacques Delors turned an auspicious opportunity to develop a supranational network of cooperation and mutual support into a train wreck. The institutions whose creation he inspired and (along with successors) shaped have malfunctioned from the first, and each subsequent attempt to set things right has only made them worse, wrought havoc on a broader scale, and eventually cast Europe into an avoidable Depression. The decision to adopt the euro as a single currency marks the point of no return. Structurally flawed, it turned public disenchantment into disillusionment, threw the economy into reverse, stripped the EU of credibility, and fuelled national hostilities that will serve as roadblocks to cooperation for years to come. Europe has been put on a course that imperils its welfare, subverts representative government, and undermines its values.

The manifold crises facing the European Union cannot be contained as matters now stand; they feed on themselves, as policymaking in one sector clashes with that in another and contradictions within them surface. In field after critical field – IT, finance, and energy – an overambitious and unrealistic line of EU policy line has broken down as European power shrinks relative to that of China and the United States. The EU finds itself playing catch up. Troubled, disillusioned, potentially defecting Europhiles bewail Brussels' lack of vision, but their concern is off the mark. What they should worry about is the lack of a 'Plan B'.

In Autumn 2015 a process of entropy set in at Europe's would-be government. Neither endless pronouncements and professions nor grandiose gestures and snarling threats can any longer conceal the EU's powerlessness. Nor can either the IMF or the German chancellor, its heirs, stem the breach. The decisive action needed to break the downward cycle into which the EU is descending requires mass mobilization incompatible with the elitist, convoluted and dysfunctional governance machinery in Brussels. Such a popular movement must begin at the grassroots, work its way through local and representative national institutions, and eventually provide a mandate for democratically elected delegates of the EU's member-state governments to reach a new European settlement.

For Brussels the endgame has begun. It is vulnerable at many points. There are, as *Financial Times* columnist Wolfgang Münchau has said, simply 'too many crises occurring simultaneously for which the EU is unprepared'.[96] The most immediate of them is the refugee crisis that broke out in September and, in tandem with it, the threat of terrorism. Together they require, and will bring about, the end of the Schengen agreement – a fundamental EU institution, an embodiment of its highest aspirations, and (or so it once seemed) a remarkable accomplishment. This sort of institutional setback is what the EU has, at great cost to Europe – as evident above all in the refusal to reconfigure the single currency union – never before admitted possible. Speaking before the Parliament on 24 November in characteristically elliptical language, President Juncker let the cat out of the bag. Calling the agreement 'semi-comatose,' he warned that 'if the spirit of Schengen leaves us . . . we'll lose more than [a mere] agreement. A single currency doesn't make sense if Schengen fails . . . It is one of the main pillars of the construction of Europe.'⁹⁷ Juncker's statement represents official Brussels first recognition that the supposedly inexorable process of European integration can be reversed. The reigning teleology is being dethroned.

Would the 'semi-comatose' Schengen agreement set a precedent, have a sequel, and lead to more far-reaching reform? The debate surrounding Brexit may provide an answer, as public discourse will create a forum for the consideration of alternative institutional arrangements. It is chiefly the misplaced fear that none are available, which keeps the lid on the festering discontent in today's Europe. British withdrawal from the EU might well trigger an orderly reordering of international relationships. The situation is propitious. An increasingly interdependent world order requires global networks of cooperation rather than the reinforcement of old-fashioned economic and political blocs like the EU. The futility of recent Commission policy-making in key areas attests to the folly of sticking to supposedly tried and true methods that no longer work in today's world.

A debacle of unknown proportions could ensue if events outrace statesmanship and common sense. Escape from the Iron Cage by way of a Schumpeterian wave of creative destruction might still be set in motion by trans-oceanic trade pacts that remove obstacles to change and open new pathways to growth, but nobody not politically suicidal would dare advocate such a policy lest an already unstable Europe hit the skids. Incrementalism and trial and error learning is called for under present circumstances. Even if Brexit should fail and the EU somehow manages to survive the present crises, enduring problems will remain: obsolescent mindsets, malformed institutions, and a lack of democratic legitimacy may prove that Douglas MacArthur's adage about old generals also holds true for international organizations like the EU, which have had their day: they never die, but just fade away. Only time will tell how the final act plays out.

# Postscript 2016

Weakened by the events of the past year – and for the historical reasons described in this book – Brussels' fate will most likely be sealed in 2016. The EU may not disappear altogether but survive in vestigial form, yet it will no longer be central to the European conduct of affairs. As is so plainly clear today, it seldom has been during most of its six-decade history. The Delors years (1985–1995) and its aftermath, the Eastern Enlargement, were exceptional in this respect. The EU's marginality during most of its existence can no longer be denied.

The EU may for many years have been Europe's great hope but it has turned out to be a disappointment, even to its advocates. It has made notable contributions to the liberalization of the economy, the democratization of Eastern Europe, and the reconciliation of peoples, but these achievements are now threatened. Above all, there is still no European nation, nor will there be in the foreseeable future. To expect that this situation can be changed is tantamount to awaiting the eleventh round in a ten-round boxing match.

Indeed, there may be no further need for an EU. Driven by technological change, marketplace competition, and consumer demand, the process of integration in Europe and the world at large will go on with or without it. Globalization continues to erode the powers of supranational entities of which it is the leading example, and in fact has long been doing so. Alternatives to Brussels do exist and are at hand. Whether they can, or will, be grasped is, of course, another matter.

The European Union cannot manage any of the present crises it faces. The current refugee tragedy drives the point home. A million and a half or more unwanted victims of war and civil disruption, mainly from the Middle East, are expected to press at Europe's gates this year, in addition to the million that came in 2015. Such figures must be quadrupled to include family members in order to estimate the number of arriving persons, present and future, who might eventually have to be assimilated into European society – the final number will probably be no less than 10 million. An increase in terrorism, furthermore, has been the terrible accompaniment to this human influx. These interrelated problems may not be insurmountable, but they are undoubtedly immense, enduring, and far exceed the administrative capacities of the debilitated and all but immobilized institutions acting in the name of Europe.

The refugee crisis is, however, only one of several widening, lengthening, and now crisscrossing fissures – many of them caused by Brussels itself – responsible for the crumbling of the EU. The European Depression is the greatest of them. It cannot be ended unless the single currency project is abandoned. In addition, the present monetary regime must be replaced by partly restored national monies, and fiscal independence returned to the nations of Europe. Until this happens, antagonism between North and South, and (increasingly) East and West, as well as across classes and generations, can only mount. This in the end will fuel public anger with, and resentment of, Brussels. While it may take different forms of expression from country to country, the EU will be the final target of this universal ire. The European idea has turned rancid.

The chances are slight that globe-girdling mega institutions of commerce and finance like the Transatlantic Trade and Investment Pact (TTIP), now under negotiation, will come to the rescue of the EU. For that to take place Brussels must clean up its act. The Volkswagen diesel emissions scandal demonstrates how difficult this might be. The implications of this cheating must be borne in mind. VW is the leading manufacturer and recognized pace-setter in the largest and most crucial European industry – as well as an essential provider of jobs, growth, and prestige. The spillover from the company's misdeeds is immense.

The motor industry is joined at the hip with its purported regulator, the EU. Caught red-handed by US authorities for engaging in activities detrimental to the health and welfare of the European public – the spewing of noxious fumes from more than 11 million automobiles over a period of many years – the Commission (amidst professions of concern and with deeply furrowed brows) punted and did its best to evade responsibility. Unlike the US Environmental Protection Agency, it did next to nothing to curtail the foul and illegal practice making exhaust pollution hazardous – let alone punish the malefactors. Nor, to its shame, did the self-anointed conscience of eco-Europe, the so-called European Parliament based in Strasbourg; it also caved in before the vehicle manufacturers. How in the world should one expect a duplicitous EU to serve as an honest and equitable rule-maker in an organization like the one proposed by the ocean-spanning trade agreement, whose overarching responsibility would be to set, as well as enforce, international standards for products and processes?

The European Union's IT policy raises a similar issue on a still larger scale: it concerns the future rather than the present. The revolutionary fifth generation (G5) of telecommunications equipment now in view will require unprecedented resources of capital, technology, entrepreneurship, and managerial savvy. G5 will be an essential determinant, worldwide, of the future industrial cyber-economy. Consider, for instance, the self-driving automobile, which requires all but instantaneous information transfer in order to operate, a requirement only G5 can satisfy. The example illustrates, one would hope, what the term the 'Internet of Things' implies: it will change the face of the modern economy.

With this future in mind, the kind of guerrilla warfare that the Commission, the Courts (ECJ) and, in general, the European

Union wage against the American high-tech mega corporations seems futile as well as self-defeating. It can only accelerate the rate of European decline. The expectation that an enfeebled EU can force these giants to lie in a Procrustean bed of regulation is laughable. The real US adversary in the in the struggle for the future of IT is not Europe, of course, but China. In this contest, the EU is a bit player.

The example of Ireland – the one 'Asian Tiger' in today's Depression Europe – demonstrates, furthermore, that growth occurs and jobs materialize not in branches of production where costs have been driven down by the austerity policy of so-called internal devaluation but chiefly from foreign investment channelled into in new high technology fields. This thought should be pondered by the witch-hunting protectionists in the present Commission.

Other equally serious but perhaps less obvious crises loom before the EU. It is too early to assume that the threat of financial meltdown has passed. As the IMF has often protested, over the long run Greece cannot meet the terms of the current bailout, therefore something must eventually give. At the moment, however, the risk of Italy's collapse is front and centre in European concerns. The citizens and institutions, both public and private, of the country with the fourth largest EU economy, own the bulk of its huge sovereign debt. It comprises no less than half of the EMU total and is currently booked at face value and far above what it could command in the market. Once sold, the true worth (or lack thereof) of this low-quality paper would expose the desperate condition of the banking system, the most vulnerable and illiquid in Europe; cause foreclosures across the board; land Italy in the arms of the IMF; and threaten the very survival of the eurozone. To make matters worse, 18 per cent of the loans held by Italian banks, most of them to local businesses, are non-performing – by far the highest rate in Europe. Not without reason is the precariousness of Italian finance a well-kept secret.

Last December the threatened failure of only a couple of the country's many minor banks nearly toppled the present pro-EU Matteo Renzi government. Even a partial default would have been political suicide for the Italian prime minister, devastating the middle-class savers who provide his main support and thereby also standing between his fragile coalition and its powerful enemies, the anti-EU duo of the Five Star Movement and the separatist Northern League. By dint of sheer necessity, Renzi therefore devised a national bailout scheme at odds with new EMU rules requiring share- and bond-holders to take hits prior to any resolution or bankruptcy proceeding. Major fudging on the part of Brussels is called for lest its weakness as a regulator be revealed.

Although Italy's numerous midget banks have received much recent attention, the country's three giants constitute a much greater danger. All of them are in far deeper trouble than publicly acknowledged, and at least one (Monte dei Paschi di Siena) is for all practical purposes bankrupt. Their share prices all collapsed in January. Notwithstanding denials by Italian central bankers, the perilous financial state of their country could well degenerate into an *Existenzkrise* of the EU.

Portugal, like Greece and Ireland, has heretofore been a throwaway of negligible importance to the grand scheme of the EU. Yet even in respect to this fringe nation, Brussels and Frankfurt now have little leverage. In connection with the resolution of the corrupt Banco Espírito Santo and its successor, Nova Banco, the recently installed anti-austerity Socialist government of Antonio Costa, backed by the Portuguese central bank, administered a haircut to senior, mainly American, bondholders so brutal that the nation's credit rating plunged almost at once to junk status. Within earshot of thundering herds moving in the wrong direction, Brussels got the shivers.

The man now at the helm of Lisbon will not relish having his knickers twisted by Frau Merkel. But this may not be necessary. In short order Costa forced her to acquiesce in his government's anti-austerity budget, which violated EMU restrictions, and she even did so without the prior consultation required by the mandatory provisions of the new European Single Financial Market.

The German chancellor must have feared that where little Portugal has gone, big Spain could follow. The tottering Spanish banking structure is now at the mercy of political instability. Two months have passed since the December elections, which produced a stand-off between the two traditional parties of government and anti-EU populists, neither of which can command a majority due to the resurgence of Catalonian secessionism. What began as an anti-EU electoral wave is turning into a crisis of state.

No one can be more closely attuned to the fragility of Europe's financial system than the MIT-trained economist and Goldman Sachs–schooled banker who runs the ECB, Mario Draghi. He dare not, however, broadcast the disheartening news that private finance in Europe has never recovered from 2008. Carrying a trillion euros of bad debt and in serious need of capital infusions, the banks are in a state of chronic crisis. Their shares plunged nearly 20 per cent at the beginning of the year and can be expected to fall further, as rich sovereign wealth funds, their biggest investors, close out large positions.

The underlying problem European banks face, as Draghi well knows, is that the powers that be in both the public and private spheres have drawn the wrong lesson from the economic crisis: instead of introducing the up-to-date market methods of financing familiar to Wall Street and the City, they have propped up outmoded national banking communities that cannot provide the credit the economy needs for recovery. Instead, they are a bottleneck to it. With little fanfare, he is trying to mend the problem. The onerous 'official' plan for EU/EMU banking regulation (Mifid II) is effectively on indefinite hold.

Economic stagnation is not the only, or even perhaps the main, source of Europe's discontent. Disenchantment with the EU also pervades those member-states who wisely chose not to accept the trammels of the eurozone and which, as a result, have enjoyed superior economic performance – Poland, the Czech Republic, Denmark, Sweden, and Britain. The hard truth is that the EU is no less unloved in these comparatively fortunate countries than those trapped in the EMU.

Only a fool would venture to predict how the official institutions of Europe will become unglued, unravel, fall apart, or simply evaporate into thin air. The list of possible scenarios is innumerable. A reasonable guess would be, however, that Brexit will trigger the process of decomposition and reconfiguration. If past events can serve as a guide to the British referendum planned for 23 June, the tide will shift in favour of the anti-EU cause.

This was the case with other recent EU referenda: the Dutch and French rejected the constitution; the Swedish refused to enter the EMU; the Irish initially repudiated the Maastricht Treaty; and in December 2015 the Danish decided not to revise the nation's opt-out agreement. In each of these instances, establishmentarian, pro-EU campaigns heavily outgunned diffuse, underfinanced, and disorganized populist factions – and, contrary to nearly all predictions, eventually lost out to them. There is little reason to conclude that in Britain, where the sides are more evenly matched, the outcome will be much different.

It is now evident that Prime Minister Cameron has not wrested enough concessions from the EU to placate the country's wary voters – the majority of whom support his own party, in which, however, a traditional division between Europhiles and Europhobes has been replaced by a more nuanced distinction between Eurosceptics and Brexiteers. Recent polls have swung decisively in favour of the Leave campaign. Behind this shift in sentiment is a reality of awesome significance: Cameron's promise of a better deal for Britain has little meaning in respect to an EU in disarray, which is untrustworthy, falling behind economically, and unable or unwilling to deliver on its commitments. At the rock-bottom level, moreover, a sovereign national political system, like Britain's, based on the supremacy of parliament, is incompatible with the existence of a supranational entity, whose leadership remains – in spite of everything – unwavering in its determination to create a European state.

Why, finally, would anyone want to upgrade a second-class to a first-class ticket on a ship that is already slipping below the waterline? The UK need no longer be a supplicant to Europe; the shoe is now on the other foot – it has more to give, economically and politically, than it needs to take. The Stay campaign therefore clamours for Britain to come to the rescue of Europe, if only in its own best interests. Many voices on the Continent are delivering a similar message.

This is no incidental matter. Responsibility for engineering the wind-down of the Brussels institutions and their replacement with something different– and, with luck and statesmanship, better – will inevitably devolve upon him as leader of the successful reform party. The task will be daunting. Every EU member state has its own gripe list and each one of them can be counted upon, once Britain pulls out, to demand concessions from the EU and EMU or, if necessary, its successors in receivership. Let it be hoped, in such an eventuality, that an elegy would be more appropriate for the lost case than an obituary.

*Harvard Center for European Studies*
*25 February 2016*

# Notes

## Introduction: A Re-examination of the European Union

1  T. Pfister, 'The Epistemic Dimension of European Integration', *Innovation, The European Journal of Social Science Research*, 28/1 (2015), pp. 11–17.

2  E. Haas, *The Uniting of Europe: Political, Social, and Economic Forces, 1940-1957* (Stanford, 1968); A. Moravcsik, *The Choice for Europe: Social Purpose and State Power from Messina to Maastricht* (Ithaca, 1998).

3  A. Milward, *The European Rescue of the Nation-State* (London, 1993); M. Newman, 'Allegiance and the European Union', in Fernando Guirao et al., *Alan Milward and a Century of European Change* (New York, 2012), pp. 481–99.

4  T. Judt, *Postwar: A History of Europe since 1945* (New York, 2005).

## 1. A Complicated Early History

1  J. Gillingham, *Coal, Steel, and the Rebirth of Europe* (New York, 2006).

2  J. Gillingham, 'The Monnet Method: Then and Now' (Unpublished ms, University of Vienna School of Business, March 2007).

3  F. Duchene, *Jean Monnet: First Statesman of Interdependence* (London, 1994).

4  E. Roussel, *Jean Monnet 1888–1979* (Paris, 1996); Pierre Gerbet, interview.

5  P. Winand, *Eisenhower, Kennedy, and the United States of Europe* (London, 1993).

6  J. Gillingham, *European Integration: Superstate or New Market Economy, 1950–2003* (New York, 2003), pp. 32–52.

7  G. Skogmar, *The United States and the Nuclear Dimension of European Integration* (London, 2004), p. 10.

8  J. Gillingham, 'Jean Monnet et le "Victory Program" americain', in G. Boussuat and D Wilokens (eds.) *Jean Monnet et les Chemins de la Paix*, pp. 98–109; J. Gillingham, 'Jean Monnet and the New Europe', in S. Schucker (ed.) *Deutschland und Frankreich vom Konflikt zur Aussoehnung* (Munich, 2000), pp. 197–209.

9  J. Gillingham, *Coal, Steel*, pp. 97–148.

10  Ibid., pp. 1–86.

11  Ibid., pp. 299–364.

12  Ibid., pp. 348–61.

13  J. Gillingham, 'Foreign Policy as Theology: The Failure of Kennedy's Grand Design', *Beyond the Cold War: The United States and the Renewal of Europe* Conference, Bologna, Italy, 2 November 1994.

14  W. Yondorf, 'Monnet and the Action Committee. The Formative Period of the European Commission', *International Organization*, 19/4 (Autumn, 1965), pp. 885–912.

15  Skogmar, *The United States and the Nuclear Dimension*, pp. 37–61; F. Heller and J. Gillingham (eds.), *The United States and the Integration of Europe* (New York, 1996), p. 11; Gillingham, *European Integration*, pp. 29–33; A. Alexander, *America and the Imperialism of Ignorance* (London, 2011), pp. 147–53; V. Zubok, *A Failed Empire* (Chapel Hill, 2007), pp. 86–92.

16  Skogmar, *The United States and the Nuclear Dimension*, pp. 144–248.

17  Gillingham, *European Integration*, pp. 34–8.

18  D. Dinan, *Europe Recast: A history of the European Union* (Boulder, CO, 2004), pp. 76–7.

19  G. Haberler, 'Integration and Growth of the World Economy in Historical Perspective', *American Economic Review*, LIV/March 1964, Number Two, Part I; also 'Economic Aspects of a European Union', *World Politics* (July 1949), pp. 431–41.

20  J. Gillingham, *European Integration*, pp. 13–14, 223, 41–52; J. Gillingham, 'German Industry and European Competition Policy: Complements or Contradictions?', in Matthias Schulz (ed.) *Die Bundesrepublik und die europaeische Einigung: Festschrift fuer Wolf Gruener* (Stuttgart, 2005), pp. 22–44.

21  B. Eichengreen, 'The European Payments Union', in B. Eichengreen (ed.) *Europe's Post-War Recovery* (New York, 1995), pp. 169–99.

22  D. Irwin, 'GATT's Contribution to Economic Recovery in Western Europe', in Eichengreen, *Europe's Post-War Recovery*, pp. 127–50.

23  J. Gillingham, *European Integration*, pp. 44–52.

24  D. Dinan, *Europe Recast*, pp. 89–94.

25  Ibid., pp. 64–75; A. Moravcsik, *The Choice for Europe* (Ithica, 1998), pp. 156–7, 336, 337.

26  J. Gillingham, *European Integration*, pp. 12–13.

27  Ibid., pp. 6, 43, 250–8.

28  W. Yondorf, 'Monnet and the Action Committee', pp. 885–912.

29  J. Gillingham, 'Foreign Policy as Theology: The Failure of Kennedy's Grand Design' (Unpublished ms, October 1994), 28 pp.

30  J. Gillingham, *European Integration*, pp. 54–66.

31  W. Hallstein, *Europe in the* Making (London, 1972).

32  Dinan, *Europe Recast*, pp. 104–8.

33  A. Boltho and B. Eichengreen, 'The Economic Impact of European Integration', (Discussion Paper 6820, Center for Economic Policy Research, 2008); Perry Anderson, 'The Italian Disaster', *London Review of Books*, 22 May 2014.

34  J. Gillingham, *European Integration*, pp. 93–4.

35  B. Eichengree, *The European Economy since 1945* (Princeton, 2007).

36  Ibid., pp. 31–40, 45, 50–1, 93–9, 129–30.

37  Ibid., p. 200.

38  Ibid., p. 203.

39  R. Barrell and N. Pain, 'Foreign Direct Investment, Technological Change, and Economic Growth within Europe', *The Economic Journal*, 107/445 (Nov. 1971), pp. 1770–86; R.N. Cooper, 'Dollar Deficits and Postwar Economic Growth', *The Review of Economics and Statistics*, 46/2 (May, 1964), pp. 155–8.

40  W. Diebold, 'The Changed Position of Western Europe: Some Implications for United States Policy and International Organization', *International Organization*, 14/1 (Winter 1960), pp. 1–19.

41  L. Franko, *The European Multinationals: A Renewed Challenge to American and British Big Business* (Stamford, CT, 1976); R. Vernon, 'Sovereignty at Bay Ten Years After', *International Organization*, 35/3 (Summer 1981), pp. 517–29.

## 2. *The Dark Years*

1  J. Gillingham, *European Integration: Superstate or New Market Economy* (New York, 2003), pp. 81–4, 97–105.

2  D. Dinan, *Europe Recast: A History of the European Union* (Boulder, CO, 2004), pp. 157ff.

3  Karl W. Deutsch, 'Integration and Arms Control in the European Political Environment: A Summary Report', *American Political Science Review*, 60/2 (June 1966), pp. 354–65.

4  F.A. Hayek, 'The Economic Conditions of Interstate Federalism', in F.A. Hayek, *Individualism and Economic Order* (Chicago, 1948); B. Balassa, *The Theory of Economic Integration* (Homewood, IL 1961); J. Pelkmans, 'Economic Theories of flanking measures' like regional, environmental, research and development, and educational policies that could eventually produce consensus.

5  A. Modi, 'Greece and the Andre Szasz Axiom' (photocopied excerpt) (20 February 2015).

6  J. Gillingham, *European Integration*, pp. 87–9.

7  Ibid., pp. 88–9.

8 U. Everling, 'Possibilities and limits of European Integration', *Journal of Common Market Studies*, 18/3 (March 1980).

9 F. Scharpf, *Governing in Europe: Effective and Democratic?* (New York, 1999), p. 189.

10 D. Calleo, *The Imperious Economy* (Cambridge, UK, 1982), pp. 7–79.

11 R.N. Cooper, 'Economic Interdependence and Foreign Policy in the Seventies', *World Politics*, 24/2 (Jan. 1972), pp. 159–81.

12 I Krause, 'Private International Finance', *International Organization*, 25/3 (Summer 1971), pp. 523–40.

13 R. Sally, *Classical Liberalism and the International Economic Order: Studies in Theory and Intellectual History* (London, 1998); J. Tumlir, *Protectionism: Trade Policy in Democratic Societies* (Washington DC, 1985); J. Tumlir, 'International Economic Order—Can the Trend Be Reversed?', *World Economy*, 5/2 (March 1982).

14 Balassa, 'Whither French Planning?', *The Quarterly Journal of Economics*, 79/4 (November 1965), pp. 537–54.

15 C. Sautter, 'France', in A. Boltho, *The European Economy: Growth and Crisis* (Oxford, 1982), pp. 451–71.

16 H. Giersch et al., *The Fading Miracle: Four Decades of Market Economy in Germany* (Cambridge, UK, 1992).

17 P. Ginsborg, *A History of Contemporary Italy,* (London, 1990); J. Haycroft, *Italian Labyrinth* (London, 1985); G. Rey, 'Italy', in Boltho, *The European Economy*.

18 M. Surrey, 'United Kingdom', in Boltho, *The European Economy*; A. Gamble, *The Free Economy and the Strong State: The Politics of Thatcherism* (London, 1994); A. Cairncross, *The British Economy since 1945* ( (Oxford, 1995).

19 J. Gillingham, *European Integration,* pp. 127–34; S. Strange, 'The Management of Surplus Capacity: Or How does Theory Stand Up to Protectionism 1970s Style?', *International Organization*, 33/3 (Summer 1979) pp. 303–34.

20 C. Barthel, 'The 1966 European Steel Cartel and the Collapse of the ECSC High Authority', in F. Guirao et al. (eds., *Alan S. Milward*, pp. 333–50; Tsoukalis and S. de Silva Ferreira, 'Management of Industrial Surplus Capacity in the European Community', *International Organization*, 34/3 (Summer 1980), pp. 355–76.

21 J. Gillingham, 'The Minimill Challenge to European Steel in Light of the Present World Financial Crisis', (Unpublished ms, September 1998); A. Collard Wexler and J. De Locker, 'Reallocation and Technology: Evidence from the US Steel Industry', *The American Economic Review*, 105/1 (Jan. 2015), pp. 131–71; F. Giattatani et al., 'Slab Casting by U.S. Minimills: An Observation-Based Analysis', *Economic Geography*, 82/4 (Oct. 2006), pp. 401–19.

22 D. Dinan, *Europe Recast*, pp. 157–61.

23 J. Gillingham, *European Integration*, pp. 132–33; D. Dinan, *Europe Recast*, pp. 157–61.

24 M. Obstfeld et al., 'Europe's Gamble', Brookings Papers on Economic Activity, 1997/2, pp. 241–317.

25 Ibid., pp. 271–9; Eichengreen, *The European Economy*, pp. 282–90.

26 J. Rabkin, 'The European Court of Justice: A Strange Institution', in H. Zimmermann and A. Duer (eds.) *Key Controversies in European Integration* (New York, 2012), pp. 88–95.

27 K. Alter, 'Understanding the European Court's Political Power',in ibid pp. 80–8.

28 D. R. Phelan, 'Between the Single Market and the European Union', *Political Science and Politics*. 26/4 (December 1993), pp. 732–6.

29 J. Gillingham, *European Integration*, pp. 130–2.

30 H. Milner, 'Resisting the Protectionist Temptation: Industry and the Making of Trade Policy in France and the United States during the 1970s', *International Organization*, 41/4 (1988), pp. 639–65.

31 P. Hall (ed.), *The Political Power of Economic Ideas* (Princeton, 1989).

32 A. Shonfield, *Europe: Journey to an Unknown Destination* (London, 1973).

33 R. Dahrendorf, *Plaedoyer fuer die Europaeische Union* (Munich, 1971).

## Part II: Behind the Curve

1 I. Berend, 'The Economic Response to Globalization, Recovery, and Growth, The Integration of Eastern and Western Europe', *Society ad Economy*, 36 (2014), pp. 5–6.

2 G. Arrighi et al., 'The Transformation of Business Enterprise', pp. 97–150; 'Western Hegemony in World Historical Perspective', in G. Arrighi and B. Silber, *Chaos and Governance in the Modern World System* (Minneapolis, 1999), pp. 217–70.

3 D. Rodrik, 'When Ideas Trump Interests, Preferences, World Views, and Policy Innovations', *Journal of Economic Perspectives*, 28/1 (Winter 2014), pp. 189–208.

4 L. Guiso et al., 'Monnet's Error?', Working Paper No. 123, Chicago Booth Paper No. 15–23, Initiative on Global Markets, The University of Chicago Booth School of Business, April 2015, pp. 1–76.

5 G. Majone, 'The Deeper Crisis: The Collapse of the Political Culture of Total Optimism', EUI Working Paper Law 2015/10, pp. 1–16.

6 Ibid., p.1.

## 3: Neo-Liberalism

1　M. Wolf, *Why Globalization Works* (New Haven, 2004), p. 105.

2　J. Gillingham, *European Integration: Superstate or New Market Economy, 1950–2003* (New York, 2003), pp. 152–75.

3　R.F. Bartlett, *Seven Fat Years* (New York, 1992); R.C. Smith, *Comeback: The Restoration of American Banking Power in the New World Economy* (Cambridge, MA, 1993); M. Feldstein, 'Supply Side Economics: Old Truths and New Claims', *American Economic Review*, 76/2 (May 1986), pp. 26–30.

4　J. Gillingham, *European Integration*, pp. 136–44, 168–80.

5　H. Schwartz, 'Small States in Big Trouble in the 1980s', *World Politics*, 46/4 (July 1994).

6　T. Iversen, 'The Choice for Scandinavian Democracy in Comparative Perspective', *Oxford Review of Economic Policy*, 14/1 (Spring 1998), pp. 59–76; R. Cox, 'The Consequences of Welfare Retrenchment in Denmark', *Politics and Society*, 25/3 (September 1997), pp. 303–27; S. Jochem, 'Nordic Labor Markets in Transition', *West European Politics*, 50 (July 1988), pp. 115–23.

7　A. Lindbeck, 'The Swedish Experiment', *Journal of Economic Literature*, 35/3 (September 1997), pp. 1273–319; B. Silverman, 'The Rise and Fall of the Swedish Model', *Challenge* (Jan.–Feb. 1998), pp. 69–90.

8　J. Gillingham, *European Integration*, pp. 59–366.

9　M. Bull and M. Rhodes, 'Between Crisis and Transition: Italian Politics in the 1990s', *West European Politics*, 20/1 (January 1997), pp. 1–14; Mark Donovan 'Election Report: A New Republic in Italy?', *West European Politics*, 24/4 (October 2001), pp. 193–206; L. Signorini, 'Italy's Economy: An Introduction', *Daedalus*, 132/2 (1998); 'Italian Banking: Spaghetti Junction', *Economist*, 27 March 1999; J. Gillingham, *European Integration*, pp. 366–74.

10　A. Recio and J. Roca, 'The Spanish Socialists in Power: Thirteen Years of Economic Policy', *Oxford Review of Economic Policy*, 14/1 (Spring 1998), pp. 139–59; O. Encarnacion, 'Social Concertation in Democratic and Market Transitions: Comparative Lessons from Spain', *Comparative Political Studies*, 30/4 (August 1997), pp. 387–420; Victor Perez-Dias, *Spain at the Crossroads* (Cambridge, MA, 1997); S. Perez, *Banking on Privilege: The Politics of Financial Reform* (Ithaca, 1997); P. Heywood, 'Sleaze in Spain', *Parliamentary Affairs*, 48/4 (1993), pp. 726–38.

11　W. Streeck, 'German Capitalism. Does it Exist? Can it be of Service?', MPIFG Discussion Paper 95/5 (November 1995), p. 12.

12　J.Gillingham, *European Integration*, pp. 390–9; J. Gillingham, *Design for a New Europe* (New York, 2003), pp. 85–90.

13　J.Gillingham, *European Integration*, pp. 194–200.

14　Ibid., pp. 374–82.

15　Ibid., p. 158.

16  Ibid., pp. 153–157.
17  Ibid., pp. 157–163.
18  Ibid., pp. 231–3.
19  Ibid., pp. 249–59.

## 4: M. Delors' Europe

  1  F. Scharpf, *Governing in Europe: Effective and Democratic* (New York, 1999), pp. 192–3
  2  G. Ross, *Jacques Delors and European Integration* (New York, 1995).
  3  J. Gillingham, *European Integration: Superstate or New Market Economy, 1950–2003* (New York, 2003), pp. 59–294.
  4  E. Mourlon-Druol, 'Don't Blame the Euro: Historical Reflections on the Roots of the Eurozone Crisis', *West European Politics*, 37/6 (2014), pp. 1282–96.
  5  Ibid., pp. 289–94.
  6  M. Obstfeld et al., 'Europe's Gamble', Brookings Papers on Economic Activity, 997/2, pp. 241–2.
  7  M. Feldstein, 'The Political Economy of the European Economic and Monetary Union: Political Sources of an Economic Liability', *Journal of Economic Perspectives*, 11/4 (1997); P.R. Lane, 'The Real Effects of European Monetary Union', *The Journal of Economic Perspectives*, 20/4 (Autumn 2006), pp. 47–66.
  8  T. Padoa-Schioppa, *The Road to Monetary Union in Europe* (Oxford, 1994).
  9  E. Spolaore, 'What is Economic Integration Really About?', *Journal of Economic Perspectives*, 27/3 (Sumer 2013), pp. 125–44, p. 150.
 10  J. Gillingham, *European Integration*, pp. 277–84.
 11  Ibid., pp. 281–2.
 12  S. Plokhy, *The Gates of Europe* (New York, 2015), pp. 337–45.
 13  Ibid., p. 283.
 14  C. Dannreuther, 'The European Social Model after the Crisis: the end of a functionalist fantasy?', *Journal of Contemporary European Studies*, 22/3 (2014), pp. 329–41.
 15  S. Silvia, 'The Social Charter for the European Community: A Defeat for European Labor', *Industrial and Labor Relations Review*, 44/4 (July 1991), pp. 626–43.
 16  J. Gillingham, *European Integration*, p. 287.
 17  Ibid., pp. 284–93.
 18  Ibid., p. 287.
 19  C. Buster, 'European Union: Failure of the IGC – an aborted Treaty?', international viewpoint (online), 17 February 2004.
 20  J. Gillingham, *European Integration*, pp. 306–7.

21  A. Alesina and R. Perotti, 'The European Union: A Politically Incorrect View', *The Journal of Economic Perspectives*, 18/4 (Autumn 2004), pp. 27–48.

22  'Bruessels Buerokraten kassieren in der Krise', *Der Spiegel*, 2 August 2012.

23  J. Gillingham, *Design for a New Europe* (New York, 2003), pp. 4–18.

24  P. Swidlicki et al., 'Seizing the Moment: Aligning the European Union Budget with Europe's Needs', Open Europe (June 2014), pp.11–35; F. Schneider and K. Raczkowski, 'Shadow Economy and Tax Evasion in the EU', *Journal of Money Laundering Control*, 18/1 (2005), pp. 34–51.

25  J. Gillingham, *European Integration*, pp. 324–8.

26  J. Gillingham, *Design*, pp. 13–18.

27  J. Gillingham, *European Integration*, pp. 324–8.

28  Ibid., pp. 330–4.

29  Ibid., pp. 333–40.

30  D. Phelan, 'Between the Single Market and the European Union', Political Science and Politics, 26/4 (December 1993), pp. 732–6.

31  J. Gillingham, *Design*, pp. 47–53.

32  R. Adler-Nissen, 'Theorizing the EU's Diplomatic Service: Rational Player or Social Body', Academia.edu (Weekly Digest), 10–16 August 2015.

33  A. Cygan, 'The White Paper on European Governance. Have Glasnost and Perestroika Finally arrived at the European Union?', *The Modern Law Review*, 65/2 (March 2002), pp. 229–40; Gillingham, *European Integration*, pp. 346–9.

34  D. Dinan, *Europe Recast* (Boulder, CO, 2004), p. 273.

35  J. Gillingham, *Design*, pp. 184–216; Gillingham, *European Integration*, pp. 410–44.

## Part Three: Lost in the Future

1  H. Varian, 'Big Data: New Tricks for Econometrics, *Journal of Economic Perspectives*, 28/2 (Spring 2014), pp. 3–28; P. Romer and Z. Griliches, 'Implementing a National Technology Strategy with Self-Organizing Industry Investment Boards', *Brookings Papers on Economic Activity, Microeconomics*, 2 (1993), pp. 345–99.

2  E. Byrnjolfsson and A. McAfee, *The Second Machine Age: Work, Progress, and Prosperity in a Time of Brilliant Technologies* (New York, 2014).

## 5: The European Depression and Institutional Debilitation

1  U. Beck, *German Europe* (London, 2013), pp. 2,34.

2  T. Hoshi and A.Q. Kashyap, 'Will the US and Europe Avoid a Lost Decade? Lessons from Japan's Post-Crisis Experience', *IMF Economic Review*, 63/1 (2015), pp. 110–63.

3 M. Wolf, 'Confronting the Eurozone Crisis', Interview W.L. Moretti, 17 April 2012, Providence, RI.

4 M. Wolf, 'The challenges of central bank divergence', *Financial Times*, 8 December 2015.

5 A. Mody, 'Living Dangerously without a Fiscal union', Bruegel Working Paper 2015/03.

6 A. Arcelli and E. Joseph, 'The Convergence Illusion: Why Europe's Approach to the Financial Crisis Isn't Working – and What to do about it', Serie Rossa Economia, Quardino N. 89 (February 2013), p. 1.

7 P. R. Lane, 'The European Sovereign Debt Crisis', *Journal of Economic Perspectives*, 26/3 (Summer 2012), pp. 49–68.

8 A. Alesina et al., 'Austerity in 2009–2013', National Bureau of Economic Research Working Paper 20827 (January 2015).

9 Mody, 'Living Dangerously', p. 2.

10 Ibid., p. 13.

11 Ibid.

12 'Eurozone Approves New Greek Bailout', *Wall Street Journal*, 15–16 August 2015.

13 L. Balcerowicz, 'Euro Balances and Adjustment: A Comparative Announcement', *Cato Journal*, 34/3 (Fall 2014), pp. 453–82.

14 H.-W. Sinn, 'Austerity, Growth and Inflation: Remarks on the Eurozone's Unresolved Competitiveness Problem', *The World Economy* (2014), pp. 1–13.

15 Feldstein, 'Ending the Euro Crisis', NBER Working Paper 20827, 15 January 2015.

16 'Divergent Paths Set for Fed and ECB', *Wall Street Journal*, 30 November 2015; 'ECB pledges to extend easing until March 2017 or beyond', *Financial Times*, 3 December 2013.

17 H.-W. Sinn, 'Austerity, Growth and Inflation', pp. 11–13.

18 K. O'Rourke and A. Taylor, 'Cross of Euros', *Journal of Economic Perspectives*, 27/3 (Summer 2013), pp. 167–92.

19 L. Beck, *German Europe* (London, 2013), p.6

20 M. Dawson, 'New Governance in the EU after the Euro Crisis: Retired or Reborn?', AEL 2015/01 EUI, Academy of European Law.

21 'Lobbying in the EU: The cost of a lack of transparency', European Parliamentary Research Service (September 2015).

22 'Brussels Buerokraten kassieren in der Krise', *Der Spiegel*, 2 August 2015.

23 Ibid., pp. i–ii.

24 P. Mair, *Ruling the Void: The Hollowing of Western Democracy* (London, 2013).

25 R. Davison, 'Re-evaluating EU Integration: An Assessment of the Impact of the Single Market', CERC Working Papers Series, 2 (2000); A. Neven, 'Regulatory Reform in the European Community', *The American Economic Review*, 82/2 (May 1992), pp. 98–103.

26  A. Stepniak-Kuchzrska, 'Changes in the Rules for Granting State Aid to Enterprises in the European Union', (Versica), 10 2478/cei 2013–0030.

27  P. Messerlin, 'How Open are Public Procuremarkets', RSCAS 2915/89 (November 2015)

28  M. Mariniello et al., 'The Long Road towards the European Single Market', Bruegel Working Paper 2015/01.

29  E. Jones, 'European Crisis, European Solidarity', *Journal of Common Market Studies*, 20 (2012), pp. 63–7

30  Y. Meny, 'Managing the EU Crisis: Another Way of Integration by Stealth?', *West European Politics*, 37/6 (2014).

31  A. Sapir, 'Still the Right Agenda for Europe? The Sapir Report Ten Years On', *Journal of Common Market Studies* 52/S1 (Sept. 2014), pp. 57–73.

32  G. Falkner, 'Is the EU a Non-Compliance Community?', *Les Cahiers europeenes de Sciences Po*, 01 (2013), pp. 1–58.

33  G. Falkner, 'Is the European Union Losing its Credibility?', *Journal of Common Market Studies*, 51, pp. 13–30.

34  'The Rise of the Quangos', Open Europe (April 2000).

35  S. Meunier, 'Integration by Stealth: How the European Union Gained Competence over Foreign Direct Investment', EUI Working Paper RSCAS 2014/66.

36  M. van Rijsbergen, 'On the Enforceability of EU Agencies Soft Law at the National Level. The Case of the European Securities and Markets Authority', *Utrecht Law Review*, 10/5 (December 2014).

37  E. Ciclet, 'Does the Lisbon Treaty Effectively Limit the Power of the European Union', Institute of Economic Affairs (2013).

38  'EU warned on devices at center of VW scandal two years ago', *Financial Times*, 25 September 2015; 'Volkswagen emission scandal exposes EU regulatory failures', *Financial Times*, 30 September 2015; 'Study shows limits of car emissions tests in wake of VW scandal', *Financial Times*, 25 September 2015; 'Volkswagen scandal fuels fears over "death of diesel"', *Financial Times*, 29 September 2015.

39  'EU failed to heed emissions warnings in 2013', *Financial Times*, 25 October 2015; 'VW Crisis Spreads to Audi Engines', *Wall Street Journal*, 27 November 2015

40  'Europe has ducked its obligations on diesel cars', *Financial Times*, 1 November 2015;'VW fallout: How Belgium accelerated diesel's dominance', *Financial Times* 2 November 2015

41  'Sarcasm and Doubt Precede VW's Update on Cheating Inquiry', *New York Times*, 7 December 2015

42  M. Mariniello et al., 'Antitrust, Regulatory Capture, and Economic Integration', Bruegel Policy Contribution 2015/11, July 2015.

43  Ibid., p. 8.

44  M. Graetz, 'Behind the European Raid on McDonald's'. *Wall Street*

*Journal*, 4 December 2015;'EU migration wish list to DC includes intel help', *Fiinancial Times*, 30 November 2015 'EU presses Tech Giants in Terror Fight', *Wall Street* Journal, 3 December 2015.

45 R. Emmit, 'Corruption in Europe could slow recovery', Reuters, 6 June 2012; F. Schneider and K. Raczkowski, 'Shadow economy and tax evasion in the EU', *Journal of Money Laundering Control* (2015), 18/1 pp. 340–51

46 L. Barbone et al., 'Study to Quantify and Analyze the Vat Gap in the EU Member States', Case Network Reports 124/2015.

47 Ibid.

48 'Revisiting the Big Plan to Save the Euro', *Wall Street Journal*, 12 March 2015; G. Wolf, 'Euro area governance: an assessment of the "five president's report" ', Bruegel, 25 June 2015.

49 'Jean-Claude Juncker, President, European Commission', Boardroom Insiders Profiles, 8 March 2015.

50 S. Bowers, 'Jean Claude Juncker can't shake off Luxembourg tax controversy', *The Guardian*, 14 December 2014; M. Karnitschning, 'Tax Leak Pressures Top EU Official: Documents show extent of corporate tax deals brokered in Luxembourg during Juncker's tenure', *Wall Street Journal*, 7 November 2014.

51 'Future EU Commissioners Come Clean on Finances', *Wall Street Journal*, 25 September 2014.

52 T. Fairless, 'Will EU Rejig Weaken Antitrust Czar?', *Wall Street Journal*, 12 November 2014.

53 Charlemagne, 'Europe's Great Alchemist', *The Economist*, 29 November 2014; M. Myant, 'Why Juncker's Investment Plan is a Good Try but not good Enough', *Social Europe Journal*, 8/2 (Winter/Spring 2015).

54 'Jean-Claude Juncker, President, European Commission'.

55 Z. Darvas and O. Tschekassin, 'Poor and Under Pressure: The Social Impact of Europe's Fiscal Consolidation', Bruegel 2015/04 (March 2015).

56 'Jean-Claude Juncker calls for the creation of a European army', *Financial Times*, 8 March 2015; P. Sparaco, 'European Defense Blues', *Aviation Week and Space Technology*, 10 June 2013, pp. 20–3.

57 Charlemagne, 'The Battle of the Scientists', *The Economist*, 20 December 2014; 'EU Parliament up in arms against raid on research funds', *Science Now*, 20 April 2015.

58 Open Market Berlin, 'Ein ordnungspolitisches Mandat fuer die neue EU-Kommission', 8 September 2014.

## 6: *Threat of a Promising Future – or Endgame?*

1 N. Bloom et al., 'Americans do IT Better: US Multinationals and the Productivity Miracle', *American Economic Review*, 102/1 (2012), pp. 167–201.

2 J. Meltzer, 'The Internet, Cross-Border Data Flows and International

Trade', *Asia and Pacific Policy Studies* (October 2014), pp. 1–13.

3  A. McAfee and E. Brynjolfsson, *The Second Machine Age: Work, Progress, and Prosperity in a Time of Brilliant Technologies* (New York, 1994), p. 90.

4  McKinsey Global Institute, 'Global Flows in a Digital Age', (April 2014), pp. 1–4.

5  A. McAfee and E. Byrnjolfsson, *The Second Machine Age*, p. 104.

6  McKinsey Global Institute, 'The Internet of Things: Mapping the Value Beyond the Hype', (June 1915), pp. 1–14.

7  Ibid., p. 6.

8  'EU proposal on genetically modified crops satisfies no one', *Financial Times,* 22 April 2015; 'More than half of EU countries ask for GMO opt-out', *EU Observer,* 2 October 2015.

9  K. Purnhagen, 'The Behavioural Law and Economics of the Precautionary Principle and Its Impact on Internal Market Regulation', *Journal of Consumer Policy,* 37 (2014), pp. 453–64.

10  J. Gillingham, *Design for a New Europe* (New York, 2003), pp. 115–55.

11  G. Majone, 'What Price Safety? The Precautionary Principle and its Policy Implications', *Journal of Common Market Studies,* 40/1, pp. 89–109.

12  Y. Wilks, 'Brussels Cash Comes at a Terrible Price', *Times Educational Supplement,* 1 July 2010.

13  Ibid.

14  'Austerity and corporate caution erode innovation', Oxford Analytica Daily Brief Service, 1 August 2014.

15  A. Renda, 'Europe and Innovation: Is 2020 on the Horizon?', *Intereconomics* (2015), pp. 20–4.

16  Ibid.

17  Ibid.

18  'EU red tape risks new Dark Age in bioscience, warns UK minister', *Financial Times,* 11 November 2015.

19  J. Thornhill, 'Borderless world of technology threatens Europe's business base', *Financial Times,* 8 September 2015.

20  S. Greenstein, *How the Internet Became Commercial* (Princeton, 2015).

21  A. Henten, 'The telcom reform process in Europe and the upcoming challenges: overview of the issues and papers in this special edition', in A. Henten and W. Melody (eds.) *European ICT policies after 25 years: achievements, challenges, and opportunities* (29 December 2014).

22  Ibid.; E. Sutherland, 'The enterprise and the digital single market: business telecommunications', ibid.

23  E. Sutherland, 'The enterprise and the digital single market'.

24  M. Armbrust et al., 'A View of Cloud Computing', *Communications of the ACM,* April 2010; 'The Cheap, convenient cloud: Information Technology', *The Economist,* 18 April 2015.

25 T. Fairless, 'Europe Weighs new Regulator for Web Firms', *Wall Street Journal*, 23 April 2015; 'Nothing to Stand On: Europe v. Google', *The Economist*, 18 April 2015; S. Fidler, 'Europe Seeks a Model to Repel U.S. Internet Giants', *Wall Street Journal*, 21 May 2015; 'Europe's Digital Mistake', *Wall Street Journal*, 31 March 2015.

26 F. Erixon, 'The Google Case and the Promotion of Europe's Digital Economy', ECIPE Bulletin No. 1/2015.

27 'China aims to rewrite rules of global web', *Wall Street Journal*, 29 July 2015.

28 Ibid.

29 S. Hampton, 'The Case for Repealing the EU's telecommunications legislation', 17/1 (Emerald Group Publishing, 2015), pp. 3–8.

30 W. Kuan Hon et al., 'Policy, Legal and Regulatory Implications of a Europe-only Cloud', Queen Mary University of London School of Law, Legal Studies research Paper 186/2014.

31 'Google Shoots Up $65 Billion in a Day', *Wall Street Journal*, 18 July 2015.

32 F. Erixon, 'The Google Case'.

33 B. Macaes, 'A Digital Strategy for Europe', ECIPE Policy Brief, 8/2015.

34 'Europe must not create a Balkanized internet', *Financial Times*, 24 September 2014; 'EU Kills Big Data Accord with U.S.', *Wall Street Journal*, 7 October 2015.

35 'Miccosoft Nods to EU's Data-Protection Fears', *Wall Street Journal*, 12 November 2015.

36 'Bad loans at Europe banks double that of the US', 'Europe slowly de-zombifies its banks', 'Europe Unreconstructed: Italy's bank rescue shows bad old ways not forgotten', *Financial Times*, 25 November 2015.

37 'Delays risk 'half=baked' banking union, Brussels warns Italy', *Financial Times*, 25 November 2015.

38 'Bureaucracy Weighs on Bank Reform', *Wall Street Journal*, 4 October 2013.

39 Simon Nixon, 'A Union Defined by its Weakness', *Wall Street Journal*, 30 November 2015.

40 N. Veron and G. Wolff, 'Capital Markets Union: A Vision for the Long Term', Bruegel, 2015/05 (April 2015), pp. 1–48.

41 Ibid.

42 'What has delayed Europe's bank recovery?' *Financial Times* 9 November, 2015; 'European Banks Hit Road Bumps', *Wall Street Journal*, 4 November 2015; 'A Trillion in Bad Loans Stymies European Banks', *Wall Street Journal*, 28 November 2015.

43 'US Banks take the Global Lead', *Wall Street Journal*, 31 July 2015; 'Strategic Choices for Banks in the Global Age', *McKinsey Global Review*, January 2015.

44 'McKinsey warns that banks face wipeout in some services', *Financial Times*, 30 September 2015.

45 J. Hill, 'A stronger capital markets union for Europe', *Financial Times*, 29 September 2015; 'Lord Hill's capital markets union plans highlight UK concerns', *Financial Times*, 29 September 2015.

46 N. Veron, 'Europe's Capital Markets Union and the new single market challenge', Bruegel, 30 September 2015.

47 'Europe Seeks to Revive Securitization', *Wall Street Journal*, 1 October 2015.

48 'Brexit would make the UK a "supplicant" says Lord Hill', *Financial Times*, 27 November 2015.

49 P. Vigna and M. Casey, *The Age of Cryptocurrency: How Bitcoin and Digital Money are Challenging the Global Economic Order* (New York, 2015); C. Beer and B. Weber, 'Bitcoin – The Promise and Limits of Private Innovation Monetary and Payments Systems', *Monetary Policy and the Economy*, 4/14, (2006), pp. 54–66; A. Endres, 'Currency Competition: A Hayekian Perspective on International Monetary Integration', *Journal of Money, Credit, and Banking*, 41/6 (September 2009), pp. 1251–63.

50 P. Vigna and M.Casey, *The Age of Cryptocurrency*.

51 P. Stafford, 'Blockchain Initiative backed by 9 large investment banks', *Financial Times*, 15 September 2015.

52 'Technology: Banks seek the key to blockchain', *Financial Times*, 1 November 2015.

53 G. Zachmann, 'The European Energy Union: Slogan or an Important Step Towards Integration?', Bruegel, 17 September 2015.

54 'EU stuck on horns of trilemma', *Financial Times*, 13 October 2015.

55 R. Newell et al., 'Carbon Markets 25 Years after Kyoto: Lessons Learned, New Challenges', *Journal of Economic Perspectives*, 27/1 (Winter 2013), pp. 125–46.

56 R. Schmalensee and R. Stavins, 'Lessons Learned from Three Decades of Experience with Cap-and-Trade', NBER Working Paper 21742, November 2015, pp. 1–25, p.14.

57 'EU: Climate Deal will be used for global agreement', *Oxford Analytica* (29 October 2014); R. Bezdek 'Carbon Follies: The EU–ETS example', *World Oil* 235/6 (June 2014), pp. 23–4; J. Varley, 'Commission abandons binding national renewals agreement', 34/2 (February 1914), pp. 10–12; M. Mensing, 'The European Energy Union: Time to Re-open Pandora's Box', *IPW*, 3 (2015), p. 3.

58 'Only Connect', *The Economist*, 17 January 2015.

59 'European Energy Agency Faces Hurdles',, *Wall Street Journal*, 24 November 2015.

60 M. Ridley And B. Peiser, 'Your Complete Guide to the Climate Debate', *Wall Street Journal*, 28-29 November 2015.

61 'Norway urges EU assurances on gas output', *Financial Times*, 30

November 2015; 'Russia – the implications of he reset for energy markets', *Financial Times*, 19 November 2015.

62 'Ukraine Urges EU to Block Pipeline', *Wall Street Journal*, 8 December 2015.

63 Open Europe, 'Rotten Foundations: Time to reassess the Europe 2020 climate change targets', 28 January 2015; 'EU Chiefs Knock Solar Aid', *Wall Street Journal*, 12 October 2013; A. Tooze, 'Germany's Unsustainable Growth: Austerity Now, Stagnation Later', *Foreign Affairs*, 91/5 (September/October 2012), 23f.

64 S. Tagliapietra, 'Designing a new EU–Turkey strategic gas partnership', Bruegel, 1 July 2015.

65 Y. Bobylev, 'The Oil and Gas Sector's Development', *Russian Economic Developments*, 4 (2015), pp. 32–6; 'New European Energy Map will shape EU policy', *Oxford Analytica*, 8 December 2014.

66 S. Williams, 'UK Offers New Onshore Blocks for Shale Development', *Wall Street Journal*, 18 August 2015; E. Ochieng et al., 'Fresh Drivers for Economic Growth: Fracking the UK Nation', *International Journal of Energy Sector Management*, 9/3 (2015), pp. 412–31.

67 'Renewables scrutinized as oil price falls', *The Financial Times*, 8 September 2008.

68 R. Leal-Arcas and J. Alemany-Rios, 'How can the EU diversify its energy supply to improve its energy security?', Queen Mary University of London Legal Studies Research Paper 190/2015, pp. 1–21; 'Invisible fuel; Energy efficiency', *The Economist*, 17 January 2015, 12 pp.

69 W. Buiter and E. Rahbari, 'Trade Transformed: The Emerging New Corridors of Trade Power', *Citi GPS Global Perspectives and Solutions*, 18 October 2011; 'World trade heads for weakest year since 2009', *Financial Times*, 25 November 2015.

70 P. Messerlin, 'The EU's Strategy for Trans-Pacific Partnership', *Journal of Economic Integration*, 28/2 (June 2013) pp. 285–302.

71 O.-A. Colibasanu et al., 'The Trans-Atlantic Trade and Investment Partnership: A Challenge for the European Union?' (Unpublished ms., December 2014), 28 pp.

72 G. Kolev, 'TTIP: Mehr als Handelsliberalisierung', Institut der deutschen Wirtschaft IW Policy Paper /11/20/2014; R. Azevedo 'Use Trade as the Next Stimulus', *Wall Street Journal*, 31 March 2015.

73 A. Deardorff, 'Trade Implications of the Trans-Pacific Partnership for ASEAN and other Asian countries', *Asian Development Review*, 31/2, pp. 1–20(2013); R. Sally, 'Asia's Story of Growing Economic Freedom', CATO, Policy Analysis 725, 5 June 2013.

74 'Japan: End of the Rice Age', *Financial Times*, 21 September 2015.

75 'Moment of reckoning: Japan and Abenomics', *The Economist*, 6 December 2014.

76 D. Ikenson and S. Linicome, 'Beyond Exports: A Better Case for Free Trade', *Free Trade Bulletin* No. 43, 31 January 2011.

77 B. Mercurio, 'The Trans-Pacific Partnership: Suddenly a "Game Changer"', *The World Economy* (2014), pp. 1558–74.

78 Ibid., p. 1563.

79 'Obama's Pacific trade deal success poised in Atlanta', *Financial Times*, 20 September 2015.

80 M. Bauer et al., 'Trans-Pacific Partnership: A Challenge to Europe', ECIPE Policy Briefs, 9/2014.

81 B. Horvathy, 'The Transatlantic Trade and Investment Partnership: The Revival of Bilateralism', Faculty of Law and Political Sciences, Szechenyi Istvan University (2014); 'One Year into the TTIP Negotiations: Getting to Yes', *Free Trade Bulletin*, 59, 29 September 2014.

82 'US–EU trade talks reach critical stage', The Economist Intelligence Unit, 21 November 2014.

83 C. Cellerino, 'Recent Trends of common commercial policy of the European Union: from global-to-regional (and return?) in the governance of international economic order', (Unpublished ms., n.d.), p. 4.

84 Kolev, 'TTIP: Mehr als Handelsliberalisierung'; 'Transatlantic deal offers Europe a great opportunity', *Financial Times*, 17 September 2014.

85 J. Caytas, 'From shield to sword: TTIP's lessons on democratic legitimacy for international investment arbitration', Columbia University Law School Papers, November 2015.

86 'Anti-TTIP Petition Garners 1 Million Signatures, Surpassing Key Threshold', *Inside US Trade*, 12 December 2014; B. Fox, 'MEPs back US Free Trade after Socialist U-Turn', *EU Observer*, 28 May 2015; 'Trade Committee Leaders Warn of TTIP from EU Digital Market Resolution', *Inside US Trade Daily*, 1 December 2014; A. Demling, 'Jeder zweite Deutsche findit TTIP gut', *Der Spiegel*, 31 October 2014.

87 B.T. Hanson, 'Whatever Happened to Fortress Europe? External Trade Policy Liberalization in the European Union', *International Organization*, 52/1 (Winter 1998); R. Cellerino, 'Recent Trends of common commercial policy', pp. 1–19.

88 E. Benvenisti, 'Democracy Captured: The Mega-Regional Agreements and the Future of Global Public Law', Global Trust Working Paper Series 08/2015.

89 W. Muenchau, 'Paris Attacks highlight need to end the folly of a border-less Europe', *Financial Times*, 22 November 2015.

90 David Cameron, 'Speech at Bloomberg', 23 January 2013.

91 Suration Poll, 9–11 November 2015.

92 'Cameron runs out of time for EU deal this year', *Financial Times*, 25 November 2015.

93 'Britain stumbles into long EU-referendum campaign', *Financial Times*, 16 October 2015.

94 'What if . . .? The Consequences, challenges, and opportunities facing Britain outside EU', Open Europe, Report 03/2015.

95 'Danish referendum rejects further EU integration'. *Financial Times*, 4 December 2015.

96 'Europe needs a sense of strategic direction to survive', *Financial Times*, 2 November 2015.

97 'End of EU Border-Free System Could see Euro Fail, Warns Juncker', *Wall Street Journal*, 15 November 2015.

# Index

## Index

# Index

# Index

# Index

# Index